EDEN TO EDEN

FROM EDEN TO EDEN.

Eden to Eden,

A Historic and Prophetic Study.

By J. H. WAGGONER.

"All scripture is given by inspiration of God, and is profitable for doctrine, for reproof, for correction, for instruction in righteousness; that the man of God may be perfect, thoroughly furnished unto all good works."—*2 Tim. 3:16, 17.*

PACIFIC PRESS PUBLISHING COMPANY,
OAKLAND, CAL.
NEW YORK, SAN FRANCISCO, AND LONDON.

TEACH Services, Inc.

World rights reserved. This book or any portion thereof may not be copied or reproduced in any form or manner whatever, except as provided by law, without the written permission of the publisher, except by a reviewer who may quote brief passages in a review.

The author assumes full responsibility for the accuracy
of all facts and quotations as cited in this book.

Facsimile Reproduction

As this book played a formative role in the development of Christian thought and the publisher feels that this book, with its candor and depth, still holds significance for the church today. Therefore the publisher has chosen to reproduce this historical classic from an original copy. Frequent variations in the quality of the print are unavoidable due to the condition of the original. Thus the print may look darker or lighter or appear to be missing detail, more in some places than in others.

Copyright © 1994, 2017 TEACH Services, Inc.
ISBN-13: 978-1-57258-027-5
ISBN 1-57258-027-5
Library of Congress Control Number: 94-62084

Entered according to Act of Congress in the year 1890, by
PACIFIC PRESS PUBLISHING CO.,
In the office of the Librarian of Congress, Washington, D. C.
ALL RIGHTS RESERVED.

PACIFIC PRESS PUBLISHING COMPANY,
OAKLAND, CAL.,
PRINTERS, ELECTROTYPERS, AND BINDERS.

Published by

TEACH Services, Inc.
www.TEACHServices.com

PREFACE.

The reader will not find in this book any effort to prove that the Bible is inspired, and that it is the word of God. It is the office of the Scriptures themselves to convince of their own origin and authority. To those who read them reverently not a word is needed to prove that they are divine; while to those who do not read them, or who read them carelessly and without reverence, no manner or amount of proof can be given that can cause them to realize their divinity, their importance, or their beauty. To be appreciated, the Bible must be studied with an earnest desire to learn the truth.

And yet it is our hope that this work will increase the regard of every reader for the sacred Scriptures. In this age of skepticism, when the Bible is so often treated as a book that everyone may criticise, and many think they can improve, the lovers of the word of God will hail with joy and gratitude every effort to exalt its truths, and to lead its readers to cling more closely to the blessed Saviour, who died to open a way of pardon for the rebellious race, and to vindicate the covenant of his Father.

This book contains a brief exposition of some of the most interesting portions of the Scriptures, both historic and prophetic. One object kept constantly in view, has been to point out the unity of the divine plan from the creation; to show that the central idea of all dispensations has been the same, and that the truths revealed in the beginning were the same that have been constantly impressed upon the minds of the people of all ages, and that the object of all revelation, and of all God's dealings with the children of men, has been to restore what was lost in the fall, and to fulfill the original purpose in the creation of the world, and of man.

Although very brief for a work covering, as it does, the entire period of the world's history and the consummation of the plan of redemption, yet the important truths which enter into this plan are so connected in their presentation that the thoughtful reader cannot fail to see the relation of each to the others, and to realize the necessity of each as a part of the whole, brevity being rather a help in this direction than otherwise.

While, in respect to subject matter and methods, it will be found unlike any other book treating on the same subjects, it is hopefully trusted that its scrupulous conformity to, and recognition of, the plain testimony of the Scriptures upon every point, will commend it to the attention and consciences of all who sincerely love the truth.

With the earnest prayer that this book may be a benefit to the reader, and serve to glorify the Creator, Preserver, and Redeemer of man, it is sent forth to the world. J. H. W.

Basel, Switzerland, 1889.

CONTENTS.

CHAPTER I.
IN THE BEGINNING.
How came the world into existence?—Man its lord.—Did God make sin?—You shall and you shall not.—One wrong step changes the fate of a world.—What God does about it.—Why beasts were offered in sacrifice.......15-18

CHAPTER II.
THE PROMISE OF GOD TO THE FATHERS.
The richest heir reduced to poverty.—Value of faith.—How the lost came to hope.—A world-wide promise.—The gospel in a nutshell.—The promises to the fathers..19-24

CHAPTER III.
THE ABRAHAMIC COVENANT.
Divine mode of confirming it.—The field of the covenant.—The token.—The seed.—The land.—How much God promised to one righteous man.—Children that are no children.—A valuable inheritance, as a prize to win for whosoever will.—What was lost.—What must be redeemed.—The greatest purchase ever made.—Future prospects............................25-33

CHAPTER IV.
STEPS OF THE FAITH OF ABRAHAM.
Believing God.—Righteous through faith.—Circumcision a sign of righteousness.—Our relation to the law.—Moral and ceremonial precepts.—The covenant commanded.—What repentance implies.—Moral obligations in the patriarchal dispensation....................................34-46

CHAPTER V.
THE COVENANT WITH ISRAEL.
A favored family.—The reasons for it.—What law can do, and what not.—A means to an end.—A matter that concerns all the world.—A difficult question answered.—How the reader may become an heir............47-55

CHAPTER VI.
AN IMPORTANT QUESTION SETTLED.
The Place of worship.—The return of the Jews.—The conditions of the old covenant.—What God prizes...56-66

CHAPTER VII.

THE KINGDOM AND ITS KING.

The most worthy will bear sway.—The most favored ones receive a promise.—Reward of disobedience.—A man after God's own heart.—The first place of worship built after a design from Heaven.—When the Lord leaves a people their enemies triumph over them.—How low sin may bring a nation.—The true seed of David.—The central figure of Old Testament prophecy.—Prophetic imagery.—How God helps those who are true to him. —The world's history in a dream.—Earth's leading empires rise and fall in succession.—God's promised kingdom to stand forever.....................67–85

CHAPTER VIII.

THE TIME OF SETTING UP THE KINGDOM.

Man proposes and God disposes.—Transitoriness of earthly power.—A theory at variance with facts.—The only kingdom that will stand forever....
86–98

CHAPTER IX.

HEIRS OF THE KINGDOM.

Earthly kingdoms unenduring.—God's purpose in creation unchanged. —A king with two thrones in two dominions.—The throne of grace.—The throne of David.—Men will sit on the throne of Christ's kingdom with him.—How this will be brought about.—No human speculations, but based on infallible proof..99–109

CHAPTER X.

ANOTHER LITTLE HORN.

Beasts as portrayers of history.—What horns may signify.—Much in little.—Beginnings of a mighty power.—A famous letter.—The height of presumption.—The testimony of history.—The prophetic measurement of time...110–128

CHAPTER XI.

THE BEAST WITH SEVEN HEADS AND TEN HORNS.

A woman, a dragon, and other symbols.—Prophetic agreement.—Four steps to supreme power.—An unprecedented spectacle.—The world the protector of the church.—The crowning measure of iniquity.—How historians view it..129–146

CHAPTER XII.

THE THOUSAND TWO HUNDRED AND THREESCORE DAYS.

An error against which to guard.—A fall from highest exaltation.—Historical and prophetic time agree.—The healing of a deadly wound.—What will astonish the world...147–162

CHAPTER XIII.

THE BEAST WITH TWO HORNS.

A great and mighty nation which Daniel did not see in vision.—Distinguishing characteristics of the same.—What Satan is doing at the present time.—The greatest religious illusions of the present age.—A dragon in disguise.—A warning from Heaven 163-177

CHAPTER XIV.

THE HOUR OF JUDGMENT.

Proclamation of a judgment come.—When given, and through whom.—Collateral events.—Our destinies fixed forever, before the second coming of Christ.—How this can be.—The key to the whole subject.—Why even in Heaven the temple must be cleansed.—Result of this work.............178-187

CHAPTER XV.

BABYLON IS FALLEN.

Messages from God for our time.—Blind leaders of the blind.—Reliability of prophetic time.—The Christianity of to-day, in the light of prophecy. The danger at home and abroad.—Ready to clasp hands with her worst enemy..188-204

CHAPTER XVI.

THE COMMANDMENTS AND THE FAITH.

The only reliable standard of truth and justice.—Is God's law abolished?—If not, why not?—Two distinct laws.—The oldest of all institutions.—A popular counterfeit.—Acknowledgments from its own friends............205-213

CHAPTER XVII.

THE SEAL AND THE MARK.

The last merciful warning.—A mark that separates the righteous from the wicked.—Means of knowing God.—His purpose in giving the Sabbath.—The characteristic mark of the wicked.—Blasphemous assumptions..........
214-222

CHAPTER XVIII.

SIGNS OF THE SECOND COMING OF CHRIST.

We may know its approach with certainty.—A world-wide alarm.—Who will, and who will not heed it.—Counterfeits precede the genuine.—Precursors of Christ's return in the heavens.—Not to know is to be lost......
223-230

CHAPTER XIX.

THE RESURRECTION OF THE DEAD.

The change from death to life.—What did Abraham believe?—Testimonies from holy men of Old Testament times.—New Testament writers on the subject.—What is involved in the doctrine?......................231–237

CHAPTER XX.

THE RESTORATION OF THE FIRST DOMINION.

The purchased possession.—What does the punishment of the wicked consist in?—Precious promises.—Where and what is the New Jerusalem?—The investiture of the kingdom.—When will the seven last plagues be?—A city from Heaven.—The earth in the holy day garb of innocency.—An end of sorrow and crying.—Unalloyed happiness at last.................... 238–255

LIST OF ILLUSTRATIONS.

                                                                    OPP. PAGE
FROM EDEN TO EDEN ....(*Frontispiece*)
ABRAHAM OFFERING ISAAC... 23
DAVID ON HIS THRONE.. 68
DANIEL INTERPRETING THE DREAM.. 72
THE FEAST OF BELSHAZZAR.. 76
THE IMAGE OF NEBUCHADNEZZAR'S DREAM...................................... 94
THE FOUR BEASTS OF DANIEL 7...110
THE BEAST WITH SEVEN HEADS AND TEN HORNS................................131
ROME, THE SEAT OF THE PAGAN EMPIRE, GIVEN TO THE PAPACY.................138
CONSTANTINOPLE, THE NEW SEAT OF PAGANISM................................146
PIUS VI. TAKEN PRISONER...156
THE BEAST WITH TWO HORNS..164
SOME OF THE REFORMERS...194
THE DARKENING OF THE SUN AND MOON.......................................228
THE FALLING OF THE STARS..230

CHRONOLOGICAL TABLE.

	No. YEARS.	B. C.
Creation of the world		4004
Abraham called to go into Canaan	2083	1921
Covenant with Abraham, Genesis 17	60	1898
Isaac was born	1	1897
Promises renewed to Isaac	93	1804
Promises renewed to Jacob	44	1760
Jacob went down into Egypt	54	1706
Israelites left Egypt,—covenant at Horeb	215	1491
They ask for a king,—Saul is anointed	396	1095
David began to reign in Hebron	40	1056
Promises made to David and his seed	14	1042
Solomon built the temple	37	1005
The kingdom divided,—Judah and Israel	30	975
Kingdom of Israel (Samaria) entirely overthrown	254	721
Manasseh, king of Judah; carried captive to Babylon	44	677
Part of the vessels of temple, and some of the children of Judah, taken to Babylon, Daniel *et al.*	70	606
Nebuchadnezzar's dream interpreted	3	603
Zedekiah taken to Babylon, temple and city destroyed (Solomon's temple stood 417 years.)	15	588
Daniel's vision of chapter 7	48	540
Belshazzar slain; kingdom of the Medes and Persians	3	538
Alexander the Grecian overthrew the Persians	206	331
League between the Jews and the Romans	170	161
		A. D.
Jesus preached the gospel of the kingdom, Mark 1	197	27
Roman Empire divided	449	476
The Papacy established	62	538

NOTE.—For the convenience of the reader, the dates in this table are according to the chronology of the English Bible, Authorized Version. Any variation in correction of these dates cannot be so great as to affect the results. As the full year cannot always be given, there will be found an apparent discrepancy, but there is none in fact.

INTRODUCTION.

In this nineteenth century many books have been produced, with labored and scholarly arguments, to prove that the Bible is the word of God; that it is Heaven's revelation to man. And many have thought it necessary to spend much time in giving instruction concerning its authenticity, the measure of its authority, the degrees of inspiration of its several parts, etc., etc. But the Bible is a practical book; it must speak for itself. It is the word of the Spirit of God, and all the wisdom of man cannot add one whit to its force. Being practical, we should give instruction in it as we would in any other practical study. In teaching arithmetic we do not begin with essays on its study, or with evidences of its exactness and utility; but we begin with its elements, and lead the class through its problems, until they realize for themselves what it is, and what is its importance.

A recent writer in England said that Paley was an able man, as we all know that he was, and that he wrote an excellent book on the evidences of Christianity; but he did not think that Paley's writings were ever the direct means of converting a soul. Whether the statement is true or not, there is reason in this expression. People are not converted by dissertations about the Bible, but by the Bible itself; by its truths, its prophecies, and its promises.

It is a significant fact that no Bible writer or teacher ever entered into an argument, to prove that the Scriptures are true. Nothing of that kind is found in the Bible from the apostles or prophets. They stated their propositions or their message, and if the Scriptures sustained them that was the end of the matter. On this subject we have a notable example in the teachings of the Saviour. When the Sadducees thought to perplex him on the subject of the resurrection, he replied: "Ye do err, not knowing the Scriptures, nor the power of God." Matt. 22:29. The power of God is sufficient to raise the dead, and the Scriptures say he will raise the dead, and that is an end of the controversy. Philosophy and science may cavil and doubt; they have no right to reply when the word of God speaks.

In examining the teachings of the Scriptures, we would that the mind of every reader might be free from bias on one point of great importance. The idea has obtained to a considerable extent, that the different dispensations are separated by such impassable barriers that nothing can come over from one to another. And, connected with this is the obvious error that the worship in former dispensations was, comparatively at least, destitute of spirituality in both its rules and its methods; that they who lived in the dispensations preceding the present were bound in chains of legality, nearly if not quite deprived of the liberty of the children of God, which we so largely enjoy. And further, it is quite largely supposed that, before the time of the making of the covenant with the children of Israel at Sinai, there was great darkness and ignorance concerning God and his purpose toward man, as to what was required, and what were the riches of his grace.

It seems strange that such ideas should so largely obtain, when it needs but little study and reflection to convince any one that there are certain fundamental and material truths which are common to all dispensations. It needs not very much study of the Scriptures to be able to perceive that God revealed himself to man by his Spirit, by his angels, by dreams and by visions, in all ages. If we carefully trace those important truths which reveal the mysteries of godliness, which connect all dispensations into one harmonious whole, through the revelations of both the Old and New Testaments, there is little difficulty in understanding God's revelation of himself to man. In this way we may readily learn his purpose in the creation of the earth.

In regard to the inspiration of the Scriptures, it is evident that a revelation from God must be perfect, whenever and to whomsoever made. The words revealed to Adam, to Enoch, to Noah, were as truly the words of the ever-living God, as were the things spoken to Nicodemus or to Paul. The Holy Scriptures which Timothy knew from a child, were all given by inspiration of God; and in regard to inspiration we agree with Prof. Gaussen: "A word is from God, or it is not from God. If it be from God, it is not so after two different fashions." Inspiration is altogether a miracle, and is therefore beyond the comprehension of man—beyond the possibility of an explanation. "He who can explain a miracle can work a miracle." It is not the place of man to judge the word of God, but to reverently listen and obey.

If any have doubts about the ancients having the true spirit of worship, let them read the eleventh chapter of the letter to the Hebrews. It is enough that the patriarchs, the prophets, and the host of holy ones of old, are set before us as examples of the power of faith; as a "cloud of witnesses" to the certainty of God's promises; to the sustaining power of his grace through faith. That their faith was evangelical—that it took hold of the blessings of the gospel of Christ,—is proved by the fact that they endured afflictions, "not accepting deliverance, that they might obtain a better resurrection." Heb. 11:35. It is enough that Abraham is presented as "the father of all them that believe" (Rom. 4:11); that it is declared to us that "they which be of faith are blessed with faithful Abraham;" and that if we are Christ's, then are we heirs to the promises made to Abraham. Gal. 3:9, 29. It is enough that we, in these days, are exhorted to walk in the steps of that faith that our father Abraham had. Rom. 4:12.

Again, the book of Psalms is the devotional part of the Bible. It has ever been a wonder to the pious, to the tried and tempted, to the rejoicing saints, that in the Psalms there is something exactly suited to every phase of Christian experience.

There is indignation for offenses against the holiness of God, earnest confession, unrivaled penitence, thanksgiving for mercies, and triumphing in the hope of final salvation. How ardent the love, how rich the experience of the authors. May every reader, and the writer, of this, be able to say with a writer of the Psalms: "I will walk at liberty, for I seek thy precepts." Ps. 119:45.

From Eden to Eden.

CHAPTER I.

"IN THE BEGINNING."

There is but one source from which we can obtain correct information concerning the origin of the earth and its inhabitants. Thus it is written: "Through faith we understand that the worlds were framed by the word of God, so that things which are seen were not made of things which do appear." Heb. 11:2. And we learn that faith comes by hearing the word of God. Rom. 10:17. Science and philosophers have their acknowledged spheres, but they cannot reach to such a subject as this. Revelation alone can instruct us here. "In the beginning God created the heavens and the earth." Gen. 1:1. This is the rational and consistent view of the origin of things. It is thus that "the heavens declare the glory of God, and the firmament showeth his handiwork." Ps. 19:1.

Concerning the creation of this world, we read in Isa. 45:18, that the Lord "created it not in vain; he formed it to be inhabited." Accordingly, when the earth was completed, when it was fitted for the abode of man, and nature, animate and inanimate, was all prepared for his comfort and pleasure, God said to his Son (compare John 1:1-3; Col. 1:13-17; Heb. 1:1, 2.): "Let us make man in our image, after our likeness, and let them have dominion over the fish of the sea, and over the fowl of the air, and over the cattle, and over all the earth." Gen. 1:26.

Man was created upright. Eccl. 7:29. He was possessed of

rational capacities, of moral powers; but he must yet have an opportunity to develop a moral character. Powers and capacities may be conferred, but character can be formed only by the free action of moral agents. Unfortunately for Adam and for his race, he did not stand the trial; he fell from the gracious position in which he was placed by his Creator, and lost his dominion, for he lost his life.

God created the earth to be inhabited, but not by a sinful race, as we learn from his dealing with Adam after his fall. Sin could not be in the purpose of God; it was contrary to his nature. And it could not have an abiding-place in his creation without marring his purpose. As the Saviour said of the sowing of the tares: "An enemy hath done this." Matt. 13:28. And now, that God's purpose has apparently been frustrated, three ways present themselves, one of which must be pursued: (1) Relinquish his purpose to have the earth inhabited; (2) let Adam die, according to the penalty pronounced, and create a new race; or, (3) devise a plan for his restoration and redemption. The first would have been directly contrary to the object for which the earth was made; a complete relinquishment of the divine purpose. The second would have accomplished the object of creation, but it would have been contrary to the action of God in the gift already conferred. The gift was to man and to his posterity. The use of the plural noun in Gen. 1:26 proves this: "Let us make man . . . let them have dominion." And with this agree the words of Ps. 115:16, as follows: "The heaven, even the heavens, are the Lord's; but the earth hath he given to the children of men." And either of these ways, if adopted, would have been a surrender unto the being by whom sin was introduced into Paradise. The third was the only way in which God could maintain his honor, and carry out his original purpose. Man at the first was placed on probation; and therefore sin was possible, but by no means necessary. For if the necessity had been placed upon man to sin, his action would have had no character. To permit sin for a season, for the formation of the character of his creatures, finally bringing all to the test of the judgment, is perfectly consistent with the attributes and purpose of God. But to originate sin, or to perpetuate it, and give it an eternal habitation within the bounds of his government, would forever tarnish the glory of the Creator.

We must consider that God's love for the man that he had created was very great, and this would lead him to save man, if possible, from the ruin which he had brought upon himself. This was manifested in the wonderful plan that was devised for his redemption, and is shown in the constant long-suffering exercised toward the children of men.

The serpent beguiled the woman; she was deceived by his falsehood. Gen. 3:1-6, 17; 1 Tim. 2:14; Rev. 20:2; John 8:44. She was first in the fall, and her name was mentioned in the recovery. It was the seed of the woman, whose heel should be bruised by the serpent, and should bruise the serpent's head. This denoted that the serpent should wound the seed of the woman, and that he should receive a crushing, fatal wound in return. And it should be noticed, that this promise of the triumph of the seed of the woman was given before the sentence was pronounced upon Adam, thus placing him under a new probation, and, by this reprieve, permitting the race to be multiplied so that the work of redemption could be carried out in harmony with the purpose originally contemplated.

The book of Genesis, especially in the first chapters, is a very brief record of events. We cannot learn from them just how far Adam and his immediate descendants were instructed in the way of salvation; but we are led to conclude that they were well instructed, for angels continued to converse with them, and God revealed himself to them by his Spirit, as he did afterwards also to his prophets. Abel offered the same sacrifice that was required of God's people in all their services in after years. The New Testament says he offered by faith; he believed in the plan of redemption as revealed to Adam, and offered a sacrifice that proved that his faith embraced the offering of the Lamb of God. Enoch walked with God with such faithfulness and purity of life, that God translated him, making him a notable example to all generations of the righteousness of faith. But the record is so brief that we are left to draw conclusions from other scriptures—just, it is true, because inevitable—as to what was revealed to him, and what he obeyed, to develop a holy character.

Noah also offered sacrifices of the same nature, which showed his faith in the plan for the redemption of man. We know that God spoke directly to Noah, and through him warned the world of their great wickedness, and of the calamity which their sin was bringing upon them.

The assumption that in the beginning man was weak and ignorant—especially ignorant of the great moral truths which have been revealed in later ages—is an assumption without any basis, and cannot be correct. Man's relations to his Creator, as a moral agent, were created with him. In his fall we are all involved. To Adam was revealed the one only plan of salvation that was ever devised in heaven, through the seed of the woman—the Saviour of mankind. That the race is now in a fallen, degenerate state is abundantly revealed in the Scriptures. Paul says that the nations now wrapped in the deepest darkness, given to the most foolish idolatry, and addicted to the vilest practices, have been given over to this sad state because "they did not like to retain God in their knowledge." Rom. 1 : 18-28.

It must be noticed that the word "seed," in Gen. 3 : 15, does not refer to the posterity of the woman in general, but to some particular individual of her race. It was not true that her posterity in general was able to overcome the serpent, and to give him a deadly wound. That can only be effected by some one who, while he is indeed the seed of the woman, must differ very materially from the posterity of the woman in general.

CHAPTER II.

THE PROMISE OF GOD TO THE FATHERS.

When Adam transgressed the law of his Creator, he was driven out from the garden in which the Lord had placed him, and deprived of access to the tree of life. This was the carrying out of the sentence, that he should return to the dust from which he was taken. In this we see that Adam left no hope to his posterity; their only hope is in the help offered through the seed of promise. But the record in the third chapter of Genesis is so very brief that from it alone we could form no definite idea of the method of carrying out the divine plan of restoration. But we are not therefore left in the dark, in the book of Genesis, as to that plan. In the New Testament we are directed to certain promises made of God to the fathers, as the foundation of our hope. But not one of these promises is original in the New Testament. It only directed to them as they already existed. Thus Paul spoke before Agrippa: "And now I stand and am judged for the hope of the promise made of God unto our fathers." Acts 26:6. And thus again he wrote to the Hebrews:—

"And we desire that every one of you do show the same diligence unto the full assurance of hope unto the end; that ye be not slothful, but followers of them who through faith and patience inherit the promises. For when God made promise to Abraham, because he could swear by no greater, he sware by himself, saying, Surely blessing I will bless thee, and multiplying I will multiply thee. And so after he had patiently endured, he obtained the promise. For men verily swear by the greater, and an oath for confirmation is to them an end of all strife. Wherein God, willing more abundantly to show unto the heirs of promise the immutability of his counsel, confirmed it by an oath; that by two immutable things, in which it was impossible for God to lie, we might have a strong consolation who have fled for refuge to lay hold upon the hope set before us; which hope we have as an anchor of the soul, both sure and steadfast, and which entereth into that within the veil; whither the forerunner is for us entered, even Jesus." Heb. 6:11-19.

As the word of God is the sole foundation of all true faith, so is the promise of God the sole foundation of a good hope. According to the texts quoted from the New Testament, our hope rests on the promises made unto the fathers, but especially to Abraham, the chief of the fathers to whom the promises were made. Therefore if we desire to understand the unfolding of the divine plan for the recovery of a fallen race, we must go to the covenant that God made with Abraham.

In regard to these promises, we must come in contact with the three errors noticed in the introduction. To prepare the minds of the readers to appreciate the evidence of the scriptures which we shall now examine, we call attention to what will be found, fully disproving the erroneous ideas concerning the differences of dispensations, which have so largely obtained.

1. To the fathers were fully revealed the divine purposes; to them were given the promises which underlie the divine plan of restoration. It was by such means that Abraham saw the day of Christ, and rejoiced in it. John 8:56; Gal. 3:8, 9.

2. The writers of the New Testament clearly and continually teach that Abraham is the father of all who hold the faith of the gospel; that to him were given the promises on which rests our hope; and this, of itself, is sufficient proof that the several dispensations are not independent of each other, but there are essential truths coming down to us through them all, which are common to them all.

3. We are not to infer, because the Saviour did not appear in their days, but did appear in the beginning of this dispensation, therefore their faith was deficient in the elements of spirituality and faith in Christ, and that they did not enjoy the freedom which faith alone can bring. In Hebrews 11, we have a list of most remarkable instances of faith, set before us as examples, from Abel to the prophets, all before the advent of Christ. If it be said that they had to typify Christ in their sacrifices, but did not see him; we reply, that we do

not see him, but he is continually represented to us in ordinances. If it be said that they lacked the certainty in their faith that we possess, because Christ has now come, of which we have so good historic evidence; we reply, that thereby their faith is proved to have been purer and stronger than ours. They gave greater evidence of genuine faith than is given in this age, as they had not so much historic evidence to rest upon as we have. They rested only upon the word of God. Our faith is more like that of Thomas, who believed because he saw; but the Lord most highly commended the faith of those who believed without seeing. As for the genuine spirit of piety, it was abundantly shown in the experience of the fathers and prophets. As was said, the book of Psalms is the devotional part of the whole Bible.

Let us now examine the promises to the fathers, upon which, according to the Scriptures, our hope rests. In Genesis 12 we read:—

"Now the Lord said unto Abram, Get thee out of thy country, and from thy kindred, and from thy father's house, unto a land that I will show thee; and I will make of thee a great nation, and I will bless thee, and make thy name great; and thou shalt be a blessing; and I will bless them that bless thee, and curse him that curseth thee; and in thee shall all families of the earth be blessed." Verses 1–3.

Obedient to this call, he went into the land of Canaan, directed by the Lord, "not knowing whither he went" (Heb. 11: 8), and came to Sichem in the plain of Moreh. And the Lord said, "Unto thy seed will I give this land." Gen. 12: 7.

These promises embrace the following points: 1. The Lord would make of him a great nation. 2. In him all the families of the earth should be blessed. 3. The land should be given to his seed. In some form the same promises were often renewed. And the three points noted embrace all that the promises to Abraham contained. Chapter 13 says the Lord appeared to him again and said:—

"Lift up now thine eyes, and look from the place where thou art, northward, and southward, and eastward, and westward; for all the land which thou seest, to thee will I give it, and to thy seed forever. And I will make thy seed as the dust of the earth; so that if a man can number the dust of the earth, then shall thy seed also be numbered. Arise, walk through the land in the length of it and in the breadth of it; for I will give it unto thee." Verses 14-17.

Chapter 14 contains one most interesting fact, namely, that Abram paid tithes to Melchizedek, priest of the Most High God. How Abram came to understand the duty to pay tithes, or how he came to understand the character of Melchizedek, or in what light he held him, we are not informed. The writer of the book of Hebrews presents Melchizedek as the highest type of the Messiah, and no doubt Abram looked upon him in that light—as representing the seed of the woman who was to bruise the head of the serpent. In him, by faith, he saw the work of the Son of God, and he honored him accordingly.

Chapter 15 contains Abram's complaint that he had no heir, and the assurance from the Lord that he should have a son. He was instructed to prepare an offering of a heifer, a she goat, and a ram, a turtle dove, and a young pigeon. It is worthy of remark that these were samples of the beasts and birds that were required or accepted when the law of sacrifices was given to Abraham's descendants. This also shows that not only the purpose and the plan, but the unfolding and the fulfillment of that plan, were carried in one unbroken chain through all dispensations.

Abram, having pleaded with the Lord to accept Ishmael as his heir, was assured that he should have a son of Sarah, and he should call his name Isaac, and he should be his heir, and the promises made to him should be fulfilled in Isaac.

"And he said unto him, I am the Lord that brought thee out of Ur of the Chaldees, to give thee this land to inherit it." "In that same day the Lord made a covenant with Abram, saying, Unto thy seed have I given this land, from the river of Egypt unto the great river, the river Euphrates." Gen. 15:7, 18.

In every renewal of the promises, whether to Abraham, to Isaac, or to Jacob, the gift of the land always held a prominent place. In chapter 17 we learn that his name was changed from Abram to Abraham. The change was to indicate the enlargement of his blessing to the people. Other points in this chapter will be noticed hereafter.

ABRAHAM OFFERING ISAAC.

In chapter 22 is the account of the trial of Abraham's faith in the offering of Isaac. It was not merely the trial of his faith in the goodness and mercy of God in requiring such a sacrifice, or the trial of his fatherly feelings for a son whom he loved so dearly; it was a trial of his faith in the fulfillment of the promise that Isaac should be his heir—that in Isaac should his seed be called. But Abraham's faith stood even this test, and he was therefore called the friend of God.

We will quote a few more passages to show the prominence of certain points in the promises; to show in what light these promises were held by the fathers to whom they were given, and that the reader may have all the evidence before him.

When Abraham sent his servant to take a wife for Isaac, he said to him:—

"The Lord God of Heaven, which took me from my father's house, and from the land of my kindred, and which spake unto me, and that sware unto me, saying, Unto thy seed will I give this land; he shall send his angel before thee, and thou shall take a wife unto my son from thence. Gen. 24:7.

This servant was also a believer in God, and in the efficacy of prayer, as we learn from the record of his journey.

In chapter 26 we find the promise renewed to Isaac. There was a famine in the land, and Isaac went to Gerar, and thought to go down into Egypt. But the Lord said unto him:—

"Go not down into Egypt; dwell in the land which I shall tell thee of. Sojourn in this land, and I will be with thee, and I will bless thee; for unto thee, and to thy seed, I will give all these countries, and I will perform the oath which I sware unto Abraham thy father; and I will make thy seed to multiply as the stars of heaven, and I will give unto thy seed all these countries; and in thy seed shall all the nations of the earth be blessed; because that Abraham obeyed my voice, and kept my charge, my commandments, my statutes, and my laws." Gen. 26:2-5.

And when Isaac sent Jacob to his mother's kindred, because he would not have him take a wife of the daughters of the land, he said:—

"And God Almighty bless thee, and make thee fruitful, and multiply thee, that thou mayest be a multitude of people; and give thee the blessing of Abraham, to thee, and to thy seed with thee; that thou mayest inherit the land wherein thou art a stranger, which God gave unto Abraham." Gen. 28:3, 4.

As Jacob went on his way toward Haran, he lay down at night in a certain place to sleep, and he dreamed, and in his dream he saw a ladder.

"And, behold, the Lord stood above it, and said, I am the Lord God of Abraham thy father, and the God of Isaac; the land whereon thou liest, to thee will I give it, and to thy seed; and thy seed shall be as the dust of the earth; and thou shalt spread abroad to the west, and to the east, and to the north, and to the south; and in thee and thy seed shall all the families of the earth be blessed. And, behold, I am with thee, and will keep thee in all places whither thou goest, and will bring thee again into this land; for I will not leave thee, until I have done that which I have spoken to thee of." Gen. 28:13-15.

After Jacob's long sojourn in the East, he returned to Canaan, and he came to Luz, or Bethel, where the Lord had appeared to him in his dream, and there he built an altar. And again the Lord appeared unto him, and said unto him:—

"I am God Almighty: be fruitful and multiply; a nation and a company of nations shall be of thee, and kings shall come out of thy loins; and the land which I gave Abraham and Isaac, to thee I will give it, and to thy seed after thee will I give the land." Gen. 35:11, 12.

And yet again when Jacob blessed the two sons of Joseph, he said:—

"God Almighty appeared unto me at Luz in the land of Canaan, and blessed me, and said unto me, Behold, I will make thee fruitful, and multiply thee, and I will make of thee a multitude of people; and will give this land to thy seed after thee for an everlasting possession." Gen. 48:3, 4.

These are the promises which God made unto the fathers; and upon examination they will be found to contain the gospel in all its fullness. They are the foundation of the hope set before us,—sure and steadfast, because they rest upon the promise and the oath of the everlasting God.

CHAPTER III.

THE ABRAHAMIC COVENANT.

In Genesis 17 we find the promises which God made to the fathers taking the specific form of a covenant, of which circumcision was given as the seal. It was the token or sign whereby his children were to be distinguished from other people as a holy nation. "And the uncircumcised manchild whose flesh of his foreskin is not circumcised, that soul shall be cut off from his people; he hath broken my covenant." Gen. 17:14.

Now we have before us the three terms that cover the entire field of the covenant with Abraham; namely, the Land, the Seed, and the Token. We must trace these to their extent or full meaning in order to come to a complete understanding of the covenant. For the benefit of those who have never considered them as having any positive relation to each other in the gospel, we shall take them up in reverse order, examining first those which are to some extent accepted by all Christians.

1. THE TOKEN. The Lord said to Abraham, "And ye shall circumcise the flesh of your foreskin, and it shall be a token of the covenant betwixt me and you." Gen. 17:11. It is generally supposed that the great majority of the people of Israel understood the token of the covenant, circumcision, only in its most literal sense. But that may well be doubted. According to Heb. 4:1, 2, they who fell in the wilderness of Arabia had the gospel preached to them, though there are many who fail to discover wherein they could have understood the gospel. It is clearly revealed that they were taught the spiritual nature of the covenant with Abraham, and the real intent of circumcision. Thus it was said in Deut. 10:16: "Circumcise

therefore the foreskin of your heart, and be no more stiffnecked." And again in chapter 30:6, Moses said to them: "And the Lord thy God will circumcise thy heart, and the heart of thy seed, to love the Lord thy God with all thine heart, and with all thy soul, that thou mayest live." And many years after this, the same was spoken by the prophet: "Circumcise yourselves to the Lord, and take away the foreskins of your heart, ye men of Judah and inhabitants of Jerusalem." Jer. 4:4.

These scriptures show that the true intent of the ordinance was revealed to Israel; and no doubt all the faithful, devoted ones among them, all who searched to know the ways of God, well understood the subject, even as they saw the sacrifice of the Messiah in the daily offerings upon their altars; just as we see the body and blood of the Saviour in the Lord's supper. No one can doubt that Abraham understood the true nature of the covenant then made, and we are informed that he received circumcision as a seal of righteousness.

But in process of time, as traditions supplanted the word of God, and the fear of God was taught by the precept of men, Isa. 29:13, it is likely that they largely lost sight of the spirituality of the covenant, and regarded circumcision only in its outward sense.

The covenant that God made with Abraham has never been disannulled. It is the covenant of salvation from the effects of the fall. And, therefore, it is the plan for carrying out the promise made to Adam, that the seed of the woman should bruise the head of the serpent. He who does not see this relation of the Abrahamic covenant to the original promise of Gen. 3:15, reads it amiss. The token of that covenant remains, the true circumcision according to what God revealed to the children of Israel. The external has passed entirely away, as Paul said to the Romans: "Neither is that circumcision which is outward in the flesh; . . . circumcision is that of the heart, in the spirit, and not in the letter." Rom. 2:28, 29. In Rom. 4:11, circumcision is called both a sign and a seal. Therefore in Eph. 1:13, the apostle says: " Ye were sealed with that Holy Spirit of promise." Also in Eph. 4:30, he said: "Grieve not the Holy Spirit of God, whereby ye are sealed unto the day of redemption." And as it was said to Abraham, the uncircumcised shall be cut off from among his people, even so now. "If any man have not the Spirit of Christ, he is none of his." Rom. 8:9. He has not the true token or seal of the covenant; he shall be cut off.

An outward seal was given only to the males, but that distinction is put away with the passing away of the external. The true seal is applied to all, for "there is neither Jew nor Greek, there is neither bond nor free, there is neither male nor female; for ye are all one in Christ Jesus." Gal. 3:28.

That this part of the covenant with Abraham remains, in the sense in which it was spoken of by Moses and Jeremiah, no one denies. And the same may be said of the next point.

2. THE SEED. First we will notice Paul's application of that term. "Now to Abraham and his seed were the promises made. He saith not, And to seeds, as of many; but as of one, And to thy seed, which is Christ." Gal. 3:16. Some have said that the conclusion of the apostle is far-fetched, not truly in accordance with the letter of the promise. But we think not so. Whatever may be thought of the method of his argument, of his peculiar use of the grammatical number of the term, the conclusion itself is so evident that it scarcely calls for any argument. For a moment consider the similar expression in Gen. 3:15. It is here said that the seed of the woman shall bruise the head of the serpent; and no one stops for a moment to argue that this promise was not said " of many;" all perceive at once that it must be considered as spoken " of one, which is Christ." And likewise when it was said to David, "I will raise up thy seed after thee, which shall be of thy sons; and I will establish his kingdom. He shall build me an house, and I will establish his throne forever" (1 Chron. 17:11, 12), it is well understood that his seed to whom his throne shall be established forever, is Christ. Compare Luke 1:32, 33. In the promise to both Adam and David, the circumstances imperatively demand that the term "seed" be referred to Christ, and not to their posterity in general.

And so also in the case of Abraham. It is just as unreasonable to apply this word here to any but Christ, as in the other cases. But we are met with the objection that all the faithful are called Abraham's seed; that he is the father of all them that believe. True, but this gives the term one remove from its first, or first-supposed, meaning. Granted that it was for many generations mostly supposed to refer to Abraham's natural descendants only, and that it referred to all of them. Now it is readily seen that outward circumcision could not serve the purpose for which the seal was given; for, while it was said, "In Isaac shall thy seed be called," Ishmael and his posterity were circumcised, as well as Isaac and his children. The sons of Ishmael made the same boast, that they had Abraham to their father. And Esau, as well as Jacob, descended from Isaac.

The decisive fact on this point is this: Though all true believers are the children of Abraham, they are such only through Christ. "If ye are Christ's then are ye Abraham's seed, and heirs according to the promise." Gal. 3:29. If ye are not Christ's, then ye are not Abraham's seed—ye are not heirs. Christ is the true seed to whom the promises were made; he is the only one that can confer heirship; the only one who can constitute us the seed of Abraham. Being so constituted, we are "heirs of God," but only as being "joint heirs with Christ." Rom. 8:17. We are not natural heirs; we are heirs by adoption. Verse 15. We are brought nigh unto God by the blood of Christ. Eph. 2:13, 16. The promises to Abraham belong truly to Christ; he is the heir, and we, being united to him, are Abraham's seed and heirs of God. This point is quite beyond dispute.

3. THE LAND. While the truth concerning the other two points, the seal and the seed, are quite readily, or even generally admitted, it is quite as generally supposed that the gift of the land was a promise of temporary benefit, and that it was fulfilled to the literal descendants of Abraham, the twelve tribes of Israel. On this point it will be necessary to present several considerations, which clearly show that the promise remains to be fulfilled.

1. According to the argument in Hebrews, chapters 3 and 4, the land of Canaan bore the same relation to the true rest that remains to the people of God, that Moses and Joshua bore to Christ. As Christ was the prophet like unto Moses, Deut. 18:15; as he is the true leader of the Israel of God, to cause them to inherit the promise, as Joshua did in type; so the land of Canaan, temporarily possessed by the tribes of Israel, was but a type of the everlasting inheritance promised to Abraham and to his seed.

2. The promise of the land was not merely to the twelve tribes of Israel; it was to Abraham and his seed. We have seen that the seed to whom the promise was made is Christ; and it is a fact clearly set down in the Bible, that neither Abraham nor his seed, Christ, ever inherited the land that was promised to them. And therefore, if they do not inherit this land in the future, the words of Jehovah will be broken—a thing that cannot be contemplated for a moment. Of this Stephen spoke in his sermon: of Abraham he said that the Lord "gave him none inheritance in it, no, not so much as to set his foot on; yet he promised that he would give it to him for a possession, and to his seed after him, when as yet he had no child." Acts 7:5. So also it is written in Heb. 11:9: "By faith he sojourned in the land of promise, as in a strange country, dwelling in tabernacles with Isaac and Jacob, the heirs with him of the same promise."

So entirely was it true that he inherited no part of the land that was promised to him, that the only part of the land to which Abraham ever laid any manner of claim, was a cave and field in Hebron, which he bought from the Canaanites for a place to bury his dead. But this promise stands on record, as the unfailing word of Jehovah.

As with Abraham, so with his seed; Christ spent all his earthly life in the land of promise, yet himself declared that while the foxes had holes, and the birds of the air had nests, the Son of man had not where to lay his head. It is a fact, that after the time of his youthful subjection to his parents, he had no home. The coming of night found him at the homes of his friends in various parts of the country, or in the desert, or in the mountain, or over on the trackless sea. But on earth there was no place to which he could go and say he was at home. Yet he was the seed to whom the promise of the land was made, and the promise still stands in the Scriptures of truth.

Again, as we, believers in Christ, are the seed of Abraham, to be blessed with faithful Abraham, so says Paul, we are heirs according to the promise. Gal. 3:29. It is not a vain thing to be heirs of Abraham; he had a valuable inheritance by promise to bequeath to his children. Have the saints inherited the promise? No; they have not been superior in privileges to Abraham and to Christ. Jesus said to his disciples: "In the world ye shall have tribulation." John 16:22. And Peter said to his brethren, that they were strangers and pilgrims. 1 Pet. 2:11. And such they must be if they are partakers in this world with Abraham, the father of the faithful, and with the Lord Jesus Christ their example.

3. Another fact, proving that the possession of the land of Canaan was only typical of the true inheritance, is that Abraham is declared to be the heir of the world. Rom. 4:13. He and his sons, heirs with him of the same promise, "confessed that they were strangers and pilgrims on the earth." Heb. 11:17. Go where they would, they found themselves homeless; they had no inheritance here, but "died in faith, not having received the promises."

4. And as with Abraham, so with all his seed; they are all heirs of the world. Said Jesus, "Blessed are the meek; for they shall inherit the earth." Matt. 5:5. To inherit is to possess by heirship. The meek can inherit the earth only as being Abraham's seed, and heirs with him of the promise of the land—the earth. Jesus quoted this promise from Ps. 37:11, which contains a double promise, namely: "The meek shall inherit the earth; and shall delight themselves in the abundance of peace." Go to Hebrews 11, and learn whether this has been the lot of the meek in the present world. Ask the martyrs if in this world they delighted themselves in the abundance of peace. Ask them that have lived godly in Christ

Jesus whether they have inherited the earth with abundance of peace, or whether they had to suffer persecution. 2 Tim. 3:12. Tell us if Jesus did not speak the truth when he said that his followers should have tribulation in the world. But yet the promise stands, that the meek shall inherit the earth. Admit that the time is coming when Abraham, and Christ, and those who are his by faith, shall have a peaceful inheritance of the earth, and the Scriptures are clear, harmonious, and beautiful. And thus, and only thus, can the promises of God be verified.

5. Another and most decisive fact is, that the inheritance is to be redeemed. Circumcision was given to Abraham as a token, or assurance of the faithfulness of God to fulfill his promise. And thus Paul says of the true circumcision, the seal of the covenant: "After that ye believed, ye were sealed with that Holy Spirit of promise, which is the earnest [assurance] of our inheritance until the redemption of the purchased possession." Eph. 1:13, 14. Here are recognized, (1) our inheritance; (2) that it has been purchased; (3) that it remains to be redeemed; and (4) that we have the earnest of the Spirit to assure us that we shall certainly possess that inheritance. But from what is it to be redeemed? If our inheritance is just what the Scriptures say it is, namely, the earth, then the question is easily answered. It is to be redeemed from the curse which Satan was instrumental in bringing upon it. But if it is claimed that it is something else, or somewhere else, then we cannot conceive how the question can be answered. And this leads us to notice,—

6. That the misapprehension on this subject arises largely from the error of losing sight of the identity of the work of the seed of the woman, and that of the seed of Abraham; from overlooking the harmony and the unity of the divine plan for the recovery of that which was lost in the fall. "The seed," of Gen. 3:15, is identical with "the seed," of Gen. 12:7. Christ is the one individual referred to in both promises. It is Abraham's seed that shall bruise the head of the serpent; and the seed of the woman shall possess the land. What is said in either case applies also to the other. Now it is written

that the Son of God was manifested to destroy the works of the devil. 1 John 3:8. In order effectually to thwart the designs of the enemy of all righteousness, Christ must reverse every condition, and restore every loss, which resulted from the introduction of sin into Eden. By Satan's deception Adam was robbed of his innocency, by reason of which he transmitted tendencies to his posterity, and brought them under the influence of sinful surroundings. He brought a curse upon his dominion, so that the lovely earth which God pronounced very good, over the creation of which the morning stars sang together, and all the sons of God shouted for joy (Job. 38:4–7), was caused to bring forth thorns and thistles and poisonous weeds; and the animals which were made subject to man, have become wild and ferocious, and even man is the enemy of his fellow-man. The earth itself groans beneath the weight of its corruption and its curse, and the angels of Heaven weep over the triumphs of the enemy, temporary though they are. Shall Satan's triumph be forever? If so, then Christ died in vain; then were the promises made in vain.

Let us behold at a glance what was lost, and what must be done for its recovery.

Adam Lost	He Left Us	The Seed Must
1. His innocence.	1. Sinful.	1. Take away our Sin.
2. His Dominion.	2. Homeless.	2. Restore the Dominion.
3. His Life.	3. Dying.	3. Give us Life.

If there should be a failure in any of these points, then the failure would be complete, for just so far would Satan remain triumphant. But who could entertain the idea that God would suffer his purpose in creating the world to be forever frustrated by Satan? The angel said that Jesus should save his people from their sins (Matt. 1:21); and this, to the glory of his grace he is now accomplishing. And he has promised also to give unto his people eternal life (John 10:28); and this promise we all believe will be fulfilled. And he also said that the meek shall inherit the earth. Matt. 5:5. When all this is accomplished, then all the works of the devil will be destroyed. All that Adam lost will be restored by the seed of the woman; the children of Abraham shall inherit the promise; the inheritance shall be redeemed—that is, the earth shall be made new; the counsel of God shall stand; his purpose will be fulfilled; not a word of the Most High shall fail.

7. This is strongly confirmed by the following impressive fact. All admit that Christ bore the curse for man on the cross; "for it is written, cursed is every one that hangeth on a tree." Gal. 3:13. But it is not so well considered that there was a peculiar significance in his being crowned with thorns by the soldiers. They put a purple robe upon him, and a reed in his hand, thus signifying that he was a king. They also crowned him, but with thorns—the emblem of the curse put upon the earth. The curse was brought by the wile of Satan. And as they smote him with the reed, and drove the thorns into his brow, and the blood ran down his face, that blood drawn by the thorns, the curse of the earth, was the surety of the earth's redemption.

God made the world to be inhabited; he gave it to the children of men; and his purpose will not fail, for the children of men shall inherit and possess it forever, and shall delight themselves in the abundance of peace, when God shall make all things new. Rev. 21:1-5.

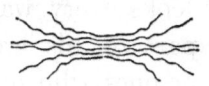

CHAPTER IV.

STEPS OF THE FAITH OF ABRAHAM.

"And Abram believed in the Lord; and he counted it to him for righteousness." Gen. 15:6.

AT first glance it might be thought one of the simplest things imaginable to believe the Lord; indeed, it might seem to be a proposition too monstrous to be entertained for a moment, that any people would not believe God. Nevertheless it is true that firm, unwavering belief in the word of God is very rare in the world. Ever since Satan instilled a spirit of distrust into the heart of the mother of our race, and led her to question the righteousness of God in defining her duties and her privileges, the human family have constantly manifested that same distrust, have ever developed that same spirit of rebellion against the word and appointments of God. And so deeply is this spirit inwoven into our natures that, while we stand astonished at the fact of this rebelliousness in the race, we ourselves live in the very atmosphere of rebellion, and our hearts are moved and our lives are fashioned by distrust.

When we consider the words of the apostle, that he that believeth not the record that God hath given, hath made him a liar (1 John 5:10), it looks every way just that God should require faith on the part of his creatures. And it seems strange that the self same ones who question the propriety of God's exacting faith in his word, consider it a grievous offense, worthy of all condemnation, for any to charge them with being liars. As if their names and their reputation were more worthy of respect than the name and word of the Most High!

But it is suggested that the Creator is so high, so exalted in his majesty and power, that we may well consider it unworthy of him, beneath his dignity, to exact belief and worship of feeble mortals. But his majesty and power, his exalted position as Governor and Judge of all, are the considerations that make it necessary that his creatures should have faith in him, and should worship him. The more exalted the Governor, the more extensive his government, the greater injury is done to the peace and welfare of his citizens if his authority is denied. When men refuse to worship God, it is because they desire either to exalt themselves in rebellion, or to transfer their allegiance to some object utterly unworthy of their esteem. Whatever may be the motive, its tendency is to anarchy—to the destruction of order and the rights of the people. All that God requires to the maintaining of his own honor and authority is for the security of justice and the welfare of his creatures.

There was a time when all the people of the earth had the knowledge of God. From the creation to the flood was one thousand six hundred and fifty-five years; of this period Adam lived nine hundred and thirty years, and until one hundred and twenty-six years before the birth of Noah. During this time lived Enoch—one of the most godly men that ever dwelt upon the earth, which shows that there were sincere and faithful worshipers of God in that age. Noah lived three hundred and fifty years after the flood, and Shem, his son, lived until Abraham was about one hundred and fifty years old; or, till about seventy-five years after Abraham was called into the land of Canaan. These things show how easily was the knowledge of God, and of the fact of creation, preserved for several thousands of years. Besides this knowledge being transmitted from a father unto his sons' sons, unto many generations, God was continually revealing himself unto his servants by visions, by dreams, by the visits of angels, etc. The flood did not come, and the Lord did not confound the language of the people, because of their ignorance. They did not sin ignorantly. These calamities befell them because, as Paul said, "They did not like to retain God in their knowledge," and, "When they knew God, they glorified him not as God, neither were thankful." Rom. 1 : 28, 21.

While almost the whole world were turning away from God, Abraham stood as a bright example, a very pattern of faith, reverently listening to every word that God spoke to him. In this respect he has scarcely been equaled in any age.

But faith is far more than mere consent; more than the easy acceptance of the statement of a fact. It is taking the word of God as an obedient and affectionate child takes the word of a loving father. It is the hearty acquiescence in the word of God, in every action and feeling. Such was the faith of Abraham. It was active and efficient in its operation. "Faith wrought with his works, and by works was faith made perfect." James 2:22.

While it is a truth clearly revealed that the blood of Christ cleanses from all unrighteousness, and it alone can cleanse from sin, it must also be true that we are justified by faith alone "for the remission of sins that are past." Rom. 3:24-28. Over past sins our future actions can have no influence. But not so in the formation of Christian character; not so in reference to our final salvation. Faith in the blood of Christ removes sin, and saves from its curse; obedience to the moral rule of right prevents sin. Inasmuch as Jesus came to save his people from their sins (Matt. 1:21), he came to put away sin (Heb. 9:26), it is evident that prevention as well as cure is incorporated into the gospel plan of salvation. Moreover, it is plainly stated that "to obey is better that sacrifice." 1 Sam. 15:22. And Jesus said they call him Lord in vain, and their faith in him is vain, who do not the will of his Father,—if they work iniquity, or, literally, lawlessness. Matt. 7:21-23. Eternal life will be given to them who patiently continue in well doing. Rom. 2:7. The same apostle who taught that we are justified by faith without works, in regard to past sins, also commanded us to work out our salvation with fear and trembling. Phil. 2:12. Another apostle said to the brethren: "Ye have purified your souls in obeying the truth through the Spirit." 1 Peter 1:22. This is what is meant by being sanctified through the truth. John 17:17. And all this fully justifies that expression of James—"Faith without works is dead." James 2:20. And yet, without faith it is not possible to please God (Heb. 11:6), for of ourselves we can do nothing. John 15:5. The grace of God through Christ is necessary in order that we may work to divine acceptance; and love to God is also necessary that our work may be acceptable Christian service as a "work of faith." 1 Thess. 1:3; 2 Thess. 1:11. And genuine Christian faith is a "faith which worketh by love." Gal. 5:6. And such a faith as this was the faith of Abraham. Of the relation of his faith Paul thus speaks:—

"And he received the sign of circumcision, a seal of the righteousness of the faith which he had yet being uncircumcised; that he might be the father of all them that believe, though they be not circumcised, that righteousness might be imputed unto them also; and the father of circumcision to them who are not of the circumcision only, but who also walk in the steps of that faith of our father Abraham, which he had being yet uncircumcised." Rom. 4:11, 12.

This is a very weighty text, fruitful of important considerations.

1. Circumcision was a sign or seal of righteousness. How different this statement from that of the multitude of theologians who assert that it was given as a means to keep the Jews a separate people from the Gentiles. It could not mark a line of separation between the children of Israel and the Ishmaelites and the descendants of Esau. And Paul declares that it was no sign at all to the unfaithful and disobedient. It was only a separating line between the righteous and the unrighteous. To Abraham it was a sign of the righteousness that he already possessed through faith. "All unrighteousness is sin" (1 John 5:17), or transgression of the law of God; "for sin is the transgression of the law." 1 John 3:4. Abraham had the righteousness of faith, but faith works by love, and love is the fulfilling of the law.

And this shows why the circumcision of the unbelieving Jews was of no value. Being given as a sign of righteousness, the sign signified nothing, if the righteousness were wanting. John says that righteousness is obedience, or the opposite of sin, and therefore Paul thus testifies:—

"For circumcision verily profiteth, if thou keep the law: but if thou be a breaker of the law, thy circumcision is made uncircumcision. Rom. 2:25.

That is, if you keep the law, or maintain the righteousness of which it was the sign, then it is profitable—it has a true meaning. But if you work iniquity, and have not the righteousness required in the law, then your sign becomes no sign; it signifies nothing, for everything is lacking which it was intended to signify.

2. He became the father of all them that believe, whether circumcised or uncircumcised, who walk in the steps of the faith of Abraham. This statement demands careful consideration.

Circumcision was given as the sign of righteousness. This righteousness was by faith. But in this, nothing avails but a "faith that worketh by love," and "this is the love of God that we keep his commandments;" and "love is the fulfilling of the law. From all this we are led to the unavoidable conclusion that the steps of the faith of Abraham consisted in obedience to the law of God; and these are the steps which we must follow to be his children indeed. And we are not left to merely draw conclusions, for on this point we have the most explicit testimony. Concerning the promises, the Lord said to Isaac:—

"Sojourn in this land, and I will be with thee, and I will bless thee; for unto thee, and unto thy seed, I will give all these countries, and I will perform the oath which I swear unto Abraham thy father; . . . because that Abraham obeyed my voice, and kept my charge, my commandments, my statutes, and my laws." Gen. 26:3-5.

We have shown that God's purposes toward man, both providential and gracious, were revealed from the beginning, and these purposes he has never changed. When man sinned and fell, then and there the Creator announced the plan of salvation which has been declared from that day to this; it has never been set aside—nor has other ever been devised. The promises made to Adam were fully explained to Abraham, as their fulfillment was to come through his seed, and these are the foundation and substance of the gospel for all ages. And it is equally reasonable, equally true, equally clearly shown in the Scriptures, that the law of God, the great moral rule of right, was also revealed in the beginning, and has been repeated from age to age, and has come down the same through all dispensations. It would be strange indeed if it were not so. Man's moral nature was conferred in his creation, and all his moral relations are a necessity of his nature. They have been neither augmented nor diminished since his creation. And the moral law is necessary in order to the development of character according to man's nature and relations. Where there is no law, says the scripture, there is no transgression; and it is equally true that where there is no law there is no obedience. Therefore without law there can be no character developed, either good or bad. If God had given man no law, he might just as well have made him an unreasoning creature, for he could have formed no more character than the brutes.

Noah was righteous before God, while the wickedness of the people was great, and the thoughts of their hearts were only evil. Gen. 6:5; 7:1. Lot also was righteous, while the men of Sodom were wicked and sinners exceedingly. Gen. 13:13. Of course Noah and Lot did righteousness, while the people around them transgressed the law of God; for they were sinners, and sin is the transgression of the law, and "sin is not imputed where there is no law." Rom. 5:13. But their sins were imputed to them. Peter says that the righteous soul of Lot was vexed with the "unlawful deeds" of the men of Sodom. 2 Peter 2:6-8. Abraham kept the law of God, even all his commandments. After speaking of the fact that all nations were to be blessed in him, Paul adds:—

"Christ hath redeemed us from the curse of the law, being made a curse for us; for it is written, Cursed is every one that hangeth on a tree: that the blessing of Abraham might come on the Gentiles through Jesus Christ." Gal. 3:13, 14.

In this scripture we notice these points: 1. Christ does not redeem us from the law, but from its curse; and the curse falls only on the transgressor. Therefore all who have an interest in the redemption of Christ, are amenable to the law of God, and are transgressors of the law. Christ came to call sinners to repentance. 2. This redemption is in order that the Gentiles, or all nations, may receive the blessing of Abraham. And this again proves that the curse of the law rests on the Gentiles. Some affirm that the Jews alone are amenable to the law, which is utterly absurd. All men are sinners; all have gone astray; when the law speaks, every mouth is stopped, and all the world stand guilty before God. Rom. 3: 9–19.

And we learn further in the scripture quoted, that they who are under the curse of the law, that is, who are transgressors of the law, cannot receive the blessing of Abraham. He received the blessing solely by faith, and no one can receive the same blessing except by faith. Christ alone can redeem any from the curse, and therefore faith in Christ alone can constitute us children of Abraham, and heirs of his blessing.

The same law that Abraham kept, was afterward declared to Israel at Sinai. The covenant with Abraham embraced these two main points, namely: 1. The promise of the land to him and to his seed. 2. The promise was given to him because he kept the commandments of God. In other words, the promises were conditional, the condition being the law of God. This we also find stated in the sacred record, as follows:—

"Be ye mindful always of his covenant; the word which he commanded to a thousand generations; even of the covenant which he made with Abraham, and of his oath unto Isaac; and hath confirmed the same to Jacob for a law, and to Israel for an everlasting covenant, saying, Unto thee will I give the land of Canaan, the lot of your inheritance." 1 Chron. 16: 15-18.

In these verses the foundations of the Abrahamic covenant are presented in brief. First, the condition; the law which he commanded to a thousand generations. Were this intended to mark a definite period, but a small part of it is yet expired; but it is probably indefinite, merely expressive of a vast or unlimited period. Secondly, the promise of the land, the lot of their inheritance. The law, the word commanded, is essentially distinct from the promise of the land. One is based upon the other.

There is in the whole Bible but one "covenant commanded," which the Lord calls *his covenant*, defined as follows:—

"And the Lord spake unto you out of the midst of the fire; ye heard the voice of the words, but saw no similitude; only ye heard a voice. And he declared unto you his covenant, which he commanded you to perform, even ten commandments; and he wrote them upon two tables of stone." Deut. 4:12, 13.

But here comes the objection, almost constantly persisted in, that this law was given to the Jews, and therefore we have no concern in it. But we have already seen that the word commanded to Abraham and Isaac was confirmed to Israel for a law, even an everlasting covenant. And the Scriptures give us complete, and of course the correct, views of the relation of those things committed to the Jews.

This law was indeed given to the Jews, and so were the adoption, and the glory, and the covenants, new as well as old (Jer. 31:31-34), and the service of God, and the promises. Rom. 9:4. For of a truth, "salvation is of the Jews." John 4:22. This was the advantage accorded to Israel, "that unto them were committed the oracles of God." Rom. 3:2. And the apostle further shows that their unfaithfulness and unbelief could not make void or of no effect that which was committed to them, for otherwise, how shall God judge the world? For he shows that it is when the law speaks that every mouth is stopped, and all the world stands condemned before God. Rom. 3:3-19. God had aforetime given the "lively oracles" (see Acts 7:38) by which he will bring every work into judgment, and every secret thing, whether it be good or whether it be evil. Eccl. 12:13, 14. Let us not slight those sacred oracles because they were committed to Israel, for Christ himself was of Israel according to the flesh. Rom. 9:5; 1:3; Acts 2:30.

But the things that were given to the Jews were not for them alone, neither were they original with or to the Jews. The new covenant was given to the Jews, and we must receive it through them; but it was given to Abraham long before their time. Gal. 3:17. Christ came of the Jews; but he was promised to the fathers, to Abraham, and to Adam from the beginning. Paul says that the service of God was given to the Jews; but it was given to many others before their day. The law was given to the Jews; but every item of it was given to the patriarchs—yes, to all the world, before it was given to the Jews. As before said, man's moral nature was given in his creation, and the moral law is but the complement, the necessary accompaniment, of his moral nature. Therefore the law was planted in the nature of man, and revealed to the head and representative of the race in the beginning. And thus Paul says, that the nations who had not the written law given to them as it was given to Israel, might yet do by nature the things contained in the law, because they had "the work of the law written in their hearts." Rom. 2:14, 15. In this same chapter the apostle shows that the secrets of men shall be judged by the same law of which he was speaking; the law in which the Jews rested, and in knowing which they knew the will of God. Rom. 2:17-23.

Of course we make a distinction between the moral and ceremonial law. To deny this distinction because the Scriptures do not use these terms, is not an argument; it partakes more of the nature of a cavil. The word probation is not in the Bible; shall we therefore deny the existence of the fact? The terms moral, morality, moral obligation, moral character, and moral agency, are not in the Bible; but who would argue from this that we do not correctly use these terms?

There is a wide distinction between moral and ceremonial or positive law. Moral law is fundamental or primary; positive law is secondary; having no force nor meaning without the primary. Take the law for the offering of sin-offerings: When an offering was brought to the priest it indicated that sin had been committed. If sin had never entered into the world, no sin-offerings would have been required. The offering was made necessary in order to forgiveness. So the relation is easily traced to its foundation. The offering indicated that sin had been committed; and the existence of sin indicated the pre-existence of the law; for sin is the transgression of the law, and where no law is there is no transgression—no sin. Hence the law of sin-offerings was given because another law, of another nature, had been violated. If that other law had never been violated, no sin-offerings would ever have been offered. The same principle is recognized at the present time, for those offerings were types of gospel facts. If sin had never entered into the world, there would have been no gospel; the gospel has the pre-existing law for its basis. Take away the law, and the gospel would be a nullity. It would be an offer of pardon without conviction. Thus it is easy to see that antinomianism is as absurd as it is unscriptural.

Look at the sermon of Peter on that Pentecost after the resurrection of Jesus. His message to those who were convicted of sin was this: "Repent, and be baptized every one of you in the name of Jesus Christ for the remission of sins." Acts. 2:38.

Repent of sin, and be baptized for its remission. Sin lies back of baptism—back of repentance; and the law lies back of sin. To ignore the law is to have a baptism without any foundation—without any significance. Now if there is no distinction between laws in their nature, then it would be reasonable and proper to command thus: Honor thy father and thy mother, for the remission of sins; Thou shalt not steal, for the remission of sins; Remember the Sabbath-day to keep it holy, for the remission of sins. Why is it not as correct to read them thus, as it is to command to be baptized for the remission of sins? Clearly because those laws are of another nature; they are moral laws, and required because their transgression is sin. But baptism is not a moral duty, and may therefore be incorporated into a system of remission. If baptism was a primary obligation, it would be required on its own account, as are the ten commandments, and then it could not possibly have any place in the gospel plan.

Ceremonial laws are made necessary by the action of man; moral law has its origin in the will of God, without any regard to human actions. Of this nature is every one of the ten commandments. And every precept was known before the days of

Moses. When the Lord told Cain that sin lay at the door, it was evidence that he knew the law; and this law certainly included the sixth commandment, which Cain broke, for he was condemned as a murderer. That crime could not have been imputed to him if there had been no law on the subject. Gen. 4:7, 10-12; Rom. 5:13. And when the Lord directed Jacob to go to Bethel, he said to his household: "Put away the strange gods that are among you, and be clean, . . . and I will make there an altar unto God." Gen. 35:2, 3. Here it was understood that they were unclean in the sight of God, not fit to approach unto his altar while the strange gods were among them. Jacob buried their idols in the earth. And the curse came upon Ham for the violation of the fifth commandment; Gen. 9:21-25; but if the law had not been known he could not have been guilty.

Numerous evidences are found in the book of Genesis that the people knew that adultery was sinful. When Abimelech would have taken Abraham's wife, not knowing that she was his wife, the Lord commanded him to restore her; and the king said to Abraham, "Thou hast brought on me and on my kingdom a great sin." Gen. 20:4-9. And when Joseph refused to comply with the immoral request of his mistress, he asked, "How then can I do this great wickedness, and sin against God?" Gen. 39:7-9. These are but a few of the evidences on this precept.

When the messenger of Joseph accused his brethren of stealing his cup, they offered proofs of their honesty towards him, and inquired: "How then should we steal out of thy lord's house silver or gold?" Gen. 44:4-9. See also chapter 31:19, 30, 32, 39. The transgression of the tenth commandment must precede the violation of the eighth, and it is as sinful to covet as it is to steal.

Nothing positive is found in the book of Genesis in regard to the ninth precept. That it was wickedly broken is a matter of record, for Joseph's mistress maliciously bore false witness against him. Likewise in the book of Genesis not a word is said concerning the sinfulness of taking the name of God in vain. But we find explicit testimony in Leviticus 18. Said the Lord to Israel: "After the doings of the land of Canaan, whither I bring you, shall ye not do." He then enumerated a list of abominable practices among which is the following: "Neither shalt thou profane the name of thy God;" and afterwards added: "For in all these the nations are defiled which I cast out before you: and the land is defiled; therefore I do visit the iniquity thereof upon it." Lev. 18: 3, 21–25. Profanity was sinful in the nations of Canaan; and because of it and their other sins, the Lord visited them in judgment. But it was as true of them as of others, that "sin is not imputed when there is no law." For God is no respecter of persons. This is further proof of what Paul teaches in Romans 3, that Jews and Gentiles are and were all amenable to the same law.

The evidence in regard to the sabbatic institution is most positive and clear. The Sabbath was not only known before the law was given on Mount Sinai, but it was distinctly enforced before that time. Ex. 16 : 22, 23. We learn that a double portion of manna was gathered on the sixth day, and on that day Moses said: "To-morrow is the rest of the holy Sabbath unto the Lord." The morrow was the seventh day of the week, and it appears from the language of Moses that it was already the Sabbath, before its arrival, and therefore by a previous appointment. When the Lord expressed his intention to give them manna, he declared as an object before him: "That I may prove them, whether they will walk in my law, or no." Verse 4. When some of the people sought for manna on the seventh day, the Lord said: "How long refuse ye to keep my commandments and my laws?" Verse 28. From all this it is very plain that the Lord had a law for the observance of the Sabbath before it was given on Mount Sinai. It was called the rest of the holy Sabbath unto the Lord. How it came to be the rest of the holy Sabbath, the commandment spoken by Jehovah himself informs us: "In six days the Lord made heaven and earth, the sea, and all that in them is, and rested the seventh day; wherefore the Lord blessed the Sabbath-day and hallowed it." Ex. 20 : 11. This transaction took place at creation,—before the fall of man. Unlike the ceremonial laws for sin-offerings, it was instituted before sin existed. The Sabbath is a commemorative institution; but it commemorates the work of God—not of man. It originated in the mind and will of God himself, and was not made necessary by an act of rebellion as even the gospel was. It was an original institution, as was marriage, and as such it would have existed and continued if man had never fallen. With what propriety, then, can men call it a Jewish institution? It is so called by many, but in direct contradiction of the Bible, which plainly says: "The seventh day is the Sabbath of the Lord thy God." Ex. 20:10. These are the words of Jehovah himself, and who dares to dispute his claim? He also said of the Sabbath that it is "holiness" to the Lord. Ex. 31:15; margin. By the mouth of the prophet he called it, "My holy day." Isa. 58:13. It was consecrated from the beginning, as the commandment says and the historic record proves: "And God blessed the seventh day, and sanctified it; because that in it he had rested from all his work which God created and made." Gen. 2:3.

Thus have we identified the holy covenant of God, his word which he commanded to a thousand generations; which was given to Abraham and to Isaac, and confirmed to Israel for an everlasting covenant. The violation of this law has brought the curse upon all the world, Jew and Gentile alike, from which curse we must be redeemed by the blood of Christ in order that we may inherit the blessing of Abraham. Gal. 3:13, 14. And being thus freed from its condemnation we must " Go and sin no more," and walk in the steps of that faith which our father Abraham had, that we may do his works and be his children in truth. John 8:33–39. Jesus, the seed of Abraham, says: " Not every one that saith unto me, Lord, Lord, shall enter into the kingdom of heaven, but he that doeth the will of my Father which is in heaven." Matt. 7:21. The will of the Lawgiver is found in his law, as Paul shows in Rom. 2:17–23. Without obedience to the law of God our faith is dead, and our profession of love to God is vain, " For this is the love of God, that we keep his commandments." 1 John 5:3.

CHAPTER V.

THE COVENANT WITH ISRAEL.

The seed of the woman, who was to bruise the head of the serpent, must be some one individual to be known as of Adam's race; but how should he be known? How could he be distinguished from others of the same race? The children of men soon spread abroad upon the face of the earth, and some means must be instituted whereby the promised One should be recognized, for it was necessary that faith must receive him, and his identity must be so complete that an impostor could not be received in his stead.

Of all the families of the earth, the family of Terah, of Mesopotamia, was chosen as the one from which the promised Redeemer should come. And of the sons of Terah, Abraham was chosen. The conquering seed of the woman was to be his seed also. And of the sons of Abraham, Isaac was chosen. And of the sons of Isaac, Jacob was chosen. And of the twelve sons of Jacob, Judah was chosen.

Inasmuch as the Ishmaelites and the sons of Esau were circumcised as well as the Israelites, and called themselves by the name of Abraham, it was necessary that special means be instituted to keep the latter separate from all others. Jacob was caused to go down into Egypt; and when the iniquity of the Amorite was full (see Gen. 15:13-16), his children, grown to be a large people, were brought back to the land of Canaan. They were forbidden to make any covenant with the nations of that land, or to intermarry with them; but were required to keep themselves separate from all people. On the way to Canaan the Lord made a covenant with them; it was not the covenant made with their fathers (Deut. 5:3); though it embraced the same purpose—the one great purpose—and required the same holiness. But it differed from the covenant made with Abraham, being based solely on obedience. That covenant is found in Ex. 19:5-8. From Mount Sinai the Lord sent a message to the people by the hand of Moses, in the following words:—

"If ye will obey my voice indeed, and keep my covenant, then ye shall be a peculiar treasure unto me above all people; for all the earth is mine; and ye shall be unto me a kingdom of priests, and an holy nation."

Moses laid these words before the people, and they answered with one accord: "All that the Lord hath spoken we will do."

The condition was something that he called *his covenant*. It was connected with obeying his voice. But as yet they had not heard his voice; thus far he had spoken to them only through Moses. But three days after that time, he spoke unto them with his own voice, in the hearing of the whole multitude. Moses, afterward speaking of this, Deut. 4:12, said:—

"And the Lord spake unto you out of the midst of the fire; ye heard the voice of the words, but saw no similitude; only ye heard a voice. And he declared unto you his covenant, which he commanded you to perform, even ten commandments; and he wrote them upon two tables of stone."

The covenant that was made was one of mutual promises; the ten commandments was the condition they promised to keep. On the part of the people the promise was one of unqualified obedience. On the part of God it was of blessings to be conferred in consideration of their obedience. That the blessings to be conferred were the highest known in the word of God, may be learned by comparing the Scriptures.

1. They should be a peculiar treasure unto the Lord. Christ gave himself for us, that he might purify unto himself a peculiar people. Titus 2:14; see also, 1 Peter 2:9.

2. They should be a kingdom of priests. "Ye also are built up a spiritual house, an holy priesthood." "But ye are a chosen generation, a royal priesthood." Equivalent to a kingdom of priests. 1 Peter 2:5, 9.

3. They should be an holy nation. "Ye are a chosen gen-

cration, a royal priesthood, an holy nation, a peculiar people." 1 Peter 2:9.

There are no higher blessings contained in all the promises of God, than are contained in these scriptures; and the things set before Israel, to be gained if they kept the first covenant, perfectly coincide with the choicest blessings in the gospel of Christ. All these were theirs *provided* they had done what they promised to do.

But did they keep their promise? Did they keep his covenant, and perfectly obey his voice? They did not. Very soon after this solemn transaction was ratified, they made a molten calf, and sacrificed unto it after the manner of the worship of the Egyptians. Not one of them fulfilled the perfect righteousness indicated in the condition. They were well described in that scripture before which the world stands convicted: "They are all gone out of the way; . . . there is none that doeth good, no, not one." Rom. 3:12, 19; Ps. 14:3.

Then another question arises: If that covenant was based upon obedience only, and had not faith incorporated into it as a means of pardon, then it could afford no salvation to any who violated it; for it is impossible for law to save its own violator. That is very true; it admits of no question, for we find nothing but obedience in that covenant. "If ye will obey." And the people said, "We will do."

Are we to conclude, then, that all were lost who lived under that covenant, because they were all sinners, and it contained no power of forgiveness? By no means. A consideration of a few texts of Scripture will make this point clear.

1. Our Lord Jesus reminded his hearers that circumcision was not of Moses, but of the fathers. John 7:22. It was a token, not of the covenant made with the twelve tribes of Israel, but, of the covenant made with the fathers. They were already the covenant children of Abraham,—under a covenant of faith and grace. Hence, when the law condemned them, the law which they had so solemnly promised to obey, they were turned back as their only refuge to the covenant with Abraham. Of this covenant the true seed of Abraham, Christ the Messiah,

was the appointed mediator. In this manner the law served to bring them to Christ. Gal. 3 : 24. As they only who are sick need a physician (Matt. 9 : 12), so must the sinner be convicted of his malady before he will apply to the great Physician for healing. And as by the law is the knowledge of sin, and by the law sin is made to appear exceeding sinful (Rom. 3 : 20; 7 : 13), nothing but the law can convince anyone of his need of a Saviour, and bring him to Christ for salvation. How inefficient, then, to lead to genuine conversion, are all proposed systems of gospel teaching which ignore the law of God.

2. That this position is correct, is proved by Paul in Gal. 3 : 16, 17, where he declares that "the covenant, that was confirmed before of God in Christ, the law, which was four hundred and thirty years after, cannot disannul, that it should make the promise of none effect. Compare with Rom. 5 : 20. There were many righteous, faithful ones, of whom Paul said the time would fail him to mention, who through *faith* wrought righteousness, out of weakness were made strong, not accepting deliverance when they were tortured, that they might obtain a better resurrection. Their faith was in every respect truly evangelical; and having obtained a good report through faith, received not the promise, but saw it afar off, thus confessing, as did Abraham, and Isaac, and Jacob, that they were only pilgrims and strangers on the earth. But not one was saved by virtue of the covenant made at Horeb; their faith was the faith of Abraham, whose children they were.

The object of this covenant is further shown in the system of types or ceremonies given to them. Immediately after the covenant was ratified with the children of Israel (Ex. 24 : 1–8), God called Moses unto him into the Mount, where he gave him the system known as the ceremonial law. At the first the Lord commanded Moses to take from the people an offering of various valuable articles, and therewith to make a sanctuary, that he might dwell among them. The definition of this word as given by Cruden is as follows: "A holy or sanctified place, or dwelling place of the Most High." This is correct according to the etymology of the word, and according to what the Lord said: "Let them make me a sanctuary; that I may dwell among them." Ex. 25: 8.

The sanctuary made by the children of Israel, under the direction of Moses, was a temporary or movable building, consisting of two rooms, the first called the holy, the second the most holy. In the first were a golden lampstand with seven lamps, a table of show bread, and a golden altar of incense. In the second or most holy was an ark containing the two tables of stone on which God himself had written his covenant, or law of ten commandments. And this was the only thing that was permanently kept in the most holy place. See 1 Kings 8: 9. The order for making the ark, including its description and use, or object, is found in Ex. 25: 10-22, as follows:—

"And they shall make an ark of acacia wood; two cubits and a half shall be the length thereof, and a cubit and a half the breadth thereof, and a cubit and a half the height thereof. And thou shall overlay it with pure gold, within and without shalt thou overlay it, and shalt make upon it a crown of gold round about. . . . And thou shalt put into the ark the testimony which I shall give thee.

"And thou shalt make a mercy seat of pure gold; two cubits and a half shall be the length thereof, and a cubit and a half the breadth thereof. And thou shalt make two cherubim of gold, of beaten work shalt thou make them, in the two ends of the mercy seat. And make one cherub on the one end, and the other cherub on the other end; of the mercy seat shall ye make the cherubim on the two ends thereof. And the cherubim shall stretch forth their wings on high, covering the mercy seat with their wings, and their faces shall look one to another; toward the mercy seat shall the faces of the cherubim be.

"And thou shalt put the mercy seat above upon the ark; and in the ark thou shalt put the testimony that I shall give thee. And there I will meet with thee, and I will commune with thee from above the mercy seat, from between the two cherubim which are upon the ark of the testimony, of all things which I will give thee in commandment unto the children of Israel."

But that was not the only place in the sanctuary in which the Lord said his glory should be manifested: we read as follows:—

"This shall be a continual burnt-offering throughout your generations at the door of the tabernacle of the congregation before the Lord; where I will meet you, to speak there unto thee. And there I will meet with the children of Israel, and the tabernacle shall be sanctified by my glory." Ex. 29: 42, 43.

"There was to be a continual burnt-offering at the door of the tabernacle of the congregation, or holy place, and the priests daily went into the holy place to trim the lamps and to burn incense. Ex. 30: 1-8. But, as Paul says (Heb. 9: 7), "into the second went the high priest alone, once every year."

The order of the service in the most holy place is given in Leviticus 16. Verse 29 says this service shall take place on the tenth day of the seventh month, and from the nature of the service that day was called the day of atonement. See Lev. 23: 27, 28. Lev. 16: 11-14 describes the manner in which the high priest was to make an atonement for himself with the blood of a bullock. Verses 15, 16, describe the making of the general atonement, as follows:—

"Then shall he kill the goat of the sin-offering, that is for the people, and bring his blood within the vail, and do with that blood as he did with the blood of the bullock, and sprinkle it upon the mercy seat, and before the mercy seat; and he shall make an atonement for the holy place."

This has reference to that holy place where the ark was; see verse 2; and before we read further let us inquire, Why was he to make an atonement for the holy place? Surely the holy place had given no offense. It was not capable of action, either right or wrong. The remaining part of verse 16, and verse 19, give us full information on that point:—

"And he shall make an atonement for the holy place, because of the uncleanness of the children of Israel, and because of their transgressions in all their sins; and so shall he do for the tabernacle of the congregation, that remaineth among them in the midst of their uncleanness." "And he shall sprinkle of the blood upon it with his fingers seven times, and cleanse it, and hallow it, from the uncleanness of the children of Israel."

Thus we see that the meaning of making an atonement for the sanctuary, or the holy place, is this: The sanctuary was defiled by the sins of the people, and as it was the place where God's glory dwelt, and where he met the priests in judgment for the violations of his law, it was to be cleansed from their sins, that their uncleanness might not remain before God,— before the throne of judgment. During the whole year the work of propitiation was to be carried on in the service in the holy place, but the tenth day of the seventh month was the day of judgment, when all transgressions of his people were to be removed from before the Judge. It was the most solemn of all occasions in the religious observances of the nation. The high priest was to enter upon this service only after special preparation. Had he gone into the most holy without this preparation, or had he gone therein on any other day than the tenth day of the seventh month, he would have died. Lev. 16:1-4. And the people well understood the importance of the success of the work of the high priest on that day. Had he not strictly observed the order given he would have died. Had he died therein, the sanctuary would have been doubly defiled; and as it was death for any but the high priest to enter there, they could have devised no means for his removal. In the event of any failure on his part, no atonement could have been made, and their sins would have remained before the seat of judgment. Everything connected with the service of that day was calculated to deeply impress upon their minds the following words of the Lord:—

"Also on the tenth day of the seventh month there shall be a day of atonement; it shall be an holy convocation unto you; and ye shall afflict your souls, and offer an offering made by fire unto the Lord. And ye shall do no work in that same day; for it is a day of atonement, to make an atonement for you before the Lord your God. For whatsoever soul it shall be that shall not be afflicted in that same day, he shall be cut off from among his people. . . . It shall be unto you a sabbath of rest, and ye shall afflict your souls; in the ninth day of the month at even, from even unto even, shall ye celebrate your sabbath." Lev. 23:27-32.

All that we have here described, both the sanctuary and its service, were typical. They were illustrations of the work of Christ; and to teach the manner of his priestly work was one great object of the covenant with Israel. The book of Hebrews is mostly an argument on the priesthood, both type and antitype. After noticing the great differences between the priesthood of Christ and that of Aaron, the writer says:—

"Now of the things which we have spoken this is the sum: We have such an high priest [such as he has described], who is set on the right hand of the throne of the Majesty in the Heavens; a minister of the sanctuary, and of the true tabernacle, which the Lord pitched, and not man." Heb. 8:1, 2.

And concerning the sanctuary on earth, and priestly service therein, he says:—

"Who serve unto the example and shadow of heavenly things, as Moses was admonished of God when he was about to make the tabernacle, for, See, saith he, that thou make all things according to the pattern showed to thee in the mount." Verse 5.

And again, discoursing especially of the work of Christ as our high priest, he says:—

"It was therefore necessary that the patterns of things in the Heavens should be purified with these; but the heavenly things themselves with better sacrifices than these. For Christ is not entered into the holy places made with hands, which are the figures of the true; but into Heaven itself, now to appear in the presence of God for us." Heb. 9: 23, 24.

The old covenant has passed away; the Aaronic priesthood has ended. As the first covenant was ratified or dedicated with blood (Ex. 24: 6-8; Heb. 9: 18, 19), and on the principle that a testament is of force after men are dead (verse 17), Christ shed his blood as the sacrifice of the new covenant (see Luke 22: 20), which made the covenant of full effect, and made all the sacrifices of the old covenant effective and their further use meaningless.

When Christ came to his own, and they received him not, but despised and rejected him, and finally delivered him to death, they fully demonstrated their unfitness to be the depositaries of God's holy law. Not only had they refused to let their light shine to the people around them, but they themselves rejected the light by crucifying the Author of it. But God was still gracious to the tribe of Israel for the father's sake. They were a disobedient and gainsaying people (Rom. 10: 21); but they were the children of Abraham, from whom the Messiah must come, and so the word of salvation through the risen Messiah must be first preached unto them. Acts 3: 26; 13: 46. The work of the gospel must begin at Jerusalem. It was written by the prophet that the new covenant was to be made with the house of Israel and the house of Judah. Jer. 31: 31. And by another prophet it was declared that the seventy weeks, which reached to the manifestation of the Messiah and the full confirmation of the new covenant, was appointed to that people. Dan. 9: 24-27.

But this state of things was to continue only until the covenant was confirmed and offered to Israel. God had from the first included all mankind in the plan of salvation. His promise to Abraham was that in him all families of the earth should be blessed. Upon the lineal descendants of Abraham he bestowed the high honor of being the depositaries of his truth—of being that people who should carry the light to the world, and around whom the faithful should gather. In every age all who wished to might come into covenant relation with God. But the Jews were unfaithful to the trust committed to them. They not only neglected to carry the light to others, but they themselves rebelled against God. Even after they had, by severe captivity, been turned from idolatry, and had made a strict profession, they took away the key of knowledge, and would not enter into the kingdom themselves, nor suffer others to. It was because of this disposition that God cut them off. He bore long with them, but could not suffer them always to stand in the way of his plan to send the truth to all the world. In accordance with the promise, the Messiah came to them, and the gospel was first preached to them, that they might have one more opportunity to fulfill their mission. But they neglected Christ and the gospel, and so the kingdom was given to a nation that should bring forth the fruits thereof. Others received the word gladly, and proclaimed it to the ends of the earth. And so now, as was designed from the beginning, all who exercise faith in Christ are Abraham's seed, and heirs according to the promise. Gal. 3:26-29.

CHAPTER VI.

AN IMPORTANT QUESTION SETTLED.

Jesus was on his way into Galilee, and as he came to Sychar, being weary, he sat down by Jacob's well. A woman of Samaria came to draw water, and she was surprised when the stranger, whom she perceived to be a Jew, asked her to give him water to drink. The Samaritans were a mixed people, and had introduced the practices of their several nations into their worship. 2 Kings 17: 24-41. Therefore the two nations were at variance, and the Jews had "no dealings with the Samaritans." In her conversation with Jesus, the woman soon discovered that he was no ordinary man; and when he, a Jew, and an entire stranger, showed to her that her life was known to him, she confidently declared that he was a prophet. And then there immediately arose to her mind a question that had long vexed the people, and she said:—

"Our fathers worshiped in this mountain, and ye say, that in Jerusalem is the place where men ought to worship." John 4: 20.

This was a declaration intended as a question. The woman had shared in the anxiety of the godly of her nation, to have this question settled. As a question Jesus received it, and in reply he laid down a principle which corrected the erroneous ideas of both parties, both Jews and Samaritans. But in defining this principle he did not set aside any facts which had been developed concerning the plan of salvation. He very distinctly declared that "salvation is of the Jews." Not that the Jews were better than other people, or that they needed salvation more than other people, or that they of themselves had anything to confer on other people which was necessary to salvation. But it was necessary in the development of God's promise to Abraham that his posterity should be kept a separate people, for the manifestation of Messiah to the world, and salvation by Abraham's seed must come through them. Paul, speaking of the Israelites, said:—

"To whom pertaineth the adoption, and the glory, and the covenants, and the giving of the law, and the service of God, and the promises; whose are the fathers, and of whom as concerning the flesh Christ came." Rom. 9:4, 5.

All the things here enumerated were committed to them, and whosoever partakes of these blessings must receive them as coming through that channel. To them were committed the oracles of God. Rom. 3:1, 2. And not for their own sakes alone were these oracles committed to them. Stephen, in that memorable sermon which cost him his life, said that Moses, who stood in behalf of the people, "received the lively oracles to give unto us." Acts 7:38. But these facts do not exhaust the subject, nor do they make necessary the perpetuation of the forms and ceremonies which were given to them. As has been seen, the great object of the hope of the people of Israel was the manifestation of the Messiah to the world, and the law of ceremonies was to illustrate his work; but the Messiah having come, the time had arrived when the principle above referred to could be declared. Therefore Jesus answered the woman of Samaria thus:—

"The hour cometh, when ye shall neither in this mountain, nor yet at Jerusalem, worship the Father." John 4:21.

He certainly did not mean that the Father should not be worshiped in those places; but he did mean that it was not necessary to go to those places to worship the Father, for thus he continued:—

"But the hour cometh, and now is, when the true worshipers shall worship the Father in spirit and in truth; for the Father seeketh such to worship him. God is a Spirit, and they that worship him must worship him in spirit and in truth." John 4:21, 23.

And this was the settlement of the question thus far; the worship of God is no longer to be considered a matter of localities, nor of nationalities. In all places, and by all peoples, he may be worshiped to acceptance, wheresoever and by whomsoever he is worshiped in spirit and in truth.

But in the minds of some, the question may arise: How can it be that this is not a question of nationalities, if it remains true that salvation is of the Jews? Now whatever shape this query may assume, we must continue to insist that salvation is of the Jews, for the facts in reference to them can never be set aside. The Messiah came of them, and the new covenant was made with them, according to the promise. But as Jerusalem has ceased to be the special place where the Father must be worshiped, their national system must also of necessity have ceased, for they could present their offerings in no place but Jerusalem. Lev. 17: 1-6.

No one who believes the gospel will dispute the fact that that covenant has passed away. But we must always bear in mind that, as the making of that covenant did not annul the covenant with Abraham, so its abolition had no effect upon anything that was peculiar to the Abrahamic covenant. That covenant stands secure.

And inasmuch as their covenant has passed away, and their national system of worship is abolished, and Jerusalem is no longer the place where men must go to worship the Father, we cannot possibly believe that any special promises or blessings are in reserve for the Jews as a nation; neither promise nor blessing remains for them, except such as are common to all the children of Abraham by faith in Christ. And they can inherit the promises on the same condition and in the same manner that other children of Abraham shall inherit them, and in no other. We will notice some of the facts which lead us to this conclusion.

1. The declaration of Jesus, already referred to, that that arrangement has passed away by which Jerusalem was made a special place of worship, involves the abolition of their national system of worship. To restore this system would be a transgression against the gospel, according to the principle stated by Paul in Gal. 2: 18.

2. The promise that the new covenant should be made with

Judah and Israel, has been fulfilled. The covenant was made and confirmed in the blood of Christ, and by the preaching of Christ and his apostles. But the confirmation of the new covenant was the opening of the gospel to the Gentiles, and it placed all on an equality, making but one body of Jews and Gentiles. See Eph. 3: 6.

3. And this leads us to notice that the house of Israel and the house of Judah were in Palestine when the covenant was made. The promises of the restoration of Israel to their own land were twofold: (1.) Those which were made to the tribes of Israel, the children of Abraham according to the flesh, referring to their restoration after the Babylonian captivity. These have been fulfilled. It is nothing to the purpose that they who claim that literal Israel will be restored again to Palestine, quote a great many prophecies; but the truth depends, not in the number of texts quoted, but in the correct application of them. It is of no possible avail to quote scripture unless it is correctly applied. We mean no disrespect to any, but illustrate our remark by referring to the fact that Satan himself quoted the scriptures correctly, but that which he quoted had no reference to that time or occasion. The Saviour repulsed him by quoting texts which had an application then and there. We will briefly notice some of the evidences that the twelve tribes were there when the new covenant was made.

a. The prophets, except Malachi, all wrote between the years 534 and 800 B. C. The decree of Cyrus for the return of the children of Israel was made in B. C. 536, and that of Artaxerxes in 457. Hence, there is no chronological necessity for referring to any future time or event, those prophecies which speak of their returning to Palestine. In truth the whole weight of chronology is against that view.

b. The decree of Cyrus was liberal, and was proclaimed throughout all his realm. He said:—

"Who is there among you of all his people? his God be with him and let him go up to Jerusalem." "And whosoever remaineth in any place where he sojourneth, let the men of his place help him with silver, and with gold, and with goods, and with beasts." Ezra. 1: 1-4.

Artaxerxes, in his decree, said:—

"I make a decree, that all they of the people of Israel, and of his priests and Levites, in my realm, which are minded of their own free will to go up to Jerusalem, go with thee." Ezra 7:13.

Further, that the prophecies referred to a restoration from the captivity in Babylon, is proved in the most positive terms:—

"For thus saith the Lord, That after seventy years be accomplished at Babylon I will visit you, and perform my good word toward you, in causing you to return to this place. . . . I will turn away your captivity, and I will gather you from all the nations, and from all the places whither I have driven you, saith the Lord; and I will bring you again into the place whence I caused you to be carried away captive." Jer. 29:10-14.

While many declare that ten tribes were lost, and never returned from the captivity of Babylon, the word of God declares that he gathered them from all nations and from all places whither he had scattered them. We cannot reject the word of God, and therefore cannot receive the theory of those who teach that they were not returned. Of the time of their restoration there can be no doubt, for the Lord said it should be after seventy years were accomplished at Babylon.

c. It is assumed that only two tribes returned from that captivity, and that ten tribes were dispersed and lost. But that is only an assumption, for which there is no shadow of foundation in fact. The Persian empire, in the days of Ahasuerus, was divided into one hundred and twenty-seven provinces (Esther 1:1); and the Israelites were scattered throughout the empire; and the decree for their defense and deliverance from the malice of Haman went to every province in the empire. Esther 9:17. The decree of Cyrus for their return was proclaimed throughout his whole realm. Artaxerxes, also, addressed his decree to all the people of Israel in all his kingdom. All returned who were willing to return. And they were not hindered by reason of any disability on their own part, for the king commanded the people to assist them with money, goods, and beasts. Thus did the Lord, in his providence, make every provision for the fulfillment of his promise. There is no promise that he would bring them back against their will.

d. Although critics mostly discredit the statement of Josephus in regard to the origin of the Septuagint, it seems that his testimony is entitled to more consideration than is generally given to it, inasmuch as their objections are solely of a critical, and not at all of a historical, nature; while he sets it down as a historical fact, even giving the very words of the correspondence between the parties. He says that Ptolemy Philadelphus sent a request to the Jews to send six men out of every tribe for the purpose of translating the law into the Greek. When they were sent, word was returned to Ptolemy thus: "We have chosen six men out of every tribe, whom we have sent, and the law with them." He says that seventy-two were sent, seventy being engaged in the work, from which number of translators the name of the Version is derived. Thus twelve tribes were represented. See Josephus' Antiquities, B. 12, chap. 2, sec. 4-7.

e. This evidence of the presence of the twelve tribes is corroborated by the Scriptures. That the tribe of Levi was represented in the return from the captivity is evident, for all the priests and servants of the temple were of that tribe. Of the priests alone, of the family of Aaron, Ezra gives the number who returned to Palestine under the decree of Cyrus, 4,289. Ezra 2:36-39. And he further says:—

"So the priests, and the Levites, and some of the people, and the singers, and the porters, and the Nethinim, dwelt in their cities, and all Israel in their cities." Ezra 2:70. "And when the seventh month was come, and the children of Israel were in their cities, the people gathered themselves as one man to Jerusalem." Ezra 3:1; Neh. 7:73.

And most decisive is the testimony of Ezra concerning the dedication of the temple, built after the return from Babylon.

"And the children of Israel, the priests, and the Levites, and the rest of the children of the captivity, kept the dedication of this house of God with joy; and offered at the dedication of this house of God an hundred bullocks, two hundred rams, four hundred lambs; and for a sin-offering for all Israel, twelve he goats, according to the number of the tribes of Israel." Ezra 6:16, 17. "The children of those that had been carried away, which were come out of the captivity, offered burnt-offerings unto the God of Israel, twelve bullocks for all Israel, ninety and six rams, seventy and seven lambs, twelve he goats for a sin-offering." Ezra 8:35.

If ten tribes were absent, it is truly strange that no mention was made of it, when a sin-offering was made for the twelve tribes; for "all Israel" which dwelt in their cities. And is it not strange that people will persist in setting forth the idea that all Israel were not in their cities, when the proof is so strong that they were, and not a hint in all the Scriptures to the contrary?

There is also another class of promises concerning the gathering of Israel, but these are not spoken of "Israel after the flesh," but, of the true Israel, who are the seed of Abraham by faith in Jesus Christ. These promises are found in both the Old and New Testaments. Thus spoke the Lord:—

"And it shall come to pass in that day, that the Lord shall beat off from the channel of the river unto the stream of Egypt, and ye shall be gathered one by one, O ye children of Israel. And it shall come to pass in that day, that the great trumpet shall be blown, and they shall come which were ready to perish in the land of Assyria, and the outcasts in the land of Egypt, and shall worship the Lord in the holy mount at Jerusalem." Isa. 27:12, 13.

With this compare the words of the Saviour:—

"And then shall appear the sign of the Son of man in heaven; and then shall all the tribes of the earth mourn, and they shall see the Son of man coming in the clouds of heaven with power and great glory. And he shall send his angels with a great sound of a trumpet, and they shall gather together his elect from the four winds, from one end of heaven to the other." Matt. 24:30, 31.

The time of the gathering of the elect of God is fixed by these words of the Saviour; it will take place at his coming. He shall send his angels with a great sound of a trumpet to gather them,—when the great trumpet shall be blown, as Isaiah says. Compare 1 Cor. 15:51-54; 1 Thess. 4:16, 17. With these agree the following words of the apostle:—

"Now we beseech you, brethren, by the coming of our Lord Jesus Christ, and by our gathering together unto him." 2 Thess. 2:1.

But one may inquire, Can the gathering of the elect, the Israel of God by faith, at the coming of Christ, consistently be called the gathering and the return of Israel unto their own land? Most assuredly it can; and it is so called by the express word of the Lord himself. That the resurrection of the just will take place at the coming of Christ, all will admit. Then we read the following:—

"Prophesy and say unto them, Thus saith the Lord God: Behold, O my people, I will open your graves, and cause you to come up out of your graves, and bring you into the land of Israel. And ye shall know that I am the Lord, when I have opened your graves, O my people, and brought you up out of your graves, and shall put my Spirit in you, and ye shall live, and I shall place you in your own land; then shall ye know that I the Lord have spoken it, and performed it, saith the Lord." Eze. 37:12-14.

The opening of the graves of all Israel shall take place "when Christ, who is our life, shall appear." It is his voice that will raise the dead. When the Son of man comes, the great trumpet will be blown, and the elect of God will be gathered from the four quarters of the earth. This is the only gathering of Israel that remains to be fulfilled. And, all ye saints of God, partakers of the faith of your father Abraham, rejoice, for that day is near to come, and the angels will gather every one who, by living faith, is united to Christ, the heir of the promise.

4. The whole nation of Israel broke the covenant made with them at Horeb, by which means they forfeited all blessings promised to them under it. And for this reason that covenant was entirely done away. Jer. 31:31-34; Heb. 8:6-12. It is a manifest absurdity to say that they have any claim to promises under a covenant that was abolished because they had forfeited all rights under it.

5. It must be admitted that if the Israelites have any claim to the fulfillment of special promises, or if special blessings remain to be conferred upon them, by virtue of the covenant made at Horeb, then the abolition of that covenant was derogatory to their rights and privileges. If there are unfulfilled promises and national rights still existing under that covenant, then it should not have been abolished until these were honored. That is to say, that they who teach that the Jews have national rights and special privileges by virtue of that covenant, virtually charge God with the injustice of abolishing an instrument in which their rights were vested. But if there was no injustice done to them in abolishing that covenant—if they had no claim under it when it was abolished; if they had forfeited all the promises in that covenant by disobedience,—from

what source have they derived the rights and privileges which are now claimed for them? We confidently affirm that the whole Judaizing system is as contrary to the principles of justice as it is to the facts of the Bible; it is as unreasonable as it is unscriptural.

6. This conclusion may not be evaded by saying that the promises to be fulfilled to them as a nation, are not matters of rights that they can claim, but of gracious promises which the Lord made to them. But the covenant at Horeb was based solely on obedience, as has been shown; and when they disobeyed, the promises were a nullity, for the covenant itself was made void. See Heb. 8: 8, 9:—

"Behold, the days come, saith the Lord, when I will make a new covenant with the house of Israel and with the house of Judah: not according to the covenant that I made with their fathers, in the day when I took them by the hand to lead them out of the land of Egypt; because they continued not in my covenant, and I regarded them not, saith the Lord."

God had said that they would be a peculiar treasure above all people and a holy nation, if they would obey. But they did not obey, and he regarded them not. There is no work of grace for any people except in the gospel, and the gospel is not national. But two covenants were made with Judah and Israel—the covenant at Horeb, and the new covenant. But the first is done away, and in the second there is no national work of grace known; and it is by faith alone that the promises of the new covenant may be inherited.

7. Nor can it be said that the promises will be fulfilled to the Jews as a nation, by their turning to Christ, and accepting him as the Messiah and their Saviour; for in Christ all are on an equality. When the apostle Paul said: "And if ye are Christ's then are ye Abraham's seed, and heirs according to the promise," he also said: "For ye are all the children of God by faith in Christ Jesus. . . . There is neither Jew nor Greek, there is neither bond nor free, there is neither male nor female; for ye are all one in Christ Jesus." Gal. 3: 26-29. It is in respect to this very point of being Abraham's seed, and heirs according to the promise, that all national distinctions and privileges are

obliterated. For he says in another place: "That the Gentiles should be fellow heirs, and of the same body, and partakers of his promise in Christ by the gospel." Eph. 3:6. See also Eph. 2: 11–19; Matt. 3: 9; John 8:38–44.

In all this it is not denied that there were conditions made to Israel in the covenant at Horeb, and by the mouths of the prophets, which were never fulfilled. But the scriptures herein quoted show that by their transgressions they forfeited the blessings expected, so that their bestowment was impossible. The only promises now remaining to be fulfilled to the children of men are those set forth to Adam, found in Gen. 3, and fully presented in the covenant with Abraham. Not to be fulfilled to any people by reason of their natural descent, but to all of all nations who are Abraham's seed by faith in Christ.

Conditional promises were given to them by Ezekiel, especially in the latter chapters of his book; but the conditions were not regarded, and of course they could no more be fulfilled than those noticed. So the Lord promised to bring the Israelites, who were suffering in Egypt, into the land of Canaan. But the whole generation, with barely two exceptions, fell in the wilderness because of their unbelief and rebellion. For an illustration of God's method of dealing with the subjects of his promises, take the case of Eli. The Lord sent this message to him:—

"I said indeed that thy house, and the house of thy father, should walk before me forever; but now the Lord saith, Be it far from me; for them that honor me I will honor, and they that despise me shall be lightly esteemed." 1 Sam. 2:30.

The principle upon which the Lord acted towards the Jews is set forth in Jer. 18: 7--10.

"At what instant I shall speak concerning a nation, and concerning a kingdom, to pluck up, and to pull down, and to destroy it; if that nation, against whom I have pronounced, turn from their evil, I will repent of the evil that I thought to do unto them. And at what instant I shall speak concerning a nation, and concerning a kingdom, to build and to plant it; if it do evil in my sight, that it obey not my voice, then I will repent of the good, wherewith I said I would benefit them."

Now to Israel the Lord said he had all the day long stretched out his hands to a disobedient and gainsaying people. And as he spoke by the mouth of Jeremiah, so will he do by Israel, and by all people. The Lord Jesus said directly to the Jews: "The kingdom of God shall be taken from you, and given to a nation bringing forth the fruits thereof." Matt. 21:43. The words of the forerunner of Christ to the Jews were: "Think not to say within yourselves, We have Abraham to our father; for I say unto you, that God is able of these stones to raise up children unto Abraham." Matt. 3:9. It is not accident of birth which finds favor with God, it is not because of honored ancestors that his blessing abides with us. He prizes above all things "the upright heart and pure," and his blessing abides with those whose characters are forming by faith in Jesus Christ according to his revealed will. And all will find their labor vain who try to make void the word of the Lord.

CHAPTER VII.

THE KINGDOM AND THE KING.

God made the earth to be inhabited by the children of men. Isa. 45:18; Ps. 115:16. When the intention was expressed to make man, it was said: "And let them have dominion over the fish of the sea, and over the fowl of the air, and over the cattle, and over all the earth, and over every creeping thing that creepeth upon the earth." Gen. 1:26. More may have been implied than is here expressed. There is order in Heaven; some are appointed to higher stations than others, but all is harmony, for all delight to do the will of their Creator. When the earth is freed from the curse, there will be different orders among the children of men. Rev. 21:24. How natural to suppose that, had Adam remained innocent, as the earth was filled with his posterity, great respect would always have been shown to him, the head of the race. But now that glory and honor will be borne by the second Adam.

In addition to the gift of the land, and the blessing of the nations, the Lord said to Abraham: "And kings shall come out of thee." Gen. 17:6. The same words were repeated to Jacob. Gen. 35:11. And the idea of royalty is incorporated into the covenant at Horeb. "Ye shall be unto me a kingdom of priests." Ex. 19:6.

In the days of Samuel the prophet the people asked for a king. The motive that actuated them was not good; they wanted a king that they might be like all the nations. 1 Sam. 8:19, 20. The Lord had given directions for their conduct, with a view to keeping them separate from, and unlike, the nations. He was their ruler, their guide, and protector. Doubtless the heathen who knew not God, held them in derision because they had no king, no visible ruler; and this may have had an ill effect upon them. But God, while he disapproved of their request, listened to them, only reserving to himself the right to choose their king for them. He did not resign the right to rule over them; he was still their actual sovereign, guiding and directing their kings in the government of the kingdom.

Samuel was directed to anoint Saul, the son of Kish, of the tribe of Benjamin. When Saul had reigned sixteen years, he disobeyed the word of the Lord, who had before appointed Amalek to utter destruction for their sins. Ex. 17: 8-14; Deut. 25: 17-19. Therefore the Lord rejected Saul, and took the kingdom from his house. Samuel was sent to Bethlehem, and there anointed David, the youngest son of Jesse, of the tribe of Judah. This was about seven years before the end of Saul's reign. In the year 1055, B. C., David was made king over Judah, and reigned in Hebron seven years. At the end of that period all Israel sought after him; and he reigned in Jerusalem thirty-three years.

In the thirteenth year of his reign, David expressed his intention to build a house for the ark of the Lord, which had always rested under curtains from the time the tabernacle was made by Moses in the desert of Arabia. But the Lord would not suffer him to build a temple to his name, because he had been engaged in many wars; but the promise was then made that his seed should build a house for the Lord, and should be established upon his throne forever. The language of the promise was very expressive:—

"I will raise up thy seed after thee, which shall be of thy sons; and I will establish his kingdom. He shall build me an house, and I will establish his throne forever. I will be his father, and he shall be my son; and I will not take my mercy away from him, as I took it from him that was before thee; but I will settle him in mine house and in my kingdom forever; and his throne shall be established forevermore." 1 Chron. 17: 11-14.

Thus the Lord said to David, he shall be thy seed and my son. As in the promise in Gen. 3: 15, and also in that to Abraham, we shall find in this to David, that this promise to his seed does not refer to his posterity in general, nor to his

DAVID ON HIS THRONE.

immediate son, but to one remote, namely, to Christ. He alone is at once the seed of David and the Son of God.

But even as the children of Israel possessed the land of Canaan, so Solomon built a temple for the sanctuary of God. This, of course, was a type of the real temple, "the true tabernacle" (Heb. 8:2), which the seed of promise was to build.

This promise, dwelt upon in Ps. 89, is as follows:—

"I have made a covenant with my chosen, I have sworn unto David my servant, Thy seed will I establish forever, and build up thy throne to all generations." "His seed also will I make to endure forever, and his throne as the days of Heaven." "His seed shall endure forever, and his throne as the sun before me." Ps. 89:3, 4, 29, 36.

Solomon enjoyed a peaceable reign of forty years, but when his son, Rehoboam, took the kingdom, there was a revolt, and the kingdom was divided into two branches of Judah and Israel. This was 975 years B. C. The kings of Israel, in order to separate themselves entirely from Judah, and thus maintain a separate supremacy, corrupted their worship, and during its entire existence there was not one truly pious king in Israel. Nearly two hundred and sixty years after this division took place, the king of Assyria utterly overthrew the kingdom of Israel, taking the people captive and scattering them in his own dominions, and peopling Samaria with strangers. 2 Kings 1:7. About forty years after this, 677 B. C., the king of Assyria took Manasseh, king of Judah, captive, and carried him to Babylon, for he had done very wickedly, and the Lord delivered him into the hand of his enemy. And thus in 677, B. C., the twelve tribes were without a king in either house.

To those who cannot look beyond this present state or dispensation for a fulfillment of the promises to David, this seems to be a sad commentary on those promises of everlasting glory to his throne and kingdom. There was temporarily a change in the condition of the kingdom of Judah. Manasseh humbled himself, and they restored him to his throne; and kings reigned in Jerusalem about the space of seventy-five years longer, when the king of Babylon took Jerusalem, and put kings over Judah according to his own mind. He exalted

Zedekiah to be king, but Zedekiah rebelled against him, and the king of Babylon took him captive and put out his eyes, and destroyed the temple and the chief houses in Jerusalem. This was 588 years before Christ. 2 Kings 25 : 4–10; 2 Chron. 36 : 14–20.

The temple built by Solomon stood 417 years, from 1005 to 588 B. C. But before the utter destruction of the city, in the days of Jehoiakim, B. C. 606, Nebuchadnezzar came and took the king captive, and carried away some of the vessels of the house of God, and some of the goodliest of the children of Judah he took to Babylon, to be instructed in the learning of the Chaldeans. Compare Dan. 1 : 3, 4; 2 Kings 20 : 16–18; Isa. 37 : 5–7. Among the captives were Daniel and his three brethren, Hananiah, Mishael, and Azariah, of the children of Judah.

It was only about five years before the captivity of Zedekiah, and the destruction of the temple and the city, that the prophet Ezekiel spoke of the utter subversion of the kingdom, and also of its future restoration, as follows:—

"And thou, profane wicked prince of Israel, whose day is come, when iniquity shall have an end, thus saith the Lord God: Remove the diadem, and take off the crown; this shall not be the same; exalt him that is low, and abase him that is high. I will overturn, overturn, overturn it, and it shall be no more, until he come whose right it is, and I will give it him." Eze. 21 : 25–27.

The kingdom, the crown, had passed under various changes. After many wars it was taken by the king of Babylon, who set rulers in Judah according to his will. But under Zedekiah, a most rebellious prince, the prophet said, "it shall be no more" —it shall be utterly cast down, "until he come whose right it is." And whose is the right to the kingdom and throne of David? It is the right, by an unfailing promise, of that certain one of the seed of David, who, said the Lord, "shall be my son." In his right it shall endure as the sun, even as the days of Heaven. And more than a hundred years before this time, another prophet spoke of this:—

"And thou, O tower of the flock, the stronghold of the daughter of Zion, unto thee shall it come, even the first dominion; the kingdom shall come to the daughter of Jerusalem." Micah 4 : 8.

The first dominion was that which was given to Adam—dominion over all the earth. The tower of the flock is no other than the seed of the woman—the seed of Abraham. He is heir of the world, and through him shall the kingdom come to the daughter of Jerusalem. This is a most interesting prophecy, connecting the first dominion—the original gift of the earth—with the kingdom which the seed of David shall inherit. All prophecy, all promise, all hope, centers in the stronghold, the tower of the flock. As the seed of the woman, he will bruise the head of the serpent, and recover the lost dominion. As the seed of Abraham he is the heir of the world, and a blessing to all nations. As the seed of David, he will possess the kingdom forever, and his throne shall endure as the sun, even as the days of Heaven. As the Son of God, he will save his people from their sins, and restore life to the race of Adam; to all who accept his salvation. All blessings come through him. Let all blessing and honor and glory be paid to him.

About fifteen years before the destruction of the city of Jerusalem and the temple, in the third year of the captivity of Daniel and his brethren, a prophecy of the restoration of the kingdom was given by means of a dream to Nebuchadnezzar, and its wonderful interpretation by Daniel. This is of greater interest than the prophecies that had preceded it, inasmuch as it gives a series of events easily understood by all, thereby beginning to open to us the time of the restoration of the kingdom and throne of David. This dream was given to Nebuchadnezzar by the Lord, for the express purpose of making known what shall be in the last days. Dan. 2:28. The king was reflecting upon the future, with a strong desire to look into its secrets; and the Lord caused him to understand according to his desire.

The interpretation of this dream was given under very peculiar circumstances. The dream troubled the king, though he could not remember it. This resembled a freak of the mind with which we are all acquainted. We are often troubled or perplexed over our inability to call to mind that which seems so near to our remembrance, but still eludes its grasp.

In this dilemma the king resorted to his wise men, many of whom professed knowledge which, if they had possessed it, should have served them in this emergency. He demanded that they should both tell him the dream, and give him the interpretation. Some have denounced this as a most unreasonable demand. But when we consider the pretensions of the astrologers and soothsayers, for such were some of them, we cannot call the demand unreasonable. They asked him to tell them the dream, promising then to give the interpretation. The king was apparently so disappointed in them, that he lost all confidence in their professions and promises. Perceiving the character of their pretensions to superior wisdom, he accused them of having "prepared lying and corrupt words;" for if he should tell them the dream, it would not require any great amount of ingenuity to invent some kind of interpretation. "Tell me the dream," said he, "and then I shall know that ye can show me the interpretation thereof." Dan. 2:9. If they failed to do this, he decreed that they should all be put to death. The alternative was terrible, but they were compelled to confess that they could not do it; that it required a wisdom greater than was possessed by any that dwelt on the earth. There was no chance for them to practice their wonted deception; they well knew that they could not invent anything that the king would recognize as his dream.

Daniel and his brethren had not been directly appealed to by the king, but inasmuch as they were counted among the wise men of Babylon, the officer who was appointed to execute the king's decree sought them to put them to death. But Daniel desired time, which was granted, and the young captives betook themselves to prayer, and the Lord revealed to Daniel both the dream and its interpretation. This saved not only the lives of Daniel and his brethren, but of all the professedly wise men; for the matter being revealed, the king was content to let them all live.

The dream was related to the king in the following words:—

"Thou, O king, sawest, and behold a great image. This great image, whose brightness was excellent, stood before thee; and the form thereof

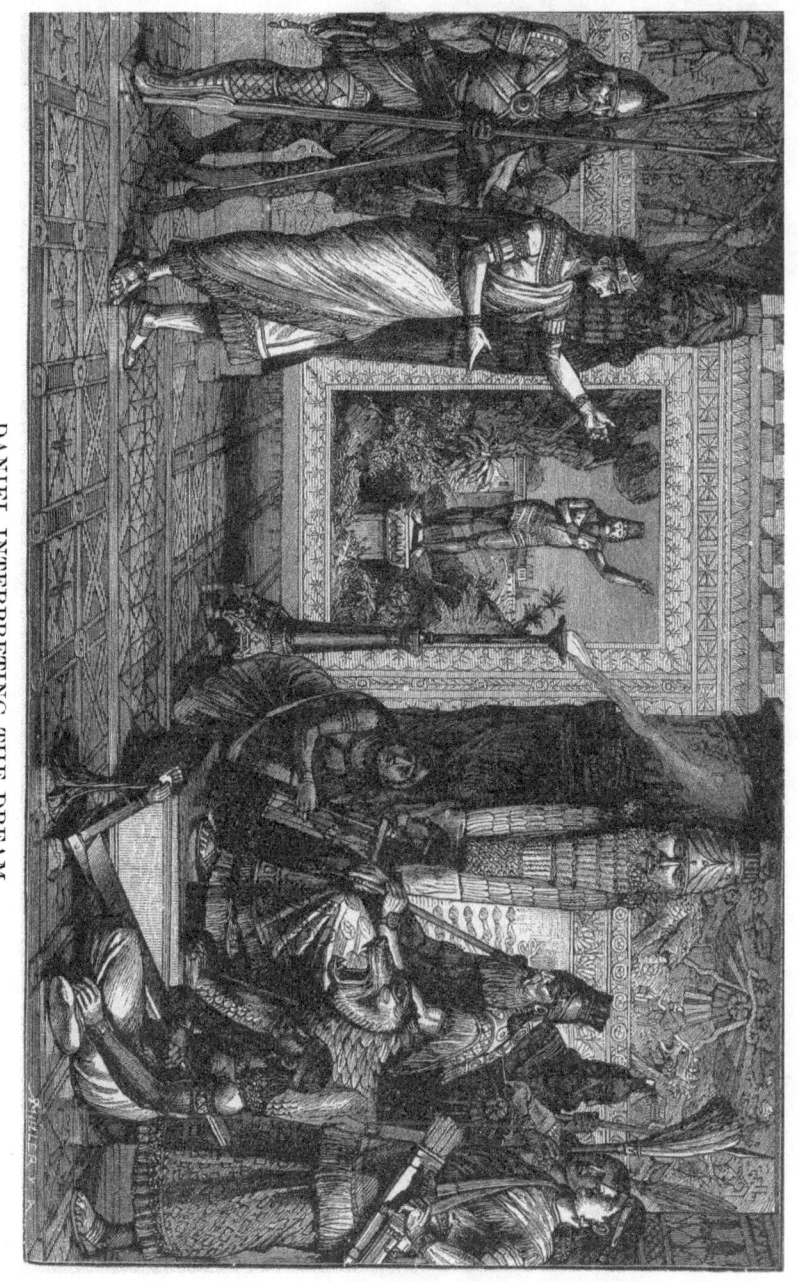

DANIEL INTERPRETING THE DREAM.

was terrible. This image's head was of fine gold, his breast and his arms of silver, his belly and his sides of brass, his legs of iron, his feet part of iron and part of clay. Thou sawest till that a stone was cut out without hands, which smote the image upon his feet that were of iron and clay, and brake them to pieces. Then was the iron, the clay, the brass, the silver, and the gold, broken to pieces together, and became like the chaff of the summer threshing floors; and the wind carried them away, that no place was found for them; and the stone that smote the image became a great mountain, and filled the whole earth." Dan. 2:31-35.

The test that the king put upon the wise men was a severe one, but here it was perfectly met. How must the great king have been struck, as the young Hebrew captive—a mere boy—stood before him and declared to him his secret thoughts, and every particular of his dream, which he had forgotten. Now it all flashed clearly upon his mind; he knew that that was what he saw in his dream, and he had all confidence that this young captive was capable of giving him the correct interpretation.

But Daniel disclaimed having any wisdom to reveal the king's secret. He said also that neither astrologer, magician, nor soothsayer, could make it known.

"But there is a God in Heaven that revealeth secrets, and maketh known to the king Nebuchadnezzar what shall be in the latter days." " But as for me, this secret is not revealed to me for any wisdom that I have more than any living, but for the intent that the interpretation may be made known to the king, and that thou mightest know the thoughts of thy heart." Dan. 2 : 28, 30.

The margin of the English Version is here copied, it being the correct reading. Dr. Barnes says: "The margin is the more correct rendering, and should have been admitted into the text." The Revised Version has adopted it.

The common English rendering of verse 30 is not only incorrect, but it does great injury to the prophecy as being a revelation from God of what shall be in the last days. The common reading implies that the matter was made known for the sake of those who should interpret it, which is altogether a wrong idea. It would effectually make it of private interpretion. Prophecy is not given to answer any personal ends. The whole matter, both the dream and the interpretation, was for the purpose of making known what shall be in the last days, and when the kingdom of Israel, that was being subverted, should be restored, and the throne and the crown given to him whose right it is.

And being such, it was not for Nebuchadnezzar alone, nor for those of that age. It is the beginning of one of the most important chains of prophecy in all the Bible. All the circumstances give the most undoubted assurance that the Lord has therein made known to all his people what shall be in the last days. In examining the interpretation each particular will be noticed as we pass.

Verse 36. "This is the dream; and we will tell the interpretation thereof before the king."

In verse 30, Daniel frankly declared that he had no wisdom above others to tell the dream; he gave all the honor to the God of Heaven. Here he says: "We will tell the interpretation," including his brethren in making known the interpretation. It was in answer to their united prayer that it was made known to Daniel.

Verses 37, 38. "Thou, O king, art a king of kings; for the God of Heaven hath given thee a kingdom, power, and strength, and glory. And wheresoever the children of men dwell, the beasts of the field and the fowls of the heaven hath he given into thine hand, and hath made thee ruler over them all. Thou art this head of gold."

Several interesting points are here presented for consideration.

1. The God of Heaven had ordered the kingdom of Babylon for purposes of his own. He selected Babylon to chastise his people for their sins. He made it a surpassingly glorious kingdom, to represent the gradation of events and kingdoms in the world, even to the last days. It was the most glorious kingdom that has ever existed, being fairly represented by its capital city, the like of which never existed, either before or since.

2. Nebuchadnezzar was king over the kings of the earth. In describing his greatness and the extent of his rule, the words of Daniel, in a most striking manner, agree with the terms of the original gift of the dominion to Adam, namely, over the beasts

of the field, and the fowls of the heaven, wheresoever the children of men dwelt, that is, over all the earth. In this we get the first idea of the full intent of this revelation, as more clearly set forth in the interpretation in verses 44, 45, as will be noticed when we come to those texts.

3. By comparison of the Scriptures we learn that in all cases the king represents the kingdom over which he rules; and Nebuchadnezzar was the head of gold, inasmuch as he stood at the head of an empire which was well symbolized by the most precious metal. The distinction of empire and kingdom is not known in the Scriptures.

Verse 39. "And after thee shall arise another kingdom inferior to thee."

The succession was not merely of a king, but of a kingdom. This next kingdom is represented in the dream by the breast and arms of silver. What this kingdom was may be easily learned from this book of Daniel's prophecy. In chapter 5 we read that Belshazzar, king of Babylon, made a great feast to a thousand of his lords; and while drinking wine before them, he commanded to bring the vessels which his father (grandfather) Nebuchadnezzar, had taken from the temple in Jerusalem, "that the king, and his princes, his wives, and his concubines, might drink therein." While committing this act, they "praised the gods of gold, and of silver, of brass, of iron, of wood, and of stone." The circumstances of that night, not related in the Scriptures, but well known in history, must be briefly noticed.

The royal houses of the Medes and the Persians were united by marriage. There was war between the Medes and the Babylonians, and Darius, king of the Medes, was aided by the Persians under Cyrus, their prince, the nephew of Darius. Cyrus was an able general, and the whole empire had submitted to his arms, except Babylon, the imperial city. This he besieged. But the city was so well prepared for a siege, that it could have held out for an indefinite time if it had been faithfully guarded. History informs us that there were provisions within the city for a siege of twenty years, while the squares were so spacious that very large gardens were found everywhere. There was much land within the walls available for raising provisions, and it was exceedingly productive. The walls were very high and strong, the entrances being guarded by heavy gates of brass. From their high walls the Babylonians laughed their besiegers to scorn, considering any means of defense useless, aside from the security offered by their walls, and believing that the besiegers would in time become convinced of the folly of their efforts.

But wickedness almost invariably attends upon the steps of worldly prosperity; and Babylon had filled up the cup of her iniquity, and the Lord had spoken by his prophets, saying that it should be not only overthrown, but utterly destroyed. To all human appearance, no power could overthrow it. Infidels might scoff at the prophecy, but no word of the prophets of God has ever failed, however improbable its fulfillment appeared at the time it was given. While Belshazzar and his proud princes were in the midst of their drunken revelry, praising the gods of their own making, and insulting the God of Israel, defying him by the sacrilegious use of the vessels consecrated to his service in Jerusalem, suddenly they were startled by the appearance of the fingers of a man's hand writing upon the wall of the royal banqueting house. Instantly their boasting was turned to consternation, and the king was so affrighted that "his knees smote one against another." The astrologers, the Chaldeans, and the soothsayers were called, but they could not make known that which was written. It appears that, in the changes of rulers, Daniel was neglected if not forgotten; but when the queen called attention to his having made known the dreams of Nebuchadnezzar, he was sent for, and read the writing to the king.

But first he uttered a most fitting rebuke to the proud and insolent Belshazzar. He reminded him of the benefits which God had conferred on his grandfather, Nebuchadnezzar, and of his having been driven from his kingdom because of his forgetfulness of God. "And thou, his son, O Belshazzar, hast not humbled thine heart, though thou knewest all this; but

THE FEAST OF BELSHAZZAR.

hast lifted up thyself against the Lord of Heaven." He then read the writing upon the wall, as follows:—

"And this is the writing that was written: MENE, MENE, TEKEL, UPHARSIN." Dan. 5: 25.

Many conjectures, all quite useless, have been indulged in, as to the character in which these words were written. Implicit reliance upon the record must lead us to believe just what it says, "This is the writing that was written;" the words set down in the record must have been the identical words upon the wall. The words are Chaldaic, but this is so closely related to the Hebrew, that the words, very much alike, are found in both languages. If they were written in the same form in which they are transmitted to us, it would make the truthfulness of the interpretation more directly apparent to all who heard Daniel speak. As in the case of the dream of Nebuchadnezzar, where the test put upon the wise men was such as to make sure to the king that the interpretation was correct, so here, if the words were those which were common to the Chaldeans, it would show to all present that the interpretation had a close relation to the words that were written. On the other hand, if they were written in some form not at all known to those present, the interpetation would lack the certainty, in their minds, which would attach to it if they had a knowledge of the words.

The wise men were unable to explain them, which is the sense in which their inability to read them should be taken. No one, except he were inspired of the God of Heaven, could possibly tell what was meant by the words themselves. Certainly, Daniel, by his own wisdom, could no more tell that MENE, which simply means "he hath numbered," meant that God had numbered and finished the kingdom, than he could tell what the divisions meant in the image of Nebuchadnezzar's dream. And the same may be said of TEKEL, which only means weighed, or, "he has weighed." Inspiration was necessary to determine that it meant, "Thou are weighed in the balances, and art found wanting." And no less difficulty attends the word UPHARSIN. The prefix U (sound of oo), is the conjunction, and *Pah-ras* means, he divided; *parsin* is the same word, with the Chaldaic plural termination. The change in the form of the words which Daniel made in the interpretation would certainly lead to the conclusion that is here adopted, namely, that he was examining words in their own language, just as they are written. With a different pointing, and thereby with a different pronunciation, this last word means the Persian. But there was no reference, by any construction, to the Medes, though there was to the Persians. Yet the hearers could readily see the force of the interpretation when it was said the kingdom was numbered, and finished, and divided, for they all knew that the united forces of the Medes and Persians were at that moment surrounding the city. And thus, as has been remarked, the interpretation was much more forcible and convincing if the words were written with the characters known at least to the wise men who were present; and of course the more generally they were known, the more effect would the interpretation have on the minds of the vast assembly.

Now turn again to the facts of history. Cyrus caused a new channel to be made for the Euphrates, and made excavations on the plain, to receive the waters when he wished to divert them from the channel that ran under the walls and through the city. Yet all this labor would have been useless to him had the city been continually guarded with diligence and care; for, inside the city, walls were built on the banks of the river, so that if any passed the outer wall and followed the bed of the river inside the city, they would still be as effectually shut out from communication, with the city or from entering it, as if they were entirely outside, unless the gates were open which led to or across the river. But the prophet of God had spoken the word that Babylon should be destroyed, and Providence was on the side of the besieging army. An occasion was soon offered to Cyrus to take advantage of the preparation that he had made. Rollin, in his "Ancient History," thus speaks of it:—

"As soon as Cyrus saw that the ditch, which they had long worked upon, was finished, he began to think seriously of the execution of his vast design, which as yet he had communicated to nobody. Providence soon furnished him with as fit an opportunity for this purpose as he could desire. He was informed that in the city a great festival was to be celebrated; and that the Babylonians, on occasions of that solemnity, were accustomed to pass the whole night in drinking and debauchery." Vol. 1., p. 30, Harpers, 1865.

Knowing all this, Cyrus judged that diligence in guarding the city would be relaxed; and those within deemed it impossible for the enemy to pass the main or outer walls. Turning the waters into the new channels that he had cut, the river bed under the walls and through the city was soon dry enough for the soldiers to pass within. Xenophon, quoted by Dr. Barnes, Notes on Dan. 5 : 30, said that Cyrus and his generals had an idea that the gates inside the city would be left open, as all inside the city would naturally join in the revelry. He said:—

"And indeed those who were with Gobryas said that 'it would not be wonderful if the gates of the palace should be found open, as the whole city that night seemed to be given up to revelry.' He then says that as they passed on, after entering the city, of those whom they encountered, part, being smitten, died, part fled again back, and part raised a clamor. But those who were with Gobryas also raised a clamor as if they also joined in the revelry, and going as fast as they could, they came soon to the palace of the king. But those who were with Gobryas and Gadates being arrayed, found the gates of the palace closed, but those who were appointed to go against the guard of the palace fell upon them when drinking before a great light, and were quickly engaged with them in hostile combat. Then a cry arose, and they who were within having asked the cause of the tumult, the king commanded them to see what the affair was, and some of them rushing out opened the gates. So when they who were with Gadates saw the gates open, they rushed in, and pursuing those who attempted to return, and smiting them, they came to the king, and they found him standing with a drawn sword. And those who were with Gadates and Gobryas overpowered him; and those who were with him were slain—one opposing, and one fleeing, and one seeking his safety the best way he could. . . . When it was day, and they who had the watch over the towers learned that the city was taken, and that the king was dead, they also surrendered the towers."

The result is thus briefly stated in Dan. 5 : 30, 31 : "In that night was Belshazzar the king of the Chaldeans slain. And Darius the Median took the kingdom."

Thus ended the kingdom of the Chaldeans, the empire represented by the head of gold in the great image of Nebuchadnezzar's dream. The overthrow took place B. C. 538—sixty-five years after the dream was given; sixty-eight years after the captivity when Daniel and others were brought to Babylon; sixty-one years after Nebuchadnezzar made Zedekiah king of Jerusalem; and fifty years after the temple and the city of Jerusalem were destroyed. Thus wondrously does God fulfill his word, and thus plainly do the Scriptures and history agree in giving the succession of empire, showing that the breast and arms of silver, in the image of the dream of Nebuchadnezzar, represented the united houses of the Medes and the Persians.

We now return to the words of Daniel in the interpretation.

Dan. 2:39. "And another third kingdom of brass, which shall bear rule over all the earth."

This third kingdom answered to the body of the image which was of brass, the third metal mentioned. And the identity of this kingdom is as easily determined as that of the Medes and Persians. In chapter 8 is the record of a vision that Daniel had in the third year of the reign of Belshazzar, He was in Elam, which had been an independent kingdom, and as a province of Babylon preserved its capital and palace. See Dan. 8:2. Daniel said that in this vision he saw a ram which had two horns, and one was higher than the other, and the higher came up last. And the ram became great and did according to his will. And then he saw a he goat which came from the west, which ran unto the ram in the fury of his power and brake his two horns, and stamped upon him; and the goat became very great. Other points in the history of these beasts are passed by for the present, as it is only the purpose here to show what they represent. The angel Gabriel was commanded to explain the vision to Daniel, and of these beasts he said: "The ram which thou sawest having two horns, are the kings of Media and Persia. And the rough goat is the king [or kingdom] of Grecia."

Here it is seen that the Medes and Persians, represented by the breast and arms of silver in the image, were overthrown by Grecia, which of course is represented by the next metal, the body of brass of the image. That the kingdom of the Medes and Persians was overthrown by the Grecians, is so well known that it is unnecessary to quote history to further show the fulfillment of the prophecy in this particular. Thus we have three parts of the image well and clearly explained, namely, the gold, the silver, and the brass—Babylon, Medo-Persia, and Grecia.

Dan. 2:40. "And the fourth kingdom shall be strong as iron; forasmuch as iron breaketh in pieces and subdueth all things; and as iron that breaketh all these, shall it break in pieces and bruise."

It will be noticed that the dream of Nebuchadnezzar, and its interpretation, show that just four great empires should rule over the earth. And it appears that the first, the gold, was to be the most glorious, while the fourth, the iron, was to be the strongest. The first three are named in the prophecy, as we have seen. The fourth is not; but it is brought to view in other scriptures, and abundantly identified in history. Thus we read in Luke 2:1, that their went out a decree from Cæsar Augustus that all the world should be taxed. Cæsar Augustus was emperor of Rome, and Rome was the only empire that has existed since the rise and fall of the kingdom of Alexander the Grecian, that had power to tax the world. This expression proves universality of dominion, such as was held by Babylon, Persia, and Greece, the first three parts of the great image. No king can tax beyond his jurisdiction, and no part of the whole world could resist the power of Rome.

The description of the action of this empire, as given by Daniel, is very expressive. "As the iron that breaketh all these, shall it break in pieces and bruise." Its rise to universal supremacy was emphatically by a breaking and bruising process. Its rise was not by a sudden overthrow of a ruling empire, as was the case with the Persians and the Greeks. The empire of Alexander was already divided into four parts, as was prophesied in Daniel 7 and 8. Of course no one of four kingdoms could be as strong as one universal kingdom. These divisions caused the Romans to carry on their conquests in almost every direction, and almost everywhere; and this again led to their having a closer supervision over all parts of the world than did their predecessors. On this text, Dr. Barnes says:—

"Nothing could better characterize the Roman power than this. Everything was crushed before it. The nations which they conquered ceased to be kingdoms, and were reduced to provinces, and as kingdoms they were blotted out from the list of nations."

Concerning the strength and extent of the Roman empire, and the watchfulness which the emperors exercised over this vast domain, Gibbon thus testifies:—

"But the empire of the Romans filled the world, and when that empire fell into the hands of a single person, the world became a safe and dreary prison for his enemies. The slave of imperial despotism, whether he was compelled to drag his gilded chain in Rome and the Senate, or to wear out a life of exile on the barren rock of Seriphus, or the frozen banks of the Danube, accepted his fate in silent despair. To resist was fatal, and it was impossible to fly. On every side he was encompassed with a vast extent of sea and land, which he could never hope to traverse without being discovered, seized, and restored to his irritated master. Beyond the frontiers, his anxious view could discover nothing, except the ocean, inhospitable deserts, hostile tribes of barbarians, of fierce manners and unknown languages, or dependent kings, who would gladly purchase the emperor's protection by the sacrifice of an obnoxious fugitive. Wherever you are, said Cicero, to the exiled Marcellus, remember that you are equally within the power of the conqueror." Decline and Fall, chap. 3, paragraph 37.

Dr. George Weber, professor at Heidelberg, in his "Universal History," says:—

"It was under Augustus that the Roman empire possessed the greatest power abroad, and the highest cultivation at home. It extended from the Atlantic ocean to the Euphrates, and from the Danube and Rhine to the Atlas and falls of the Nile." P. 102, Brewer & Tileston, Boston, 1853.

The Romans were well represented by the iron, not only in the strength of their empire, but in the cruelty of their dispositions. They were iron-hearted, delighting in shedding human blood. Titus was considered one of the mildest of Roman conquerors, the most benignant of Roman rulers, so that his subjects gave him the title of "the delight of the human race;" yet Josephus, speaking of his conquest of the Jews, said:—

"While Titus was at Cæsarea, he solemnized the birthday of his brother after a splendid manner, and inflicted a great deal of the punishment intended for the Jews in honor of him; for the number of those who were slain in fighting with the beasts, and were burnt, and fought with one another, exceeded two thousand five hundred." Wars, Book 7, chap. 3, sec. 1.

At Berytus, a city of Phœnicia, he celebrated the birthday of his father in a similar manner, where a great multitude perished by the same means. The reader cannot fail to be interested in the following remarks of Professor Gaussen, of Geneva, in his "Discourses on Daniel," on this subject:—

"The fourth empire was iron. Iron—no better definition than this can be given of the character of the Romans. Everything in them was iron. Their government was iron—merciless; hard-hearted, inhuman, inexorable. Their courage was iron—cruel, bloody, indomitable. Their soldiers were iron—never was their a nation more fearfully armed for battle; their breastplates, their helmets, their long shields, their darts, their javelins, their short and heavy two-edged swords, all their weapons were ingeniously terrible. . . . Their yoke upon the vanquished was iron,—heavy, intolerable, and yet unavoidable. In their conquests they crushed everything; they made Roman provinces of all the subjected countries; they left them nothing of their own nationality, and in a short time had even deprived them of their language. It was soon commanded to speak Latin not only in all Italy, but in Germany, south of the Danube, in all France, in all Belgium, in Switzerland, in Geneva, in Spain, in Portugal, and even in Africa. . . . When Julius Cæsar, who took all France, and made it a Roman province, finished the assault of the last city, he ordered that both hands be cut off from all the men that were found in it, which cruelty he proudly mentions in his Commentaries. They wanted human blood in all their joys." Vol. I, pp. 146-8, Toulouse, 1850.

Luther, in his "Introduction to Comments on Daniel," said:—

"The first kingdom is the Assyrian, or Babylonian; the second, the Medes and Persians; the third, that of Alexander the Great, and the Greeks; the fourth, the Roman. In this explanation and opinion all the world are agreed."

We now return to the words of the young prophet in the explanation of the dream.

Verse 41. "And whereas thou sawest the feet and toes part of potter's clay and part of iron, the kingdom shall be divided."

The iron kingdom was to be divided into different kingdoms, according to the number of toes on the image of a man. Daniel had a vision, recorded in chapter seven, in which he saw four great beasts, which also represent four great kingdoms the same as the four metals of the great image, and the fourth beast had ten horns, which are said to be ten kingdoms. Verse 24. The ten toes of the image represent the same ten kingdoms.

"But there shall be in it of the strength of the iron, forasmuch as thou sawest the iron mixed with miry clay."

The fourth kingdom was not overthrown in the manner in which the preceding ones were, so as to let the power or dominion pass to another territory. It was to be divided, and the iron was to remain in the divisions; the power of the same dominion was to be exercised by ten kingdoms instead of by one universal empire.

Verses 42, 43. "And as the toes of the feet were part of iron, and part of clay, so the kingdom shall be partly strong and partly broken. And whereas thou sawest iron mixed with miry clay, they shall mingle themselves with the seed of men; but they shall not cleave one to another, even as iron is not mixed with clay."

It would not be possible to find figures more appropriate than these to indicate that these kingdoms should never again be united. Go to the founders where the molten iron is poured into the clay. Sometimes the moulds are imperfect, become broken, and the iron finds its way in every direction—literally mingles with the clay; but they will never cleave to one another. When the mass cools, every particle of the iron can be picked out and separated from every particle of the clay. Partly strong and partly broken or brittle, well represents the condition of the several kingdoms which sprung up on the territory of the Roman empire. Bishop Lowth, in his "Commentary on Daniel," says:—

"The toes of the image signify the ten kingdoms who were in after times to divide the kingdom among themselves. . . . This partition of the Roman empire will divide its strength, and by consequence be a diminution of its power."

This dividing is another fact in the identification of the fourth kingdom as the Roman empire. It was not true of either of the other great kingdoms that it was broken into ten kingdoms and thus stood for a long time. The Grecian empire was divided into four parts, as will be seen in Daniel seven and eight and as noticed in all history. But the Roman empire was divided into half a score of kingdoms, most of which remain unto this day. And there would be scarcely any earthly limit to their power were it not for one thing: the word of prophecy long ago declared, "They shall not cleave one to another." They may enter into confederacies and form alliances, but they shall not stand. Ambitious men, as Charlemagne, Napoleon, etc., may think to hold the kingdoms in their own power,—to unite the nations in their own interests, to serve their own purposes; but look again, and where are they? Now proudly riding on the waves of victory, they think that they can make a map of the world which shall remain as a monument of the success of their schemes. But suddenly their schemes have perished with them.

"Iron and clay" still expresses the condition of those who occupy the old Roman dominion. But the climax, the great object of this prophecy, remains to be noticed. Thus the young captive in Babylon said:—

"Verse 44. "And in the days of these kings shall the God of Heaven set up a kingdom, which shall never be destroyed; and the kingdom shall not be left to other people, but it shall break in pieces and consume all these kingdoms, and it shall stand forever."

And thus, besides the four great empires represented by the gold, the silver, the brass, and the iron, another universal kingdom is to succeed them, represented by the stone, which shall be set up by the God of Heaven. In the dream it was shown that the stone became a great mountain and filled the whole earth. It is no other than the kingdom and throne of David restored in the hands of his seed, the first dominion recovered from the power of the enemy, and from the curse which has so long rested upon it. The prophecy concerning this kingdom, revealing its features, must yet be examined.

CHAPTER VIII.

THE TIME OF SETTING UP THE KINGDOM.

The first words of the revelation of God concerning man are these, "Let us make man in our image, after our likeness, and let them have dominion." Gen. 1 : 26. Thus the purpose was announced to make man that he might have dominion over the earth. It has been noticed that when Daniel spoke before Nebuchadnezzar of the extent of his dominion which the God of Heaven had given him, he used the same terms that were used in the first declaration of the purpose of God, and in the original gift to Adam, of dominion over all the earth.

When man was created, dominion was given to him in the following words:—

"And God blessed them, and God said unto them, Be fruitful, and multiply, and replenish the earth, and subdue it; and have dominion over the fish of the sea, and over the fowl of the air, and over every living thing that moveth upon the earth." Gen. 1 : 28.

We do not find these ideas expressed, or these terms again used, until Daniel reminds the triumphant king of Babylon of the source of his power. Thus he said:—

"Thou, O king, art a king of kings; for the God of Heaven hath given thee a kingdom, power, and strength, and glory. And wheresoever the children of men dwell, the beasts of the field and the fowls of the heaven hath he given into thine hand, and hath made thee ruler over them all." Dan. 2 : 37, 38.

The same witness was given by Daniel in speaking to Belshazzar, in the closing hours of this great empire:—

"The most high God gave Nebuchadnezzar thy father a kingdom, and majesty, and glory, and honor ; and for the majesty that he gave him, all people, nations, and languages, trembled and feared before him." Dan. 5 : 18, 19.

We have seen that the parts of the image in the dream of Nebuchadnezzar represented four great kingdoms which should bear rule over all the earth. The interpretation of the dream shows that it was given as a prophecy of the kingdom which the God of Heaven should set up. In other words, it was a prophecy of the restoration of the kingdom and throne of David, in the hands of him "whose right it is." The king in this kingdom, the seed of David, is also the Son of God; he is the seed of Abraham, in whom all nations of the earth were to be blessed; the seed of the woman who should bruise the head of the serpent, and restore what was lost by the sin of our first parents. This kingdom is the same as "the first dominion," spoken of by the prophet Micah,—dominion lost by Adam. Now it seems altogether fitting that, in the prophecy of the restoration of the kingdom of the whole earth, the way should be prepared for a full understanding of the subject, by setting forth the kingdoms upon the same territory, by which the order of succession could be made plain. In Dan. 2: 44, the characteristics of the kingdom which the God of Heaven should set up are pointed out; but these are prefaced with a declaration concerning *the time* when the kingdom shall be set up. The exact time is not revealed, either here or elsewhere; only an approximation to the time is given.

The statement on this subject is very explicit: "In the days of these kings shall the God of Heaven set up a kingdom. In the days of what kings? Some authors have assumed that it meant the Roman kings; that is, that the kingdom of Heaven should be set up in the time of the Roman empire. But there are insuperable objections to this view, and not a single good reason can be adduced in its favor. In the preceding verses the immediate antecedent of the expression, "these kings," are the ten kings that shall arise out of the fourth kingdom. If "these kings" did not mean the ten kings, then there is nothing to indicate that it refers to the kings of Rome more than to the kings of Greece, of Persia, or of Babylon. It is an evident truth that each part of the image represents one kingdom or king. In no case is either of them referred to in the plural number. The plural is not used until we come to the ten kings. Therefore if the ten kings are not referred to, it yet remains to be proved that it refers to the Roman kings rather than to those of the others of the four. Then it would mean that the God of Heaven would set up a kingdom somewhere in the days of the four kingdoms—say somewhere between the days of Nebuchadnezzar and Constantine. But such a construction is very far from the truth; it is based on an unreasonable supposition. It is not in harmony with the declaration of the prophecy. The immediate antecedent, and the only grammatical antecedent of the expression, "these kings," are the ten kings which are represented by the feet and toes of the image.

And this view is verified by the prophecy in its description of the kingdom of Heaven. It must be evident to every reader that, as Babylon was represented by the head of gold, and Medo-Persia by the breast and arms of silver, and Grecia by the body of brass, and Rome by the legs of iron, and the ten kings by the feet and toes of the image, so the kingdom to be set up by the God of Heaven is represented by the stone. Every point in the image or in the dream, has a corresponding fact in the fulfillment. The stone was cut out without hands; and the kingdom was to be set up by the God of Heaven—not by human agency. The stone broke in pieces and destroyed the image in all its parts; so the kingdom was to break in pieces and consume all the kingdoms of the earth. The stone became a great mountain and filled the whole earth; so the kingdom was to succeed all kingdoms under the whole heaven. Dan. 7 : 13, 14, 27. The history of the image is a history of the successive powers of the whole earth. Persia succeeded Babylon; Grecia succeeded Persia; Rome succeeded Grecia; the ten kings succeeded the Roman empire; and the kingdom of the God of Heaven succeeds the ten kings. It utterly destroys all the kingdoms of the earth. To show more clearly the proof that lies in this order of succession, we will examine the several parts of the image as they are presented in the successive kingdoms, in the order of their time.

THE TIME OF SETTING UP THE KINGDOM. 89

First we have the head of gold, Babylon, which we date from the time that Nebuchadnezzar took captive Jehoiakim, king of Judah, and carried him to Babylon, with part of the vessels of the house of God, and some of the children of Judah, including Daniel and his brethren. 2 Chron. 36:5-8; Dan. 1:1-7. This was before Christ 606. The dream of Nebuchadnezzar, and its interpretation, were given in the year B. C. 603, while this king was in the height of his power and glory. Therefore, at the time of this dream, only this much of the image—the head of gold—was fulfilled.

In the interpretation of the dream Daniel said to the king, "Thou art this head of gold. And after thee shall arise another kingdom inferior to thee." It was another kingdom that was to arise after him, —not merely another *king*. As the kingdom which was to succeed Babylon did not appear for half a century after this time, of course only the head of gold had an existence in the days of Nebuchadnezzar. But when Belshazzar was slain—when Darius the Median took the kingdom, Dan. 5:30, 31,—the second part of the image appeared in view, namely, the breast and arms of silver. Then two of the great divisions of the image were fulfilled, and the fulfilled parts stood as shown on page 90: the head of gold and the breast and arms of silver.

Belshazzar was slain in the year B. C. 538; therefore from the time of the dream of Nebuchadnezzar to the rise of the second kingdom, was sixty-five years. And in this manner the first two parts of the image stood for more than two centuries.

The first two kingdoms are identified in the clearest manner in the scriptures already noticed. The kingdom of Nebuchadnezzar was expressly declared to be the head of gold (Daniel 2); and the Babylonian kingdom ceased at the death of

Belshazzar, and was succeeded by the kingdom of the Medes and Persians. Dan. 5:30, 31. These were represented by the gold and silver of the image. "And another third kingdom of brass, which shall bear rule over all the earth," continued the prophet. And this third kingdom is as clearly revealed in the Scriptures as are the first and second. The first, Babylon, is named in Daniel 2; the second, Medo-Persia, is named in Daniel 8; and the third, Grecia, is also named in Daniel 8, as we have seen. The ram was said by the angel to be the

kings of Media and Persia. The kings of the Medes and Persians are counted one kingdom; that which came into power on the death of Belshazzar. The rough goat overpowered the ram, and became very great, and of him the angel said: "The rough goat is the king [or kingdom, see verse 22] of Grecia."

It was in the year B. C. 331 that Alexander the Grecian overthrew the Persians, and thus brought into existence another part of the image. From that time three parts stood in view, as shown on the next page. Thus it stood until the fourth, or strong kingdom, arose, more than a century and a half afterwards.

We have before remarked that the Romans did not rise to supreme power by one great victory, as was the case with the Persians and the Grecians. The rise of the Roman empire was very peculiar in this respect. It conquered the world by degrees, never yielding what it had gained, and sometimes gaining by the fears of other people, who peacefully resigned themselves into the hands of those who were everywhere triumphant, rather than to risk the chance of a destructive warfare, which they were assured would terminate in their own overthrow. Nothing stood before the people who were so well represented by the legs of iron of the image of Nebuchadnezzar, and by the fourth beast of Daniel 7, which was dreadful and terrible, and strong exceedingly.

Becker's History of the World, Vol. IV., p. 1, speaks thus of the gradual rise of the Roman power:—

"The Roman people had, through the wars of four centuries, subjected to its authority the most beautiful parts of the then known world; the terrible internal wars, in which, since the bloody days of Glaucia and Saturninus until the time of the battle of Actium, the dying republic had wasted her strength, could not check the competition of the Roman world-wide dominion."

Gibbon presents a feature of the policy of the Romans in extending their dominion, as follows:—

"It was customary to tempt the protectors of besieged cities by the promise of more distinguished honors than they possessed in their native country. By such means they not only conquered their enemies, but turned them into honored citizens, cemented and strengthened the empire wherever they went."

The Grecian empire was already divided into four kingdoms, which, however, were counted as so many parts of that kingdom. See Dan. 7:6. But these divisions made it necessary for the Romans to carry on their conquests in many directions in order to bring all the world into subjection.

As we count the beginning of the empire of Nebuchadnezzar, not from its foundation, but from the time when the kingdom of Israel was entirely subverted and subjected to it, so we date the beginning of the Roman empire from the time when the Jews, restored by the united action of Cyrus, Darius, and Artaxerxes (Ezra 6:14), made a league with the Romans. Nations are brought prominently into prophecy when they are brought into close relations with the people of God. We therefore take the date of this league, B. C. 161, for the beginning of this empire as related to the prophecy. Here the tribes of Israel were merged into the Roman kingdom, and their land became a Roman province by their own consent. And from this time onward for several centuries after Christ, the image stood thus nearly complete, having the head, breast and arms, body, and legs of iron, in full view. And what is the next event in the order of the prophecy? A correct answer to this question is of the greatest importance, for upon it depends a true understanding of all the rest of the prophecy. As the introduction of one wrong figure into an extended calculation makes every part of the process wrong from that point, and renders a correct result impossible, so a mistake in one point in the interpretation of the whole prophecy, leads the inquirer in a wrong direction, and turns the interpretation of the whole prophecy into a wrong channel.

Many affirm, and with much apparent confidence, that the next event is the setting up of the everlasting kingdom by the God of Heaven. But this is not the order of the prophecy. That kingdom is represented by the stone; but when did the stone make its first appearance? Not when the legs of iron were developed, but when it smote the image upon the feet. But where were the feet at the time of the advent of the Son of God to this earth? Where were they on the day of Pentecost, when it is affirmed that the kingdom was set up? They were not in existence. Look at the representation of the image

THE TIME OF SETTING UP THE KINGDOM.

as far as it was fulfilled up to nearly five hundred years this side of the beginning of the Christian era. The feet and toes did not make their appearance at all for nearly five centuries after the legs of iron were upon the stage of action. The stone did not smite the image upon the legs. Its first appearance was when it smote the image upon the feet; and this, in the interpretation, is explained as meaning that in the days of the kings thus smitten shall the God of Heaven set up a kingdom.

And this is confirmed by the further declaration that when the kingdom of God is set up, it shall break in pieces and consume all the preceding kingdoms; and as the clay, the iron, the brass, the silver and the gold, were all broken to pieces together, and became like the chaff of the summer threshing floors, and they were driven away so that no place was found for them, even thus were all the kingdoms of the earth to be consumed by the kingdom of the God of Heaven. And the image was not fully developed, as is shown, with the feet and toes standing upon the earth, until the Roman kingdom was divided into ten parts, as foretold in Daniel 2 and 7, which was not until near the close of the fifth century.

The difficulty with current interpretations of this prophecy is this: The setting up of the kingdom is confounded with the introduction of the new covenant, or the preaching of the gospel by Christ and his apostles. But that view is very far from being the correct one. The preaching of the gospel is preparatory to the setting up of the kingdom. The gospel is intended to call out of the world and prepare a people who shall be fitted by grace to inherit the kingdom when it is set up. There is nothing in the description of the setting up of the kingdom which can reasonably be applied to the preaching of the gospel. Dr. Barnes clearly saw this difficulty, and stated it as follows :—

"Two inquiries at once meet us here, of somewhat difficult solution. The first is, how, if this is designed to apply to the kingdom of the Messiah, can the description be true? The language here would seem to imply some violent action, some positive crushing force; something like that which occurs in conquests when nations are subdued. Would it not appear from this that the kingdom here represented was to make its way by conquests in the same manner as the other kingdoms, rather than by a silent and peaceful influence? Is this language, in fact, applicable to the method in which the kingdom of Christ is to supplant all others?"

These questions are well calculated to cause the advocates of that theory solemnly to reflect upon the violence that they are doing to the plain language of the Scriptures. We confidently answer the questions put forth by the learned doctor in the affirmative; this language is, in fact, applicable to the manner in which the kingdom of Christ is to be introduced. But it is not at all applicable, as the doctor plainly says, to the theory that makes the kingdom set up by the mildness of the introduction of the gospel. There is not a text in all the Bible which speaks of the kingdom of God supplanting all other kingdoms by mild means; everywhere it is said to break and destroy them. This description can be true,—it is true,—and there is no necessity to force the language to make it mean

THE IMAGE OF NEBUCHADNEZZAR'S DREAM.

something entirely contrary to what it says. And this is by no means the only scripture that must be perverted to make that theory appear consistent. Turn to Ps. 2:7-9:—

"Thou art my Son; this day have I begotten thee. Ask of me, and I shall give thee the heathen for thine inheritance, and the uttermost parts of the earth for thy possession. Thou shalt break them with a rod of iron; thou shalt dash them in pieces like a potter's vessel."

Strangely enough, this second psalm has been construed into a prophecy of the conversion of the world! What is the position of the Son during the preaching of the gospel? He is a priest, sitting at the right hand of his Father in Heaven. Heb. 8:1, 2. Now read Ps. 110:1, and there we learn the condition of the world when he leaves that position as a priest, as he prepares to return the second time to this world. "The Lord said unto my Lord, Sit thou at my right hand, until I make thine enemies thy footstool." And thus the author of the book of Hebrews says he is seated at the right hand of the Father, from henceforth expecting till his enemies shall be put under his feet. When his priesthood is finished, then he will leave his position at the right hand of the Father; then his enemies will be put under his feet; then he will come to take vengeance on them that know not God, and obey not the gospel. 2 Thess. 1:6-10. Then will the kings of the earth, the great men, the mighty men, try in vain to hide from the wrath of the Lamb, crying, "The great day of his wrath is come, and who shall be able to stand?" Rev. 6:15-17. Then he will break them with a rod of iron, and dash them in pieces as a potter's vessel; and then will Dan. 2:34 and 44 be literally fulfilled. Rev. 11:16-18 says that when it is announced that the kingdoms of this world are become the kingdoms of our Lord and of his Christ, then it is also said that the nations were angry, and the wrath of God is come, and the time to judge the dead, and to give reward to all his people, and to visit with destruction all those who corrupt the earth. And thus the question which appeared so perplexing to Dr. Barnes is easily solved, and the language of the prophecy is seen to apply naturally to the facts in the case. There is nothing in Daniel

2, when most literally construed, at all inconsistent with the other scriptures; and more might be quoted of like import.

We come down three centuries this side of our Saviour's advent. In Northern Europe there were great numbers of people, restless for new countries in which to settle, or to conquer for spoil. The empire of the Romans was losing its former strength and power. Describing these people of the North who were seeking new countries to inhabit, Machiavelli said:—

"These colonists have destroyed the Roman Empire, by the error of the emperors, who, having abandoned Rome, the true seat of the empire, to dwell at Constantinople, have, by this conduct, rendered the western part more feeble, not being able so well to defend it." History of Florence, Book 1., p. 2.

A certain writer said that when Constantine removed his capital to Constantinople, he virtually left the seat of the Cæsars to the bishops of Rome. One thing is certain: the power of the emperors over Rome decreased in exactly the proportion that the power of the bishops increased. A history of the "Papal Supremacy," published in Dublin in 1810, says: "It is most certain that if the emperors had continued to reside at Rome, the bishops never would have usurped a supremacy." This is reasonable; it is conclusive. Early in the fourth century, the Northern Barbarians, as they have been called, made inroads upon some of the fairest portions of the empire, in Central Europe and along the Rhine. And before the close of the fifth century the empire was broken up into ten kingdoms, as before noticed. The Ostrogoths took possession of Italy, and ruled in Rome, until they were driven out by the army of Justinian, under Belisarius, in 538.

Now we take our stand near the beginning of the sixth century, and we behold these fragments of the Roman empire, exactly as pointed out by Daniel in the interpretation of the dream of Nebuchadnezzar. And there the image stands complete, as represented in the engraving. Not before this time could the stone smite the image, for it was to smite it upon the feet, and nowhere else. The stone is not introduced into the prophecy before that time.

What then? Was the kingdom set up at that time? It

was not. In this and other prophecies, where the history of the world is briefly outlined, the ultimate—the setting up of the kingdom of God—is introduced, without in each instance, filling up all the particulars. As prophecy follows prophecy, we find more and more of these particulars inserted, but the ultimate is always the same,—the establishing of the kingdom of God; the restoration of what was lost in the fall, closes up this world's history, and introduces the eternal state.

In Dan. 2:47, speaking of the ten kingdoms, it is said: "They shall mingle themselves with the seed of men; but they shall not cleave one to another, even as iron is not mixed with miry clay." These words plainly indicate that after these kingdoms arise, some time will elapse before they are smitten and destroyed; some time is allotted to their mingling and undergoing changes. How long this time would be, the second chapter of Daniel gives no intimation; it might be very short for all that we can learn in this chapter. But Daniel 7 gives additional facts in the history of the kingdoms of the world, and describes the coming up of another power after the rise of the ten kings, before whom three of the ten were plucked up. And it is shown that this other power wears out the saints, and prevails against them a long time before the kingdom is given to the saints of the Most High. The order of these events is marked out very plainly in Dan. 7:21, 22.

"I beheld, and the same horn made war with the saints, and prevailed against them; until the Ancient of days came, and judgment was given to the saints of the Most High; and the time came that the saints possessed the kingdom."

We have seen that the ten kingdoms were not fully developed until the latter part of the fifth century after Christ. The horn that rose after them, which became stronger than they, and that persecuted the saints, was not fully established until the sixth century. For many centuries he wore out the saints; he is still opposing himself to the free worship of God; still declaring that it is his fixed principle not to tolerate freedom of conscience toward God where he has the power to put down every religion that opposes itself unto him. And still the saints are waiting; judgment has not yet been given to them; and the time has not yet come for them to possess the kingdom.

The stone has not yet smitten the image. The kingdoms of this world still occupy their places; they are not yet broken and driven away as the chaff; but they are fast filling up the cups of their iniquity. Pride and the love of worldly power fill their hearts. Their greatest ambition seems to be the making of abundant provision for shedding human blood. A slight pretext is sufficient for them to engage in the most unjust and destructive enterprises, if an extension of territory or an increase of power is to be the result: yes, the most mischievous schemes are often carried out to serve the interest of a party. Where is the exception to these declarations? Alas for the world! Peace has flown away; equity and the love of their fellow-men are not found among the great of the earth. And among the professed people of God, with very small exceptions, formality has usurped the place of the power of godliness, and the fear of God is taught by the precept of men. Surely, God will yet visit for these things.

CHAPTER IX.

HEIRS OF THE KINGDOM.

"And the kingdom shall not be left to other people, but it shall break in pieces and consume all these kingdoms, and it shall stand forever." Dan. 2:44.

HERE is presented a strong contrast between this kingdom and its predecessors. The Babylonian empire was mighty and magnificent. Its capital has never been equaled by any city on the earth. But it became exceedingly wicked, and the same Being who gave this dominion to Nebuchadnezzar, declared that it should be utterly destroyed. Belshazzar and his thousand lords, and his hosts of mighty ones, laughed to scorn the efforts of their invaders; they mocked and insulted the true and living God. But the sure word of prophecy was spoken against Babylon, and that word has never failed—it cannot fail. To show how wonderfully the prophecies of God are fulfilled, we will give quotations from two prophets in regard to the destruction of Babylon.

Isaiah spoke of this in the year 712 B. C. This was just about one hundred years before Nebuchadnezzar overthrew Jerusalem, when Babylon was the rising power of the earth. It was one hundred and seventy years before its conquest by Cyrus. Thus said the prophet:—

"And Babylon, the glory of kingdoms, the beauty of the Chaldees' excellency, shall be as when God overthrew Sodom and Gomorrah. It shall never be inhabited, neither shall it be dwelt in from generation to generation; neither shall the Arabian pitch tent there; neither shall the shepherds make their fold there. But wild beasts of the desert shall lie there; and their houses shall be full of doleful creatures; and owls shall dwell there, and satyrs shall dance there. And the wild beasts of the island shall cry in their desolate houses, and dragons in their pleasant palaces; and her time is near to come, and her days shall not be prolonged." Isa. 13:19-22.

When we consider that the city was then becoming the glory of the Chaldees' excellency, exceedingly strong, that the situation was desirable, and the land very productive, it seemed highly improbable that it should ever become so utterly desolate—even a place to be avoided—as the prophet said. But every word has been literally fulfilled. Generation after generation has passed, and the place of the glorious city continues in the very condition described by the prophet.

And very wonderful are the words of Jeremiah, spoken in the year 595 B. C. This was eleven years after Daniel was carried captive into Babylon; eight years after the dream of Nebuchadnezzar. Therefore the solemn words of this prophecy were sent of God when this mighty monarch was reigning in the greatest pride of his glory. It was fifty-seven years before Babylon fell. The following are a part of the words of this prophecy:—

"Prepare against her the nations with the kings of the Medes, the captains thereof, and all the rulers thereof, and all the land of his dominion. And the land shall tremble and sorrow; for every purpose of the Lord shall be performed against Babylon, to make the land of Babylon a desolation without an inhabitant. The mighty men of Babylon have forborne to fight, they have remained in their holds; their might hath failed, they became as women; they have burned her dwelling places, her bars are broken. One post shall run to meet another, and one messenger to meet another, to show the king of Babylon that his city is taken at one end.

"And Babylon shall become heaps, a dwelling place for dragons, an astonishment, and a hissing, without an inhabitant.

"And I will make drunk her princes, and her wise men, her captain, and her rulers, and her mighty men; and they shall sleep a perpetual sleep, and not wake saith the King, whose name is the Lord of hosts. Thus saith the Lord of hosts: The broad walls of Babylon shall be utterly broken, and her high gates shall be burned with fire; and the people shall labor in vain, and the folk in the fire, and they shall be weary." Jer. 51 : 28-31, 37, 57, 58.

No one can intelligently read the words of the prophets without becoming convinced of the correctness of the apostle Peter's statement, "We have also a more sure word of prophecy; whereunto ye do well that ye take heed, as unto a light that shineth in a dark place, until the day dawn, and the day star arise in your hearts." 2 Peter 1 : 19.

Babylon fell, and the kingdom passed into the hands of the

Persians. In like manner was it transferred to the Grecians and then to the Romans. These "masters of the world" thought they had secured a sure supremacy; but they were as vicious as they were powerful, and a rude people became their conquerors. One generation after another passes away, and wars change the boundaries of the kingdoms of the earth. But of the fifth kingdom the word stands sure: It shall not be left to other people; it shall break in pieces and consume all these kingdoms, and it shall stand forever. They who possess it shall possess it forever and ever.

Considering that the very intention to make man was connected with the gift of a dominion, and the first gift to man was a dominion, we cannot be surprised that the restoration of the kingdom becomes especially prominent in the promises of God to man. Nor need we be surprised if he who was instrumental in robbing man of his first dominion, puts forth every effort to obscure and pervert this great and important truth. As to its importance and interest, we notice:—

1. The first proclamation of the forerunner of Christ, was concerning the coming kingdom: "Repent ye for the kingdom of Heaven is at hand." Matt. 3:1, 2.

2. The beginning of the preaching of Jesus Christ was the same proclamation: "Now after that John was put in prison, Jesus came into Galilee, preaching the gospel of the kingdom of God, and saying, The time is fulfilled, and the kingdom of God is at hand; repent ye, and believe the gospel." Mark 1: 14, 15.

3. The first of the beatitudes pronounced by the Saviour in the sermon on the mount, was concerning the kingdom: "Blessed are the poor in spirit: for theirs is the kingdom of Heaven." Matt. 5:3.

4. The first petition of the Lord's prayer was for the coming of the kingdom: "Thy kingdom come." Matt. 6:10.

5. When Jesus sent forth his disciples to preach the gospel, this was the burden of their commission: "And as ye go, preach, saying, The kingdom of Heaven is at hand." Matt. 10:7.

6. Jesus said: "This gospel of the kingdom shall be preached

in all the world for a witness unto all nations; and then shall the end come." Matt. 24:14. The object of the present dispensation is the preaching of the gospel of the kingdom to prepare a people to inherit it when it shall be set up.

7. And finally, when the Saviour comes in his glory, for the full redemption of his people, then will he say to the saints: "Come, ye blessed of my Father, inherit the kingdom prepared for you from the foundation of the world." Matt. 25:34.

Some have showed their firm belief in the theory that the kingdom has already come, by saying the Lord's prayer is not appropriate for this dispensation; it was given to the disciples before he had set up his kingdom, but now it is unfitting to pray that his kingdom may come. But as the subject of the prophecy of Daniel 2, and of the promises, it certainly has not come. Nothing has yet come, or been set up, which has restored the first dominion; which has caused the meek to inherit the earth; which has restored the kingdom and the throne of David. The promises remain to be fulfilled. Neither Abraham nor his seed has inherited the earth. Neither David nor his seed has seen the promised restoration and everlasting triumph of his reign.

But the question will perhaps be asked: Is not Jesus, the son of David, already exalted to a throne? Is he not on a throne at the present time? Truly, he is; but *not as the son of David*, because he is not on the throne of David. We must bear in mind that there are

TWO THRONES AND TWO KINGDOMS.

Listen to what the Lord Jesus says: "To him that overcometh will I grant to sit with me in my throne, even as I also overcame, and am set down with my Father in his throne." Rev. 3:21. Of the present position of the Saviour, read again: "We have such an high priest, who is set on the right hand of the throne of the Majesty in the Heavens." " Is set down at the right hand of the throne of God." Heb. 8:1; 12:2, and others.

While he is on the throne of his Father in Heaven he is a

priest; a *priest-king*, after the order of Melchisedec. But note this important point: *in his priesthood he has no genealogy.* See the argument in Hebrews, chapter five to seven. He is a priest after the order of Melchisedec, whose genealogy is not recorded. But the priesthood will have an end. He will leave that position on the throne of his Father. When he comes to take vengeance on his foes, he will no longer plead the power of his blood in their behalf. When the great day of his wrath is come he will no longer be an advocate. His Father called him to sit at his right hand until his enemies are put under his feet. Ps. 110:1. And so the apostle writes: "But this man, after he had offered one sacrifice for sins forever, sat down on the right hand of God; from henceforth expecting till his enemies be made his footstool." Heb. 10:12, 13.

With these scriptures before us it is easy to correct an error into which many have fallen, namely, that one great object, if not *the* great object, of the reign of Christ, is to subdue his enemies, or put them under his own feet. That is a work that Christ will never do. 1 Cor. 15:23-28, is often quoted to uphold that view, whereas it teaches the very opposite of that. It reads thus:—

"Christ the firstfruits; afterward they that are Christ's at his coming. Then cometh the end, when he shall have delivered up the kingdom to God, even the Father; when he shall have put down all rule and all authority and power. For he must reign till he hath put all enemies under his feet. The last enemy that shall be destroyed is death. For he hath put all things under his feet. But when he saith all things are put under him, it is manifest that he is excepted, which did put all things under him. And when all things shall be subdued unto him, then shall the Son also himself be subject unto him that did put all things under him, that God may be all in all."

This scripture clearly shows that Christ possesses a kingdom which he will sometime resign. The time is located at or near his coming. Then he will have delivered up the kingdom; he will have left the throne of the Majesty in the Heavens, where he is now sitting as a kingly priest. Verse 28 says: "And when all things shall be subdued unto him, then shall the Son also himself be subject unto him that put all things under him, that God may be all in all." The Son does not subdue all things unto himself; he does not put all things under his own feet. If he did, how could he become subject to him that put all things under him? The Father said: "I will give thee the heathen for thine inheritance, and the uttermost parts of the earth for thy possession." "Sit thou at my right hand, until I make thine enemies thy footstool." And 1 Cor. 15:27 says: "But when he saith all things are put under him, it is manifest that he is excepted which did put all things under him."

Wrong ideas on this text are easily imbibed from overlooking the manner in which the pronouns are applied. "For he [the Son] must reign until he [the Father] hath put all things under his [the Son's] feet." This is not arbitrary; it is necessary. See again: "And when all things shall be subdued unto him [the Son] then shall the Son also himself be subject unto him [the Father] that did put all things under him [the Son], that God may be all in all." Notice the several events here brought to view:—

1 The coming of Christ.

2. Then comes the end.

3. Then he shall have delivered up the kingdom to the Father.

4. He must reign until all things are put under his feet by the Father.

5. When all things are put under him, he himself becomes subject to the Father,—he resigns that throne, and delivers up that kingdom.

6. The Father then becomes all in all: sole occupant of that throne in the Heavens.

This is the kingdom—that is the throne which he will deliver up at the end of his priestly work. Then probation will have ended; then the saints will have been sealed unto full redemption; and they that are unjust must remain unjust still. Rev. 22:11, 12. Then will the Son break his enemies with a rod of iron, and dash them in pieces like a potter's vessel.

Then the day of the wrath of the Lamb will have come, the image will be smitten on the feet, and all the dominions of the earth be destroyed.

What has here been stated concerning the throne of the Father in Heaven is well known, and will be readily admitted by all. Let us briefly examine some of the facts of Scripture concerning

THE THRONE OF DAVID.

Jesus says he is set down on his Father's throne, and will grant to the overcomer to sit down with him in his throne. Of this latter throne the angel said to Mary:—

"He shall be great, and shall be called the Son of the Highest; and the Lord God shall give unto him the throne of his father David; and he shall reign over the house of Jacob forever; and of his kingdom there shall be no end." Luke 1:32, 33.

The throne which he now occupies is the throne of the universe, and it can in no sense be called the throne of David. The difference between his occupancy of the two can be readily seen.

1. He inherits this throne as the son of David. On the throne of his Father in Heaven his genealogy is not reckoned.

2. David had no priesthood; and Christ will have no priesthood on David's throne. In Heaven only, as the antitype of Melchisedec, is he a priest.

3. He shall sit upon the throne of David forever, and of his kingdom there shall be no end. But he will resign the throne of his Father in Heaven, and of his priestly kingship there will be an end; he will deliver up that kingdom.

Now we may confidently appeal to every reader: To which of these thrones and kingdoms will the promises and prophecies apply, which we have been noticing? Which of these kingdoms will destroy the kingdoms of this world, and fill the whole earth? To which of these thrones will the saints be exalted? Will Jesus destroy his enemies while he sits a priest at his Father's right hand, or after he leaves that position, and takes possession of his own throne? He will sometime say to the righteous, Come ye blessed of my Father, inherit the kingdom prepared for you from the foundation of the world; will he say this while he is on the Father's throne, or when he shall come again, in his own kingdom? See Matt. 25:31-41. James says: "Hath not God chosen the poor of this world rich in faith, and heirs of the kingdom which he hath promised to them that love him?" James 2:5. This describes the present position of the saints, and their relation to the kingdom. They who are rich in faith, and love God, are *heirs* of the kingdom, and not yet in possession. Indeed, they cannot inherit the kingdom in their present mortal state; for if they did they would leave it to other people at their death.

Some may doubt the correctness of this, thinking that it conflicts with the words of Paul in Rom. 8:38, 39; but it does not. Death cannot separate us from the love of Christ, for he is Lord both of the dead and the living. Rom. 14:9. He will redeem us from the grave, which is the land of the enemy; for death is an enemy. Jer. 31:15-17; 1 Cor. 15:26. But surely, when we are in the land of the enemy, under the dominion of death and the grave, we are not in the kingdom of Christ.

On this point we have the most decisive testimony in the words of Paul in 1 Cor. 15:50: "Now this I say, brethren, that flesh and blood cannot inherit the kingdom of God; neither doth corruption inherit incorruption." Flesh and blood is an expression denoting a corruptible state, such as we all possess in this world of mortality. In this state we cannot inherit the kingdom of God. And why not?—Because the kingdom of God is an everlasting kingdom; of the reign of Christ there will be no end. Being an incorruptible kingdom, only incorruptible subjects can inherit it; otherwise they would die and leave it to other people. From this point the apostle goes on to explain how we may inherit that kingdom. "For this corruptible must put on incorruption, and this mortal must put on immortality." This will take place at the sounding of the last trump, when the dead shall be raised incorruptible, and the living shall be changed. At that time the Lord himself shall descend from Heaven "with a shout,

with the voice of the archangel, and with the trump of God."
1 Thess. 4:14–17. Then the dead in Christ will arise immortal, and the living will be caught up to meet the Lord in the air, and so be forever with the Lord.

Of this time the Lord Jesus speaks in Matt. 25:31–34. The Son of man will come in the glory of the Father, and all the holy angels with him. His voice will raise the saints, immortal, incorruptible; and then he will say to them: "Come, ye blessed of my Father, inherit the kingdom prepared for you from the foundation of the world." This is "the first dominion," for it was prepared from the foundation of the world. And that will be the first moment that the saints could inherit it, for until that time they are mortal, corruptible, and cannot inherit the incorruptible kingdom of God. The gospel of the kingdom is still being preached, and concerning it the prayer of faith is still ascending: "Thy kingdom come. Thy will be done in earth, as it is in Heaven."

Here we may emphasize the facts already noticed in regard to the true heirs. For purposes which have been considered, the children of Jacob had especial privileges for a season, and they might have occupied a high place in the fulfillment of the purposes of grace; but, as Jesus said, they would not. Matt. 23:37. For this unfaithfulness, for their oft despising the messengers of God's love and mercy, and finally for maliciously putting to death his only-begotten Son, their house was left desolate, and the kingdom of God was taken from them to be given to a nation bringing forth the fruits thereof. Matt. 21:33–43. From the first announcement of the gospel, this truth began to be given to them. John the Baptist said to them:—

"Think not to say within yourselves, We have Abraham to our Father; for I say unto you, that God is able of these stones to raise up children unto Abraham." Matt. 3:9.

Do any think this was a hard saying? If so, why? He who could make a living soul of the dust of the ground, and can bring the dead from the earth, and would cause the very stones to cry out if necessary to have the words of the prophet fulfilled (Gen. 2:7; Luke 19:38-40), could make living beings of the stones of the valley of the Jordan, and make them children of Abraham through faith in Christ. And Jesus said that the literal descendants of Jacob, who did not believe in him, were not the children of Abraham, but were the children of the devil. John 8:39-44; compare Matt. 13:38, 39; Rev. 3:9.

The apostle Paul might have gloried because of his descent, yet he considered it all loss for Christ. Phil. 3:5, 7. How many have lost the treasures of the riches of God's grace in his covenant with Abraham, because of their vain boasting of their birth, proud of the accident of being born in a certain line, never accepting the word made plain to everyone, that they must be born again or they could never see the kingdom of God! Paul emphatically says they are not Jews; they are not the children of promise, and their circumcision is not circumcision (Rom. 2:28, 29); they have been broken off, so that they no longer belong to the stock of Israel, and they can only be restored by being grafted in again by faith in Christ (Rom. 11:23); while the Gentiles by birth, who have accepted Christ, are no longer strangers; they are no more foreigners, but citizens of the commonwealth of Israel. Eph. 2:11-19.

Having traced the promises of the kingdom of David to their fulfillment, and having seen that it will be as extensive as, and identical with, the inheritance promised to Abraham and his seed, we are prepared to notice a query that has seemed to puzzle many minds. Seeing that the Scriptures declare that Abraham was the heir of the whole world, why was he taken to the hill country of Palestine to be shown his inheritance? He was led from Mesopotamia to near the present site of Jerusalem, and there the Lord said to him, "Unto thy seed will I give this land." Why was not the promise made in the rich valley of the Euphrates? or why was he not taken to the land of Goshen, in Egypt?

Let us illustrate our reply by a supposition. The empire of Russia is very large. Suppose that an individual were taken to some far-away corner of this empire, and told that he and his posterity should possess all the land that he could see, it might prove to be an inconsiderable gift. But take him to St. Petersburg, to a position overlooking the city, its palaces, and all the treasures of the empire; then tell him that all that he can see shall belong to him and his children after him, and that would be quite a different thing. So God took Abraham to the spot where the capital of the earth is to be located; where the city which hath foundations, for which Abraham looked, will come down from Heaven. Here Abraham offered Isaac; here the True Seed of promise died to purchase the inheritance of the children of Adam; and here will the triumphant Saviour descend to redeem the purchased possession. Here will David see his Son sit upon his glorious throne. Here will Adam recover his long-lost garden, and again delight in approaching unto the tree of life. There was good reason why Abraham was led to this land, to the seat of the future capital of the whole world, to receive the promises. The great wonders of God's power and grace have been here displayed; and here will the full fruition of his gracious purpose be accomplished. Here Christ suffered; here he will triumph; here he will reign forever and ever.

> "To the land where the Saviour of sinners once trod,
>   Where he labored, and languished, and bled;
>   Where he triumphed o'er death, and ascended to God,
>   As he captive captivity led."

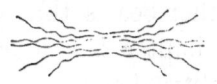

CHAPTER X.

"ANOTHER LITTLE HORN."

In the year 540 B. C., just sixty-three years after the dream of Nebuchadnezzar was given and interpreted, Daniel had a vision, which is recorded in the seventh chapter of his prophecy. In this vision he saw the four winds of Heaven striving upon the great sea, and four great beasts came up from the sea. In verses 17, 18, an explanation of the beasts is given as follows:—

"These great beasts, which are four, are four kings, which shall arise out of the earth. But the saints of the Most High shall take the kingdom, and possess the kingdom for ever, even for ever and ever."

These words show that this vision embraces the same great facts that are presented in the dream of the king, namely, four great kingdoms to be followed by a kingdom that the saints shall possess forever. Then the object of this vision is the same as that of the dream, to acquaint us with the facts of history preceding, and leading to, the setting up of the kingdom of God.

Verse 4. "The first was like a lion, and had eagle's wings; I beheld till the wings thereof were plucked, and it was lifted up from the earth, and made stand upon the feet as a man, and a man's heart was given to it."

The lion is called the king of beasts, and it bears about the same relation to the other beasts that gold bears to the other metals of the image of chapter 2. "Eagle's wings" adds something to the same quality, denoting the rapidity with which the empire rose to its wonderful greatness in the seventh century before Christ. But its wings were plucked, and the lion's heart was taken away. We must bear in mind that this beast, as the head of gold of the image, represented the empire of Babylon, and not any one emperor or king. The glory of

THE FOUR BEASTS OF DANIEL SEVEN.

the kingdom declined from the days of Nebuchadnezzar—so transitory is the glory of this world. Under the reign of Belshazzar there was left the qualities of neither the lion nor the eagle.

Verse 5. "And behold another beast, a second, like to a bear, and it raised up itself on one side, and it had three ribs in the mouth of it between the teeth of it; and they said thus unto it, Arise, devour much flesh."

This is a strikingly correct representation of the kingdom of the Medes and the Persians, the same as the breast and arms of the image. In chapter 8, the kings of Media and Persia are represented by a ram (compare Dan. 8: 3, 4, 20), having two horns, and one was higher than the other, and the higher came up last. The Medes were the leading power in the war against Babylon; for Cyrus, the real leader of the armies, gave himself entirely to the service of his uncle, "Darius the Median," who took the kingdom when the city of Babylon was overthrown. Of Darius but little need be said, except that he was ruler over a mighty empire that was presented to him by his nephew, for he gave no evidence of capability of subduing such an empire to himself. "The higher came up last." The Persian branch of the empire flourished under Cyrus, who was really one of the greatest generals that profane history presents to us; not merely because he could lead great armies, and subdue kingdoms, but he was lenient to his captives, considerate of the comfort and welfare of his soldiers and confederates, and just towards all. He went forth to war, not from a love of conquest, or because of indifference for human life, but in defense of the rights of those who were assailed. Added to all this, in his personal habits he was a model of temperance and benevolence. How well the bear represented the united houses of the Medes and Persians—it raised up itself on one side.

In describing the symbol of this kingdom in Daniel 8, the prophet said he saw the ram pushing westward, and northward, and southward. These are the directions in which the Medes and Persians pursued their conquests; and the three ribs in the mouth of the bear doubtless denote the same thing.

Verse 6. "After this I beheld, and lo another, like a leopard, which had upon the back of it four wings of a fowl; the beast had also four heads; and dominion was given to it."

The leopard represents the third great kingdom, the same as the body of brass of the image, or the rough goat in chapter 8,—the kingdom of Grecia. There is a twofold symbol to denote the speed with which Alexander conquered the world, namely, the body of a leopard, with four wings of a fowl. The love of conquest was his ruling passion. Merely to gratify a senseless ambition, he made war without cause or provocation, upon those who would gladly have remained in peace with him. Seneca said: "Alexander, who is justly entitled the plunderer of nations, made his glory consist in carrying desolation into all places, and in rendering himself the terror of mankind." See Rollin, Book 15, sec. 18. It seems a reflection on humanity to give such a man the title of "the Great."

To fully appreciate the description given in Daniel 7:7, it is necessary to notice further the symbol of Grecia in Dan. 8:5-9. The goat had a notable horn between his eyes, which, the angel said, was the first king, that is, Alexander. "The he goat waxed very great; and when he was strong, the great horn was broken; and for it came up four notable ones toward the four winds of heaven."

The kingdom of Alexander had suffered no decline when he died. He was in the full tide of victory, not having had time to prepare for himself a capital, when he fell, slain not in war, but by his depraved and ungovernable appetite,—broken in his strength. And for it came up four notable horns toward the four winds of heaven. The angel said, "Four kingdoms shall stand up out of the nation, but not in his power." Dan. 8:22.

Alexander died B. C. 323. His death was sudden and unexpected, he being in the prime of life; and no provision had been made for a successor. There were many aspirants for power, among the chief of whom was Antigonus. Lyman, in his Historical Chart, has given a view of the kingdom after the death of Alexander, in a few forcible words:—

ANOTHER LITTLE HORN. 113

"The empire was divided into thirty-three governments, distributed among as many general officers. Hence arose a series of bloody, desolating wars, and a period of confusion, anarchy, and crime ensued, that is almost without a parallel in the history of the world. After the battle of Ipsus, 301 B. C., in which Antigonus was defeated, the empire was divided into four kingdoms—Thrace and Bythinia under Lysimachus; Syria and the East under Seleucus; Egypt under Ptolemy Soter; and Macedonia under Cassander."

Two points are worthy of remark in this symbol and its fulfillment: (1) The prophecy takes no note whatever of this period of anarchy and confusion. It was a period of internal dissensions, in which there was neither time nor opportunity to establish kingdoms on anything like a permanent footing. (2) The four kingdoms which arose toward the four winds of heaven are considered but parts of the same Grecian kingdom. They are no doubt regarded a continuation of the same dominion because the four kings named entered into agreement to divide the kingdom among themselves; they reigned by mutual consent, and not in opposition to one another. This is marked in Dan. 7: 6, by the simple expression, "The beast had also four heads."

Verse 7. "After this I saw in the night visions, and behold a fourth beast, dreadful and terrible, and strong exceedingly; and it had great iron teeth; it devoured and brake in pieces, and stamped the residue with the feet of it; and it was diverse from all the beasts that were before it; and it had ten horns."

The likeness of the fourth kingdom, represented by the legs of the image in chapter 2, is readily seen in this beast. The fourth kingdom of iron was to be stronger than those preceding it; so this beast was strong exceedingly, and it had great iron teeth. "As iron breaketh in pieces and subdueth all things, and as iron that breaketh all these, shall it break in pieces and bruise," was said of the fourth kingdom, represented by the legs of the image; and so of this beast: "It devoured and brake in pieces, and stamped the residue with the feet of it."

And it had ten horns, which are said in verse 24 to be ten kings that shall arise. These ten kings were represented by the feet and toes of the image,—the ten kingdoms rising out of

8

the Roman empire when it was broken up by its invaders from the north and northeast. Thus far the facts presented in the vision of these four beasts are identical with those of the image in the dream of Nebuchadnezzar.

Chapter 2:43 says of these ten kingdoms, "They shall mingle themselves with the seed of men; but they shall not cleave one to another." This shows that these kingdoms were not smitten by the stone as soon as they arose; there must be a time for the mingling—for efforts at consolidation, for changes to take place—before the kingdom and dominion shall be given to the saints of the Most High.

This statement in chapter 2:43, in regard to their mingling, and yet not cleaving to one another, contains but a faint hint of all the changes which should take place before the closing scenes. The same idea is presented in verse 34. After the image was presented complete, Daniel said: "Thou sawest till that a stone was cut out," etc.; as if he continued to observe the image until the stone appeared. And we shall see that each succeeding vision, whether of Daniel or John, contains some additional events to precede the setting up of the kingdom of God, and the destruction of all the nations and kingdoms of this world. The additional facts in chapter 7 are principally brought to view in—

Verse 8. "I considered the horns, and, behold, there came up among them another little horn, before whom there were three of the first horns plucked up by the roots; and, behold, in this horn were eyes like the eyes of man, and a mouth speaking great things."

In all the Scriptures a horn is the symbol of power, without regard to the nature of the power. And there was an extraordinary power rising into notice just at the time when Western Rome was broken into these fragments or kingdoms. Verse 24 says, "He shall be diverse from the first." And this was diverse from the others in that it arose as a religious, a professedly Christian, power. Although it arose as a little horn, so that it did not at first take its place among the kingdoms of the earth, it became very strong, for its "look was more stout than its fellows." And it is so well known that it passes without proof, that the Romish Church kingdom became stronger than the strongest kingdoms of the earth. The heads of this system, the popes of Rome, claimed it as their right to rule over the kings, and to absolve subjects from their allegiance to any king who refused submission to their will. On this point Professor Gaussen, of Geneva, gave the following pointed and truthful testimony:—

"Daniel tells us (verse 20) that though this horn was the least, his 'look was more stout than his fellows.' The pomps of Charlemagne, Charles V., Louis XIV., and Bonaparte were very great; but were they comparable to that of the Roman pontiff? The greatest kings must hold his stirrup, serve him at table (what do I say?) must prostrate themselves before him, and kiss his feet; and even put their necks under his proud foot. Go yet this year to view him in the Vatican, as I myself have done. You will see hanging in the royal hall, where all the ambassadors of Europe pass, a picture representing the great emperor, Henry IV., uncovered before Gregory VII. You will see in another picture the heroic and powerful emperor Frederick Barbarossa upon his knees and elbows, before Pope Alexander III., in the public square of Venice; the foot of the pope rests on his shoulder; his scepter cast to the ground; and under the picture, these words: 'Frederick, a suppliant, adores, promising faith and obedience.' You must see with your own eyes this priest-king in his palaces and temples, to form an idea of his pomps, and to understand the full meaning of these words of Daniel: 'His look was more stout than his fellows.' What Eastern king was ever borne like him upon men's shoulders, decked with the plumes of the peacock? Incense is burnt before him as before an idol; they kneel on both knees before him; they kiss the soles of his feet; they worship him." Lecture in Geneva College, 1843.

Such was his rise, and such is his appearance. "And before whom three [kings] fell." All who are acquainted with the history, religious and secular, of the fourth and fifth centuries, are aware that the Arian controversy was the leading cause of dispute, not only in the churches and councils, but among kings. The Gothic kings were Arians; and in those days the people professed the faith of their kings. But the Church of Rome was the representative of the Trinitarian faith. This faith was indorsed by the Council of Nice, where the primacy was conferred upon the bishop of Rome. This forever bound the bishop of that see to that faith. The primacy and the doctrine of the Trinity were inseparable. That church was the chief support of what was then called the orthodox faith, while the Goths were held to be heretics.

The Heruli, under Odoacer, who were also Arians, took possession of Italy. Gibbon says:—

"Odoacer was the first Barbarian who reigned in Italy, over a people who had once asserted their just superiority above the rest of mankind. . . . Like the rest of the Barbarians, he had been instructed in the Arian heresy; but he revered the monastic and episcopal characters; and the silence of the Catholics attest the toleration which they enjoyed." Decline and Fall, chap. 36, paragraphs 32, 33.

In this respect the conduct of the Barbarian heretics was in strong contrast with that of the orthodox or Catholics, for these never failed to persecute the Arians when they had the power. And the spirit of persecution was so strongly entrenched in them that when they could not persecute those whom they consigned to perdition as heretics, they fell to quarreling among themselves. In them worldly ambition seemed to have entirely supplanted the spirit of Christianity. Of the time of Odoacer, Gibbon, in the same place, further says: "The peace of the city required the interposition of his prefect Basilius in the choice of a Roman pontiff." That is to say, that the election of a pope was accompanied with such party strifes that the authority of the Barbarian heretic was necessary to preserve the peace of the city, and to prevent bloodshed; for such an election was sometimes the occasion of fatal quarrels. It was also customary to purchase votes in the seclection of the pope, and the Arian king was obliged to use his authority to put an end to this scandal.

Upon the death of Pope Simplicius, in 483, the people and clergy assembled for the election of a new bishop for Rome. Then occurred that interference of Odoacer of which Gibbon spoke, as quoted above. Bower's History of the Popes says:—

"But while they were assembled for that purpose, in the Church of St. Peter, Basilius the *præfectus prætoria*, and lieutenant of King Odoacer, entered the assembly; and, addressing the electors, that is, the people, the senate, and the clergy, expressed great surprise at their taking upon them to appoint a successor to the deceased bishop, without him; adding, that it belonged to the civil magistrate to prevent the disturbances that might arise on such occasions, lest from the church they should pass to the State. . . . He then declared all they had done without him to be null; and ordered the election to be begun anew, though it was already near concluded. But, in the first place, he caused a law to be read in the name of Odoacer, forbidding the bishop, who should now be chosen, as well as his successors, to alienate any inheritance, possessions, or sacred utensils, that now belonged, or should for the future belong, to the church; declaring all such bargains void; anathematizing both the seller and the buyer; and obliging the latter, and his heirs, to restore to the church all lands and tenements thus purchased, how long soever they may have possessed them." Under Felix II.

"From this law," says Bower, "it is manifest that great abuses must have prevailed at this time in Rome, in the management of the goods belonging to the church." Indeed, it was well known that candidates for the chair of St. Peter had freely pledged the property of the church to procure votes in the "sacred college." where an infallible successor to St. Peter was to be chosen.

This might be called the first great humiliation that the popes of Rome were compelled to bear at the hands of an Arian king. Felix II. filled the papal chair by tolerance of Odoacer, and under restrictions placed upon him by one whom he esteemed an accursed heretic; for the law, read by order of the king, restrained the newly-elected pope, as well as his successors, from a practice which had been common with his predecessors. If any think that this was not a humiliation to one occupying the papal chair, let him read the life of Leo the Great, and consider what was already claimed as the right and proper authority of him who filled that position. As long as the Heruli possessed Italy, so long must the pope consider himself under the hateful supervision of those who were held to be enemies to the church and to the true faith. But to remedy this state of things was not an easy matter. From the time of Constantine, the emperors had assumed the oversight of the church, and the bishops, especially of Rome, the chief city of the empire, were elected and installed only by imperial consent. When the Barbarians ruled in Italy, their kings assumed the same right; and indeed, it became necessary for them to take the control of the important matters of the church, that the peace of the kingdom might be preserved. As Gibbon said, the peace of the city required their interposition. But it was irritating in the extreme to the ambitious popes, that they must hold their seats under the restraints imposed by a heretical king. True, they were not at all restrained from exercising jurisdiction in all matters spiritual; but that was not all that they demanded. But for the time being their demands were not only unheeded, but held in check. Of course it became an object to all who were of the Catholic faith, to have Italy freed from the rule of the Heruli.

Bower says that Theodoric, king of the Ostrogoths, then reigning in Pannonia, had served under the emperor, but "afterwards, thinking himself ill-used by that prince, not only quitted his service, but, at the head of his Goths, made war on the empire, till he was persuaded by the emperor to turn his arms against Odoacer, who reigned in Italy." Vol. 1, p. 283, note. Zeno, who was weak and inefficient, served a twofold purpose in turning Theodoric against the Heruli. Machiavel, in his "History of Florence," thus stated the case:—

"Zeno, partly by apprehension and partly wishing to drive Odoacer from Italy, consented that he should go against him and take possession of Italy. Theodoric immediately started from his States, where he left the Gepides, people with whom he was on friendly terms, and having come into Italy, he killed Odoacer, with his son; and according to the already established custom, he took the title of king of Italy." Vol. 1, pp. 15, 16, French edition of Desborkes, Amsterdam, 1694.

Zeno was orthodox, that is, in full sympathy with the Roman pontiff, and by his connivance, one of the ten kingdoms was plucked up, and an important step was thus taken to free the pope from Arian domination. But, although it was absolutely necessary that the king of the Heruli should be removed, it was soon found that one dictator of the pope was vanquished to give place to another. Theodoric, as had Odoacer before him, in no manner opposed the free action of the Roman bishop in any matter coming legitimately under the jurisdiction of the spiritual head of the church. But he took the same oversight of the church, and compelled the orthodox to do justice to the Arians, who were being subjected to severe persecutions by Justin, the emperor of the East, who was as inefficient as Zeno before him, and more radical in his devotion to the Catholic cause. This brings us to the second humiliation of the popes by the Arians.

Gibbon attributes this persecution, not to Justin but to Justinian, who was already associated in the government. The conduct of Justinian when he became emperor fully justifies the judgment of the historians. These are his words:—

"After the death of Anastasius, the diadem had been placed on the head of a feeble old man; but the powers of government were assumed by his nephew Justinian, who already meditated the extirpation of heresy, and the conquest of Italy and Africa. A rigorous law, which was published at Constantinople, to reduce the Arians by the dread of punishment within the pale of the church, awakened the just resentment of Theodoric, who claimed for his distressed brethren of the East the same indulgence which he had so long granted to the Catholics of his dominions. At his stern command, the Roman pontiff, with four illustrious senators, embarked on an embassy, of which he must have alike dreaded the failure or the success." Decline and Fall, chap. 39, paragraph 17.

In reading the above it must be borne in mind that, though Justinian was publicly proclaimed associate emperor only four months before the death of Justin, " the powers of government were assumed " by him, as Gibbon says, before that time; he really controlled affairs under his superannuated uncle.

Bower has given a minute account of the embassy of Pope John I. to the court of Constantinople. The Arians in the East appealed to Theodoric to procure, if possible, a mitigation of the horrors into which they were consigned by the action of the emperor. Theodoric was too humane to retaliate without an effort to have the edict reversed by more gentle means. But by what means his purpose could be accomplished, it was difficult to determine. Bower says:—

" He thought of many ; weighed and examined many ; and at last fixed upon one, which he apprehended could not fail of the wished-for success. He knew what weight the advice and counsels of the pope had with the emperor ; how much the emperor deferred to the judgment of the bishop of Rome, in all matters of religion and conscience; and therefore did not doubt that the persecution would soon be at an end, could the pope by any means be prevailed upon to espouse the cause of the persecuted Arians."

"The king was sensible that it was only by menaces, by force, and compulsion, that the pope could be brought to act such a part; and resolved, accordingly, to employ them at once, that no room might be left for delays and excuses. Having therefore sent for him to Ravenna, he complained to him with great warmth of the unchristian spirit and proceedings of the emperor; . . . comparing the happy situation of the heretics, meaning the Catholics in his dominion, with the unhappy condition of the Catholics in those of the emperor, he added: 'But I must let you know that I am determined not to sit as an idle spectator on such an occasion. I am, you know, and I have often declared it, an enemy to all kinds of persecution; I have suffered not only the inhabitants of Italy, but even my Goths, to embrace and profess, undisturbed, which of the two religions they thought the most pleasing to God; and, in the distribution of my favors, have hitherto made no distinction between Catholic and heretic. But if the emperor does not change his measures, I must change mine. Men of other religions the emperor may treat as he pleases, though every man has a right to serve the Creator in the manner which he thinks the most acceptable to him. But as for those who profess the same religion which I profess, I think myself bound to employ the power which it has pleased God to put into my hands for their defense and protection. If the emperor therefore does not think fit to evoke the edict, which he has lately issued against those of my persuasion, it is my firm resolution to issue the like edict against those of his; and to see it everywhere executed with the same rigor. Those who do not profess the faith of Nice are heretics to him; and those who do are heretics to me. Whatever can excuse and justify his severity to the former will excuse and justify mine to the latter. But the emperor,' continued the king, ' has none about him who dare freely and openly speak what they think, or to whom he would hearken if they did. But the great veneration which he professes for your see leaves no room to doubt but he would hearken to you. I will therefore have you to repair forthwith to Constantinople, and there to remonstrate both in my name and your own, against the violent measures in which that court has so rashly engaged. It is in your power to divert the emperor from them; and till you have, nay, till the Catholics, the Arians, are restored to the free exercise of their religion, and to all the churches from which they have been driven, you must not think of returning to Italy.'" History of the Popes, under John I.

Some authors say that there was a disagreement between the pope and the king in regard to the terms of the embassy, and that the king took him prisoner, and was about to convey him away. Bower says: "However that may be, certain it is that the pope undertook the embassy, not out of any kindness to the Arians, with which he has been by some unjustly reproached, but to divert the storm that threatened the Catholics in his dominions." And, in all the history of Rome, this is the only occasion on which her bishops ever endeavored to mitigate the cruelty of persecutions against those whom they considered heretics. And in this embassy, though he procured a reversal of the inhuman edict of the emperor, the evidence points towards a conspiracy against the king for the overthrow of the Arians, for the pope was made a prisoner on his return. Some, however, think that his imprisonment was caused by a failure to procure all that Theodoric required in the way of justice to the Arians in the East, as he did not doubt that the emperor would have granted all if they had pressed it, as they had been commanded. On this point the exact truth may never be known; but whatever the cause, the pope died in prison under the Arian rule.

The popes, from the days of Constantine, had assumed most arrogant airs; and especially from the time of Leo the Great. And John himself was not a whit behind them in his pretensions. Of his forced visit to Constantinople, Bower says:—

"The patriarch invited the pope to perform divine service in the great church, together with him. But he would neither accept the invitation, nor even see the patriarch, till he agreed not only to yield him the first place, but to seat him on a kind of throne above himself. It is observable that the pope alleged no other reason why he should be allowed this mark of distinction than because he was bishop of Rome, or of the first city." *Ib.*

We can but faintly imagine what must have been the feelings of this arrogant bishop, when sent on an embassy to intercede for those whom he declared heretics, and whom he would gladly have seen exterminated. But when he returned to his own see, in the first city, he was as helpless and dependent as the meanest citizen. And this humiliation the popes were obliged to bear as long as the Arian Ostrogoths possessed Italy.

But this was not the only humiliation which the primate, the head of the orthodox faith, had to suffer. The Vandals were in possession of Africa, and they also were Arians. Emulating the spirit of the orthodox or Catholic emperor, they were bitterly persecuting the Trinitarians in their dominions. The pope was compelled to intercede in behalf of the Arians in the East, and to put a stop to the persecutions which were raging against them; but he had no power to check the persecution which those of his own communion were suffering in Africa.

Justin died A. D. 527. Speaking of the persecution in the time of Justin, Gibbon said that Justinian "already meditated the extirpation of heresy, and the conquest of Italy and Africa." His effort to put down heresy in the East was foiled by the king of Italy; and now there remained no way to check its sway, but by the conquest of Africa and Italy. Until this was done, the pope was constantly humiliated. For this purpose the emperor sent Belisarius, an able general, against Africa, in 534. Of the capture of Carthage, the Vandal capital, Gibbon says:—

"The defeat of the Vandals, and the freedom of Africa, were announced to the city on the eve of St. Cyprian, when the churches were already adorned and illuminated for the festival of the martyr, whom three centuries of superstition had almost raised to a local deity. The Arians, conscious that their reign had expired, resigned the temple to the Catholics, who rescued their saint from profane hands, performed the holy rites, and loudly proclaimed the creed of Athanasius and Justinian. One awful hour reversed the fortunes of the contending parties." Chap. xli, paragraph 9.

The king of the Vandals collected his scattered and feeble forces, and engaged in the final struggle not far from Carthage. Both armies were small, and Gibbon thus speaks of the results of this battle:—

"Yet no more than fifty Romans, and eight hundred Vandals, were found on the field of battle; so inconsiderable was the carnage of a day, which extinguished a nation, and transferred the empire of Africa." Id., paragraph 10.

Thus was the second of the ten kingdoms removed to serve the interests of the papacy. The king of the Vandals was not taken, however, until the year 535, when he was brought to grace the triumph given to Belisarius in Constantinople.

Yet the tide of prosperity was not altogether smooth for Justinian in his own territory. Although the Trinitarians were free from opposition by the heretics, they could not agree among themselves as to the terms in which their faith should be expressed. In other words, they quarreled about the method of defining a doctrine which none of them understood.

And this very condition was the occasion of more strife and bloodshed than any other cause that troubled the church. The Nestorians and Justinian were in open opposition to each other, and the monks resolved to appeal to the pope, where they counted on an easy triumph, inasmuch as their definition had been declared by a preceding pope, in the same terms that they used. But Justinian appealed to the pope also: and his appeal was accompanied by the weighty argument of a gift to St. Peter, consisting of several chalices, and other vessels of gold, enriched with precious stones. This, with his confession of faith, Justinian sent to the pope, with a most obsequious letter, lauding the pope in the most courtly terms, and proceeding to declare that he, the pope, was the head of all the churches; that he, the emperor, had subjected to his see all the churches of the whole East; and that the pope was the effectual corrector of heretics. It was a trying time for the pope: it was difficult for him to declare against the express words of his predecessor, and still more difficult to decide against the emperor, and all the bishops of the East who favored him. After much consultation, had, no doubt, to avoid giving offense to those of the West, it was decided in favor of Justinian.

This was indeed an eventful time for the professed see of St. Peter. Gibbon speaks thus of the action of Justinian, after the triumph of Belisarius in Africa:—

"He received the messengers of victory at the time when he was preparing to publish the Pandects of the Roman law; and the devout or jealous emperor celebrated the divine goodness, and confessed in silence, the merit of his successful general. Impatient to abolish the temporal and spiritual tyranny of the Vandals, he proceeded, without delay, to the full establishment of the Catholic Church. Her jurisdiction, wealth, and immunities, perhaps the most essential part of episcopal religion, were restored and amplified with a liberal hand; the Arian worship was suppressed; the Donatist meetings were proscribed; and the synod of Carthage, by the voice of two hundred and seventeen bishops, applauded the just measure of pious retaliation." Decline and Fall, chap. xli, paragraph 11.

Belisarius was next sent to subdue the Goths in Italy. He was delayed by the jealousy and ill-will of the emperor; but he entered Rome in 536, and sent the keys of the city to Justinian as the sign that he was master of the city. But the victory was not by any means complete, as the Barbarians under Vitiges besieged Rome with Belisarius in it. The siege lasted over a year. See Gibbon and Bower. But the siege became disastrous and unprofitable to the Barbarians. Finally, unfavorable news from Rimini caused the Gothic leader to risk one more effort before leaving the vicinity of the city; but the attack was disastrous to the besiegers, and they retreated, not soon to return. Italy was rescued to the emperor, and the third kingdom was taken away to relieve the Catholic Church, and the popes, from their heretical masters. It is true that Barbarians from time to time renewed their efforts to recover what Belisarius had taken from them. Their retreat was in 538, at which time the letter of Justinian to Pope John I., in which all the churches were subjected to his authority, became more than a hope, which it had hitherto been to the pope, for the emperor was now able to give effect to the gracious promises which he had made to the pontiff.

The prophet Daniel said of the little horn, which came up after the ten, that before him "there were three of the first horns plucked up by the roots." This we have seen was accomplished between the years 493, when Odoacer was defeated and slain, which ended the reign of the Heruli, and 538, when Italy was recovered from the Ostrogoths.

Dan. 7: 25. "And he shall speak great words against the Most High, and shall wear out the saints of the Most High, and think to change times and laws; and they shall be given into his hand until a time and times and the dividing of time."

Four specifications are here presented, and each has been most faithfully fulfilled by the papacy. Not a power, not a prerogative, not a title, was ever given to, or claimed by, the Most High God but has been claimed by, and given to, the pope of Rome. Indeed, under the name of "that man of sin," Paul has described him as exalting himself above all that is called God or that is worshiped. 2 Thess. 2: 1–9. That he has worn out the saints of the Most High, all history attests. The Judgment-day alone will reveal the number of the victims who perished by fire, by the sword, by wild beasts, by the tortures and in the dungeons of the Inquisition. The Scriptures will never fail; the description of that power by St. Paul was written by inspiration, and has its perfect fulfillment. And what power ever fulfilled it by exalting itself as the papacy has done? What power ever wore out the saints of the Most High as that apostate church literally wore them out for long centuries? What other power ever continued long enough to hold dominion over the saints, and to make them the victims of its religious hatred and unbounded ambition, as long a time as is here given to this horn? "And they shall be given into his hand until a time and times and the dividing of time."

This expression is easily explained. In Dan. 4:16, 23, 25, and 32, the expression "seven times" is used. These seven times were to pass upon Nebuchadnezzar, king of Babylon, during which he should be shut out of his kingdom, and live with the cattle, because of his pride. And Josephus, book 10, chap. 10, sec. 6, says that Nebuchadnezzar was driven out from his kingdom for seven years. And he is not the only authority for applying the word "time" to a year.

In other scriptures this period of three times and a half is so numbered that it is necessary to ascertain how many days we must count for a year. No exact measurement ever has been or ever can be adopted, from the fact that, in computing the days of the revolution of the earth around the sun, a fraction remains. In the course of years these fractions amount to a considerable sum—sufficient to disarrange the seasons. For this reason intercalary periods have to be used; that is, the years are counted of unequal length, and days or longer periods are thrown in to rectify the discrepancy. In our present computation the months have no certain length, an arbitrary number of days being given to each, and the fraction remaining is nearly accounted for by adding a day to February every four years. Yet exactness requires that another be added at much longer periods.

But the computation given in the Scriptures is entirely different. Twelve months, with thirty days to the month, were counted for a year, giving a round number of three hundred and sixty days,—five less than in the present method. While we add one day to every fourth year, their deficiency being greater, they had to add longer periods, which they called a month. The twelfth month was called Adar, and the intercalated month was called *Veadar*—literally, And-Adar; equivalent to, Another-Adar. But as we commonly call a period of three hundred and sixty-five days a year, taking no note of the intercalated days, so they called the year three hundred and sixty days, not noting the intercalated month. That thirty was the number of days counted to a month, we learn in Genesis, chapters 7 and 8. In Gen. 7:11 it is said that the flood came upon the earth in the second month, the seventeenth day of the month. In chapter 8:4 it says the ark rested the seventh month, the seventeenth day of the month. And from the seventeenth day of the second month to the seventeenth day of the seventh month is just five months. And chapter 7:24 says that the waters prevailed upon the earth an hundred and fifty days. An hundred and fifty days divided between five months give thirty days to the month. And twelve months of thirty days to the month make a year of three hundred and sixty days. This point is clear; a year, or a literal time, contains three hundred and sixty days.

It has already been shown that a time is equal to a year, and a time and times and half a time would make twelve hundred and sixty days. Thus: one time, three hundred and sixty days; two times, seven hundred and twenty days; and half a time, one hundred and eighty days, together equal to twelve hundred and sixty. And this computation is verified in Revelation 12. Verse 14 says that the woman fled into the wilderness, where she was nourished for a time and times and half a time from the face of the serpent. And verse 6 says she was in the wilderness a thousand two hundred and threescore days—1260. This is the period in which the little horn had power to wear out the saints of the Most High, according to Dan. 7:25.

But 1260 days make only three and a half years, while the papacy wore out the saints for many centuries. How are we to understand this? It is true that in Daniel 4 we found that seven times made just seven years, which is literal time, because that was a period relating to the life of a single man. He was driven out from his kingdom for seven years, but that did not destroy his kingdom. It stood ready for him, and he ruled in it when his reason was restored to him. But the little horn does not represent a man or a single individual; it is the symbol of a power that stood and acted through many centuries. When applied to a symbol, time is always counted a day for a year. This rule is laid down in Eze. 4:1–6. The prophet was to represent the siege of Jerusalem, by lying as many days as the city was to be besieged years. Said the Lord, "I have appointed thee each day for a year." And this again is shown in Daniel 9, where seventy weeks are given unto a certain event, which are known to be weeks of years— seven years to a week. This is recognized by all. And this fact, that each day is counted for a year, answers the query about the length of time the little horn had power over the saints; it was 1260 years, instead of 1260 literal days. As this time is more particularly spoken of in the book of Revelation, the evidence as to its beginning and ending will be examined in connection with an examination of some prophecies in that book.

Thus briefly have the several parts of the vision been examined; the climax, "the effect of every vision," Eze. 12:23, is again presented in verse 27:—

"And the kingdom and dominion, and the greatness of the kingdom under the whole heaven, shall be given to the people of the saints of the Most High, whose kingdom is an everlasting kingdom, and all dominions shall serve and obey him."

According to the current theories of men, the saints possessed the kingdom long before this little horn arose, even before the Roman kingdom was divided. But the Scriptures always speak in a different manner. This is the period of their tribulation. Here all that live godly in Christ must suffer persecution. Here death and the grave hold them in their embrace. But a change is coming, the saints will get the victory over all their foes, and possess the kingdom forever and ever. The order of events is again given in Dan. 7: 21, 22:—

"I beheld, and the same horn made war with the saints, and prevailed against them; until the Ancient of days came, and judgment was given to the saints of the Most High; and the time came that the saints possessed the kingdom."

This testimony is unmistakable and sure. This is the consummation of all prophecy. The saints are yet the Lord's waiting ones. The promises to Abraham and his seed have not yet been fulfilled. The meek have not yet inherited the earth; they have never had the privilege of delighting themselves in the abundance of peace in the land of Abraham's sojourning. The throne of David is not yet given to his seed, "whose right it is." He is yet seated upon the throne of the Majesty in the Heavens, expecting till his own throne—his throne by birth of the line of Judah—shall be given him. Rev. 3:21; Luke 1: 32, 33. Still the longing ones, the believing ones, who wait for the fulfillment of the promises of the Lord, earnestly pray, "Thy kingdom come."

CHAPTER XI.

THE BEAST WITH SEVEN HEADS AND TEN HORNS.

The twelfth and thirteenth chapters of the Revelation so naturally follow the seventh of Daniel that some facts in Daniel's prophecy are passed over for the present, in order to follow out this chain. The thirteenth chapter of Revelation is, indeed, the complement of the seventh of Daniel; but a brief notice of Revelation 12 is necessary as preliminary to the study of chapter 13.

In chapter 12 are presented two prominent objects:—

1. A woman, which is a symbol of the church of Christ. She was clothed with the sun—the rising glory of the new, or gospel, dispensation. And the moon was under her feet—the paler glory of the dispensation just passing away. All the institutions of the Mosaic economy borrowed their light from the coming Messiah, the Son of God, the antitype of all its sacrifices, as the moon borrows her light from the sun. She had a crown of twelve stars—the twelve apostles of the Lamb. That this woman represented the church of God is evident from this circumstance, that to the woman was born a son, who was to rule all nations with a rod of iron, and who was caught up to God and his throne. This will apply to the Lord Jesus Christ and to no one else. Again, in the seventeenth chapter of this book, a woman represents the apostate church, the church of antichrist. Thus the two churches—that of Christ and that of antichrist—are represented by women.

2. The other prominent object in this chapter is a great red dragon. Two views are held in regard to this: (1) That the dragon is Satan. This view has this advantage, that the dragon

is called the devil and Satan in verse 9, and is there represented as the leader of the angels that fought against Michael, who is the Archangel, Jude 9, and his angels. And also the devil, or Satan, is called the dragon in chapter 20:2. This certainly seems decisive. (2) It is held that the dragon is a symbol of pagan Rome. In favor of this view is presented the appearance of the dragon, having seven heads and ten horns. These heads and horns are elsewhere used as symbols, and they certainly do not belong to the devil literally. Such is not the personal appearance of the devil.

Doubtless there is truth in both these views, and the whole truth seems to be comprised in the two. There is great uniformity of belief among the best authors that Satan is addressed directly as "king of Tyrus," in Eze. 28:12–19, while the reigning monarch was called the prince of Tyrus. Verses 1–10. Tyre was the great seat of commerce, the mart of nations; her merchants were princes, her traffickers the honorable of the earth. Isa. 23:3, 8. And her wickedness corresponded to her wealth and her greatness. She was Satan's chief instrument and representative in the days of her prosperity. And also of Rome. What nation or city ever served Satan so faithfully and so successfully as Rome? For many centuries it was the very seat of his service and his power. Cruelty and licentiousness were the characteristics of her people, from king to slave, under all phases of her dominion. Of this we are assured by history, yet how few of the crimes of her mighty men have come down through history. Under the circumstances, we see no difficulty in representing Satan as that old serpent, the dragon, and then letting the dragon stand as his chief representative—pagan Rome.

The dragon sought to put the man child to death as soon as he was born. An effort was put forth to slay the infant Jesus in Bethlehem. In this effort all the children of Bethlehem two years old and under were put to death—an act worthy of Satan himself. But it was committed under the order of a Roman king; and the Lord Jesus was finally put to death by another Roman king. The dragon then persecuted

THE BEAST WITH SEVEN HEADS AND TEN HORNS.

the woman; he continued his persecution during the time and times and half, though she was protected from his power; and he will also persecute the remnant of her seed, the very last state of the church, "which keep the commandments of God, and have the testimony of Jesus Christ." Rev. 12:17. Compare chap. 19:10. These facts prove that the dragon does not leave the field of action while time endures.

In Rev. 13:1, 2 is described the rise and appearance of a beast, in the following words:—

"And I stood upon the sand of the sea, and saw a beast rise up out of the sea, having seven heads and ten horns, and upon his horns ten crowns, and upon his heads the name of blasphemy. And the beast which I saw was like unto a leopard, and his feet were as the feet of a bear, and his mouth as the mouth of a lion: and the dragon gave him his power, and his seat, and great authority."

By comparing this beast with the beasts in Dan. 7:1-7 it will be seen that it contains all the main features of all the beasts of that chapter. All rose out of the sea. In Rev. 17:15 waters are shown to represent the multitudes of people. It will yet be seen that there is a contrast presented on this point: they did not grow up; the powers they represent were not built up; they rose up by conquest and strivings among the nations.

The description of this beast gives the order the reverse of that in Daniel 7, because the two prophets stood at opposite ends of the chain. John said the beast was like unto a leopard —the third beast of Daniel 7, the symbol of the Grecian kingdom. His feet were as the feet of a bear—the second beast of Daniel, the kingdom of the Medes and the Persians. And his mouth was as the mouth of a lion—the first beast of Daniel, Babylon. Thus far the likeness is complete. But this is not all. The beast had seven heads and ten horns. There is no question ever raised against the idea that these horns are the same powers that are represented by the horns on the fourth beast of Daniel 7. Thus all the four beasts combine in this. But no theory which has ever been published concerning these heads fully satisfies the prophecy, but that does not hinder our identifying the beast itself. A comparison of its work, the time of its continuance, etc., with the same features of the "little horn" of Daniel 7, is sufficient to settle beyond all controversy that the two symbols represent the same power.

Can we see any object in the prophecy thus giving to this beast every prominent feature of those beasts? Certainly we can. This beast is the actual heir to the dominion held by those four beasts. An objection against this has been offered to the intent that the dominion of the popes was so limited that it cannot be said that they inherited the dominion of the great monarchies. This objection is based on wrong views of the papal power, as to both its nature and extent. On this point verse 2 says, "And the dragon gave him his power, and his seat, and great authority." This is very important ground and should be very carefully examined.

First, what is meant by the expression, "the supremacy of the papacy"? In what did the strength of the papal power consist? The word supremacy is a proper word to use in reference to the power of the popes, but not in regard to their civil power. This was not only quite limited, but variable and uncertain. Indeed, civil power is not necessary to the existence of the papacy, as all know; neither is it necessary to the exercise of the largest power ever exercised by the popes. The possession of civil power gives prestige in a certain sense, as the pope is thereby classed among kings, no matter how small his territory, and it brings him into closer relations to other governments. But it must be borne in mind that the popes never exercised power over kings by virtue of their own kingship, but always by reason of their priesthood. They never pretended to control kings, or to absolve subjects from their allegiance, by reason of their kingly power, but as being successors of St. Peter—as vicars of Christ upon earth. They claimed that, as all power was given to Christ in Heaven and upon earth, so must his vicar, the one who holds that power on earth, have a right to exercise all that power. Pope Symmachus said to the emperor of the East, that the pope was as much superior to an emperor as heavenly things are superior to earthly things. This was an admission on his part, that his supremacy was altogether in his spiritual authority; but the popes chose to overlook the acknowledged fact that their power as temporal princes took so much from their exalted position, as it made them ministers of merely earthly things in their priesthood. This is the logical conclusion, from the position assumed by Symmachus, though it is not the manner in which it has been viewed. And it should also be borne in mind that, at the time of Symmachus, he did not claim, or even directly aspire to, the exercise of civil power.

It was in their spiritual power alone that their strength and supremacy consisted. Their anathemas, their curses of kings, their control over the subjects of kings, were all by virtue of their assumed power as the high priests of the kingdom of Christ. This was exercised without any regard to the extent of their territorial jurisdiction as civil rulers, or even to the existence of such jurisdiction.

We have been thus particular on this point, as it is one of great importance. The extent of papal power deserves special attention. Because the beginning of the civil power of the papacy is veiled in considerable obscurity, it has been argued that we cannot point with certainty to any particular time for the setting up of the papacy. But this is not correct. Examining this subject with care, we shall find that *four steps* were taken, and only four, which fully established the power of the popes; and these steps are readily identified.

First, conferring the primacy upon the bishop of Rome, which was done by the Council of Nice, and confirmed by the royal commissioners. Because the title did not, *at that time*, carry with it any great weight, or confer any particular power, some have thought that the primacy, as then established, did not amount to much. But they overlook the nature of the hierarchy as established by Constantine, and the consequences that naturally grew out of this gift. Bower gives a minute account of the church establishment, and from this some extracts are here given. He first describes the churches in their original independence, and their councils, being voluntary meetings, "there being no Christian magistrates in those days to convene synods." It is a fact that from the Council of Nice onwards, the magistrates convened synods and councils. Before the emperor took the headship of the national church, there was no earthly head of the church recognized. Bower says:—

"Such was the hierarchy, such the government of the church, during the first three centuries. But in the fourth and following ages great alterations were made in both, the church adapting her government to that of the State, namely, to the new form of government introduced by Constantine, who had taken the priesthood under his immediate protection. For it was in his reign that the titles of Patriarchs, Exarchs, Metropolitans, were first heard of, or at least had any power, authority, or privileges, annexed to them. That this conformity between the civil and ecclesiastical polity may appear more plainly, I shall premise a succinct account of the former, as established by Constantine throughout the empire."

Here follows a description of the organization of the empire into prefectures, dioceses, provinces, with proconsuls, vicars, consulars, correctors, and presidents. "Each diocese had its metropolis, and likewise each province contained in the diocese." He continues:—

"Now, if we compare the civil polity thus described, with the ecclesiastical, we shall find them in most places answering each other, in every respect, and one bishop raised above the rest, according to the rank that was given in this new division to the city in which he presided. Thus, for instance, the chief cities of the five dioceses of the oriental prefecture were—Antioch, the metropolis of the oriental diocese; Alexandria, of the Egyptian; Ephesus, of the Asiatic; Cæsarea, of the Pontic; and Heraclea, of the Thracian. Now the bishops of these cities, in regard of the eminence of their sees, were exalted above all other bishops, and distinguished with the title of exarchs; nay, and by degrees they acquired, not to say usurped, a kind of authority and jurisdiction over the bishops of the inferior sees, which was afterwards confirmed to them by several councils. In like manner, the bishops of the metropolis of each province was, on account of the dignity of his see, honored with the title of metropolitan. to which were annexed certain privileges, of which I shall speak hereafter."

After further remarks and descriptions, he adds the following significant passage:—

"However, the power of the bishop of Rome far exceeded, within the bounds of his jurisdiction, that of other metropolitans, as I shall show." History of the Popes, under Sylvester.

Another historian makes the following remarks:—

"The bishop of Rome took precedence over all others of the episcopal order. Nor was this pre-eminence founded solely on popular feeling and a prejudice of long standing, sprung from various causes; but also on those grounds which commonly give priority and greatness in the estimation of mortals. For he exceeded all other bishops in the amplitude and splendor of the church over which he presided, in the magnitude of his revenues and possessions, in the number of his ministers of various descriptions, in the weight of his influence with the people at large, and in the sumptuousness and magnificence of his style of living. These marks of power and worldly greatness were so fascinating to the minds of Christians even in this age, that often most obstinate and bloody contests took place at Rome when a new pontiff was to be created by the suffrages of the priests and people." Murdock's Mosheim, Ecclesiastical History, Book 2, Cent. 4, Part 2, chap. 2, sec. 5 (London, 1845).

Now, inasmuch as the bishops were possessed of power and dignity according to the rank of the city over which they presided, as Bower says, especial dignity and the primacy were given to the bishop of Rome, because it was the imperial city. *And every step in the transformation of the pagan empire into the papal empire, proves that the higher honor conferred upon the bishop of Rome, was not because of any supposed primacy of Peter, or of any other apostle, but solely because of the imperial rank of the city.*

The Council of Chalcedon proceeded to confer prerogatives upon the bishop of Constantinople, against which the Roman delegates protested, as encroachments upon the primacy of Rome. The imperial commissioners who heard the plea, thus decided:—

"From the whole discussion, and from what has been brought forward on either side, we acknowledge that the primacy over all and the most eminent rank are to continue with the archbishop of old Rome." Schaff, Church History, Vol. 2, p. 281.

Considering that the church was just as extensive as the empire, that its officers corresponded to those of the several divisions or provinces of the empire, "the primacy over all and the most eminent rank" no longer appears to be an unimportant matter; and yet more especially, when we consider the other steps that were taken in connection with it, or soon after.

Second, Constantine conferred certain civil privileges and

powers upon the bishops, and, as usual, the highest upon the bishops of Rome. Sozomen gives the following testimony on this subject:—

"Constantine likewise enacted a law in favor of the clergy, permitting judgment to be passed by the bishops when litigants preferred appealing to them rather than to the secular court; he enacted that their decree should be valid, and as far superior to that of other judges as if pronounced by the emperor himself; that the governor and subordinate military officers should see to the execution of these decrees; and that sentence, when passed by them, should be irreversible." Ecclesiastical History, chap. 2.

It was not an idle expression of Stanley when he called the bishop of Rome "the chief Christian magistrate." All the bishops were elevated by this decree, but the bishop of Rome had the highest rank and primacy over all. Thus two important steps were taken, tending directly to the exaltation of the bishop of the imperial city; to him was given the primacy and the chief rank, and he was a civil magistrate with great authority. But little foresight were needed to anticipate the result of such steps, especially taken in connection with those which followed.

Third, Constantine removed the seat of empire from Rome to Constantinople. Following the others, this step opened the way for the gratification of the most unbounded ambition of the Roman bishop. Of the effect of this step, Stanley says:—

"According to the fable of Sylvester, Constantine retired to Greece in order to leave Italy for the pope—'*per cedera al pastor si fece Creco*.' So said the legend, and it was undoubtedly the case that, by retiring to the East, he left the field clear for the bishop of Rome In the absence of the emperors from Rome, the chief Christian magistrate rose to new importance. When the Barbarians broke upon Italy, the pope thus became the representative of the ancient republic. It is one of the many senses in which the saying of Hobbes is true, that the papacy is but the ghost of the deceased Roman empire, sitting crowned upon the grave thereof."

In a paragraph already quoted, Machiavel attributes the downfall of the Western Roman Empire to this removal of the capital. A work entitled, "A Concise History of the Papal Supremacy," published in Dublin, 1810, takes a most rational view of this move of Constantine. It says:—

"It is most certain that if the emperors had continued to reside at Rome, its bishops never would have usurped a supremacy."

This fact is so evident that it is useless to multiply words in proof. The removal of the capital not only opened the way before the bishop of Rome, but the result was almost inevitable, that with the primacy over the whole church as extensive as the empire itself, and a civil magistracy of a very high grade in his hands, with possessions and revenues above all others, presiding in the imperial city, he must of necessity rise to great worldly importance when the emperors removed their throne as remote as to Constantinople, and the empire itself was beset on every hand by invading armies, and the emperors unable to afford relief. The emperors had before taken up their residences temporarily outside of the city of Rome; but this was a permanent removal, an entire resignation of the true seat of the empire. Thus far was the scripture fulfilled: "The dragon gave him his power, and his seat, and great authority."

But the work was not yet complete. Others were ambitious as well as the bishop of Rome, and with the throne of the empire at Constantinople, that became actually the imperial city. For this reason the bishop of Constantinople thought that he should be first in rank. True, the primacy was conferred upon the bishop of Rome at the Council of Nice, but great changes had taken place since that time, and other bishops, but especially the bishop of Constantinople, strove for the highest honors. And everything seemed favorable to his purpose. An orthodox emperor, ambitious and powerful, was reigning in Constantinople. The Arians held Italy, though under a mild sway; but the neighboring country of Africa was not only under the rule of the Arians, but they were faithfully following the example set them by the orthodox or Catholic party—they were persecuting their opponents in the faith. The surroundings of the pope were every way unfavorable, while everything appeared favorable to the bishop of Constantinople. But an unexpected opportunity occurred. There were divisions in the East, and Justinian was strongly favorable to the Roman see, inasmuch as Rome was the representative of the Nicene faith, and its constant defender.

The condition of the so-called Christian world was most

deplorable. They who read the discussions of those times cannot fail to be struck by, if not disgusted with, the quarrelings over forms of expressing distinctions which the Scriptures do not notice, and which the parties did not at all understand. It not infrequently happened that the orthodox party stood in defense of the very modes of expression which it had strenuously opposed and condemned not long before. If a form of faith was held by those to whom they took a dislike, it was immediately denounced as heretical, and this was always the key-note of persecution, and often of blood-shedding. Of that very time Bower speaks:—

"The Christian worship was now become no less idolatrous than that of the Gentiles, who therefore chose to retain their own, there being no material difference between the one and the other, between their worshiping the ancient heroes, or the modern saints; and as to the articles of belief, they were now, by the cavils and subtilities of the contending parties, rendered quite unintelligible to the Christians themselves."

That to which we have previously referred must now be noticed more in detail. The expression, "One of the Trinity suffered in the flesh," was the subject of contention between Justinian and the monks of the East. That expression, though perfectly orthodox all down the ages of the church, had been condemned by Pope Hormisdas; but Justinian, who delighted in controversies on such distinctions, had adopted it. The monks, having the decision of a former pope on their side, had no doubt of an easy triumph if they appealed to the pope. But they were not as wise by experience in the devious ways of papal infallibility as they afterwards became. Bower gives the issue of the controversy thus:—

"The emperor no sooner heard that the monks were applying, than he too resolved to apply to the pope. Having therefore drawn up a long creed, or confession of faith, conta'ning the disputed article among the rest, 'one of the Trinity suffered in the flesh,' he dispatched two bishops with it to Rome, Hypatius of Ephesus, and Demetrius of Philippi. At the same time he wrote a very obliging letter to the pope, congratulating him on his election, assuring him that the faith contained in the confession that he sent him, was the faith of the whole Eastern Church, and entreating him to declare, in his answer, that he received to his communion all who professed that faith, and none who did not. To add weight to his letter, he accompanied it with a present to St. Peter, consisting of several chalices, and other vessels

of gold, enriched with precious stones. The deputies of the monks, and the two bishops sent by the emperor, arrived at Rome about the same time; and the pope heard both; but, being quite at a loss what to determine, wisely declined, for the present, returning an answer to either. He was sensible that he could not condemn the doctrine of the monks without admitting the expression, which his predecessor had rejected as repugnant to the Catholic faith. But, on the other hand, he was unwilling to disoblige Justinian, and well apprised of the consequences which he had reason to apprehend from his condemning a doctrine that was held by all the bishops of the East, and the emperor himself, as an article of faith." History of the Popes, under John II.

In this dilemma he took council of the clergy, and appealed to the wisest bishops of the time, who, after deliberation, decided that the confession of Justinian was altogether orthodox, and condemned as heretics all who denied it, or held a contrary doctrine. Thus was one infallibility contradicted by another infallibility, on a point of faith, and both remained infallible. Had the question stood the other way, had Justinian been in harmony with the decision before given by Hormisdas, the pope would not have taken a moment for consultation over the matter.

To show that the popes were conscious of their power, it may be worth while here to note that Pope Agapetus, successor of John II., was not in all things so complaisant to Justinian. The emperor wrote another courteous letter to him, and granted some favors and privileges to the pope, and asked certain favors of him in return, but these the pope denied him.

But Justinian's letter to Pope John II. is that which specially demands our attention. This was written in the year 533, the same in which Belisarius went on his expedition against the Arians in Africa. But first it may be well to notice the real effect of Arian rule and Arian toleration in Italy. The popes chafed under the restraining rule of heretics, as may be judged from the fate of John I.: but the situation as set down by the historian, Gieseler, shows the direction in which things were tending:—

"Thus, the Roman bishops were so far from being hindered by any superior power, that it proved an advantageous circumstance to them in the eyes of their new masters, that they steadfastly resisted innovations of faith made in Constantinople, till they gained a new victory over the changeable Greeks, under the Emperor Justin. The natural consequence of this was, that while the patriarchs of Constantinople were constantly sinking in ecclesiastical esteem on account of their vacillation in these controversies, the bishops of Rome still maintained their ancient reputation of being the defenders of oppressed orthodoxy.

"Under these favorable circumstances, the ecclesiastical pretensions of Roman bishops, who now formed the only center of Catholic Christendom in the West, in opposition to the Arian conquerors, rose high without hindrance. They asserted that not only the highest ecclesiastical authority in the West belonged to them, but also superintendence of orthodoxy and maintenance of ecclesiastical laws throughout the whole church. These claims they sometimes founded on imperial edicts and decrees of synods; but for the most part on the peculiar rights conferred on Peter by the Lord. After the *synodis palmaris*, called by Theodoric to examine the charges newly raised by the Laurentian party against Symmachus (503), had acquitted him without examination, in consequence of the circumstances, the apologist of this synod, Ennodius, bishop of Ticinium (511), first gave utterance to the assertion that the bishop of Rome is subject to no earthly judge. Not long after an attempt was made to give a historical basis to this principle by suppositious Cesta (acts) of former popes; and other falsifications of older documents in favor of the Roman see now appeared in like manner." Ecclesiastical History, Vol. 2, pp. 123-126.

The Encyclopedia of McClintock & Strong says that Justinian "regarded it as his special mission to compel a general uniformity of belief and practice." While the western empire was divided into many kingdoms, he was sole emperor of the East; yet he wrote, as Bower says, "a very obliging letter to the pope, . . . entreating him to declare in favor of the faith set forth by the emperor, the courtesy and the entreaty being supported by the weight of costly presents—an argument that never failed to convince the Roman bishops. This is substantial proof of the high position then already occupied by the pope.

The fourth step. The letter of Justinian to Pope John II. greatly strengthened the power of the Roman pontiff, and constituted the fourth and last step in the full establishment of the papacy. As was said by Gieseler, the pope was already "the only center of Catholic Christendom in the West," and Justinian's letter and gifts fully accomplished the same result for the pontiff, in the East. The following is a copy of that part of the letter which specially relates to this point:—

"Justinian, pious, fortunate, renowned, triumphant, emperor, consul, etc., to John the most holy archbishop of our city of Rome, and patriarch.

"Rendering homage to the apostolic chair, and to your holiness, as has been always and is our wish, and honoring your blessedness as a father; we have hastened to bring to the knowledge of your holiness all matters relating to the state of the churches. It having been at all times our great desire to preserve the unity of your apostolic chair, and the constitution of the holy churches of God which has obtained hitherto and still obtains.

"Therefore we have made no delay in subjecting and uniting to your Holiness all the priests of the whole East.

"For this reason we have thought to bring to your notice the present matters of disturbance; though they are manifest and unquestionable, and always firmly held and declared by the whole priesthood according to the doctrine of your apostolical chair. For we cannot suffer that anything that relates to the state of the church, however manifest and unquestionable, should be moved without the knowledge of your Holiness, who are the head of all the holy churches, for in all things, as we have already declared, we are anxious to increase the honor and authority of your apostolical chair." Annals of Baronius, Antwerp edition, 1584.

Then followed a statement at length of the case in dispute, in the spirit and style of theological disputes of that age. He presented his request as follows:—

"We entreat, therefore, your fatherly love, that in your letters designed for us,—and to the holy bishops of this blessed city, and to the patriarch, your brother, since he, too, of himself, through them the messenger bishops of the emperor, has written to your Holiness, hastening in all things to follow the apostolical chair of your Blessedness,—you make manifest to us, that all we rightly confess aforementioned, your Holiness accepts."

But beyond a doubt it is safe to judge that it was not altogether "of himself" that the patriarch of Constantinople professed in all things to follow the apostolical chair of his Roman rival. It was out of complaisance to Justinian. After the death of this emperor, the patriarch of Constantinople made still further efforts to secure the honors of the primacy. The act of Justinian, causing the patriarch of the imperial city to write so obliging a letter to the Roman pontiff, was an important one in the work of subjecting all the priests of the East to the Roman see.

The matter of this letter to the pope is worthy of careful consideration.

1. The emperor renders homage to the apostolical chair of Rome.

2. It was his desire to preserve the unity of his apostolical authority.

3. He subjected and united to the pope all the priests of the whole East.

4. He would not suffer anything to be done in the churches without the knowledge of his holiness.

5. He declared the bishop of Rome to be the head of all the holy churches.

6. He was anxious to increase the honor and authority of his apostolical chair.

7. He announces the submission of the patriarch of Constantinople to the pontiff.

And to this may be added that, in a letter to Epiphanius, about the same time, he declared that the pope was the "head of all bishops and the true and effective corrector of heretics." See Croly on the Apocalypse. Every sentence is strong, and the last declaration is a seal to all the others.

Let us notice in connection the four steps in establishing the complete power of the papacy.

1. The primacy of the whole church, which was as extensive as the empire of Constantine, was given to the bishop of Rome.

2. He was made a civil magistrate of the highest rank.

3. The seat of the empire was removed from Rome to Constantinople, thus virtually leaving the old capital to the pope, and which soon became a fact.

4. All the bishops and all the churches of the whole East were subjected and united to him, he being already the center of Christendom in the West.

In these steps, nothing was lacking to enable him to exercise all the power that he claimed; for in these he was granted the most complete spiritual authority, with the civil power necessary to make that authority effective.

What do historians say of the action of Justinian in behalf of the pope? That which has been quoted from Gibbon in another place is well worth repeating in this connection. Speaking of the success of Belisarius in suppressing Arianism in Africa, he said of Justinian:—

"He received the messengers of victory at the time when he was preparing to publish the Pandects of the Roman law; and the devout or jealous emperor celebrated the divine goodness, and confessed in silence the merit of his successful general. Impatient to abolish the temporal and spiritual tyranny of the Vandals, he proceeded, without delay, to the full establishment of the Catholic Church. Her jurisdiction, wealth, and immunities, perhaps the most essential part of episcopal religion, were restored and amplified with a liberal hand; the Arian worship was suppressed: the Donatist meetings were proscribed; and the synod of Carthage, by the voice of two hundred and seventeen bishops, applauded the just measure of pious retaliation." Decline and Fall, chap. 41, paragraph 11.

These words of Gibbon refer to much more than the mere letter to the pope, important as that was. Gieseler enumerates some of the particular facts of Justinian in "the full establishment of the Catholic Church." He speaks as follows:—

"The clergy, and particularly the bishops, received new privileges from Justinian. He intrusted the latter with civil jurisdiction over the monks and nuns, as well as over the clergy. Episcopal oversight of morals, and particularly the duty of providing for all the unfortunate, had been established till the present time only on the foundation of ecclesiastical laws; but Justinian now gave them a more general basis, founding them on the civil law also. He made it the duty of the bishops, and gave them the necessary civil qualifications, to undertake the care of prisoners, minors, insane persons, foundlings, stolen children, and oppressed women; and invested them with the power of upholding good morals and impartial administration of justice. It is true, that he established a mutual inspection of the bishops and the civil magistrates; but he gave in this respect to the latter considerable smaller privileges than to the former. For example, he gave the bishops a legal influence over the choice of magistrates, and security against general oppression on their part; allowed them to interfere in cases of refusal of justice; and in special instances, even constituted them judges of those official personages. In like manner he conveyed to them the right of concurrence in the choice of city officials, and a joint oversight of the administration of city funds, and the maintenance of public establishments. Thus the bishops became important personages even in civil life; and were further honored by Justinian, in freedom from parental violence, from the necessity of appearing as witnesses, and from taking oaths." Gieseler, Ecclesiastical History, Vol. 2, pp. 117-119, Clark, Edinburgh, 1848.

It is true that these privileges were for all bishops; all were, in material points, elevated above other magistrates; and in this respect, the grants of Justinian were a great enlargement of the civil powers granted by Constantine, as already noticed. By these the church was elevated far above the civil department of the government; and if such were the prerogatives of all bishops, what must have been the effect on the standing of him who was declared by imperial authority to be "the head of all bishops"? He was aptly styled "the chief Christian magistrate." And this implied much under the peculiar condition of the country, broken up by contending armies. All the steps herein noticed for the elevation of the Roman pontiff, were by authority of the emperors and councils, and not one of them was ever reversed or annulled.

It has been assumed that we must come further down, to the time of Phocas, and to his action of 606, for the full establishment of the papacy. But for this there is no just reason. Phocas, according to all history, was one of the most depraved of men, the vilest of murderers and usurpers. Gibbon gives a description of his person and crimes, which we have room to barely notice:—

"The pencil of an impartial historian [Cedrenas] has delineated the portrait of a monster; his diminutive and deformed person. . . . Ignorant of letters, of laws, and even of arms, he indulged in the supreme rank a more ample privilege of lust and drunkenness; and his brutal pleasures were either injurious to his subjects or disgraceful to himself."

After describing his murder of all the family of the Emperor Maurice, he speaks of his treatment of other victims as follows:—

"Their condemnation was seldom preceded by the forms of trial, and their punishment was imbittered by the refinements of cruelty; their eyes were pierced, their tongues were torn from the root, the hands and feet were amputated; some expired under the lash, others in the flames, others again were transfixed with arrows; and a simple speedy death was mercy which they could rarely obtain." Decline and Fall, chap. 46, paragraph 12.

Maurice, the predecessor of Phocas, favored the claim of the patriarch of Constantinople to the primacy. This, of course, highly incensed Gregory the Great, who had, until that time, been considered one of the best of Roman bishops. Upon the usurpation of Phocas, Gregory sought his friendship, hoping that through him the influence of Maurice might be counteracted. Gregory disgraced his memory by writing the most extravagant laudation of the inhuman monster, calling upon all the earth and the angels in Heaven to rejoice over the accession of an emperor so truly just and pious. Infallibility in the popes does not guarantee truthfulness and discernment of character. We see this also in the case of Leo the Great, who declared, in his letter to Dioscorus, bishop of Alexandria, that he discovered in him great love and Christian graces. Dioscorus was one of the worst bishops of his age, which is putting him very low; avaricious, ambitious, and blood-thirsty; Leo himself was compelled to depose him. More shameful yet is the case of Gregory, who professed to find almost celestial purity in Phocas. He also wrote a letter to Leontia, the wife of Phocas, who, according to history, was as vile as her husband, ascribing to her like Christian graces, and plainly asking her to make proof of her piety by remembering with favor the see of St. Peter, on whom the Saviour had conferred such blessings. Just what Gregory desired can never be known, for he had denounced the title of universal bishop, claimed by the bishop of Constantinople, as the token of heresy, the very badge of antichrist. Had the emperor transferred that title to the West, whether then he would not have found sufficient reason to change his mind, or to modify his denunciations, as Baronius has done for him, is a question; for the instance was never known of a bishop of Rome refusing anything that added to the dignity of that see.

The bearer of Gregory's letter to Phocas was a priest who afterwards became pope under the name of Boniface III. It is recorded that he was the only one base enough to applaud and flatter Phocas in the very commission of his crimes. He became the favorite of Phocas and his wife, and when he came to the papal chair he is said to have requested the emperor to deprive the patriarch of Constantinople of the title which he had claimed, and confer it upon himself and his successors in the chair of St. Peter. And this, it is asserted, Phocas did more readily because the bishop of Constantinople had resisted him in his cruelties to the wife and daughter of Maurice. But nothing was granted by Phocas that had not already been conferred. The primacy and chief rank of Rome had been declared and twice confirmed before the time of Justinian, and this emperor constituted him the head of all the churches and of all bishops, with many other privileges of which it is not claimed that Phocas said anything. And, moreover, just what Phocas did declare is a matter of doubt. Bower says: "As for the edict issued by Phocas on this occasion, it has not indeed reached our times." And Gieseler, whose reliability will not be questioned, says:—

"It is commonly asserted, and by men of the greatest learning and best acquainted with ancient history, that the Roman pontiff, Boniface III., prevailed on that abominable tyrant Phocas, who, after murdering the Emperor Mauritius, mounted the imperial throne, to divest the bishop of Constantinople of the title of œcumenical bishop, and to confer it on the Roman pontiff. But this is stated solely on the authority of Baronius; for no ancient writer has given such testimony. Yet Phocas did something analogous to this, if we may believe Anastasius and Paul Diaconus. For whereas the bishops of Constantinople had maintained that their church was not only fully equal to that of Rome, but had precedence of all other churches, Phocas forbade this, and determined that the priority of rank and dignity should be given the Church of Rome." Ecclesiastical History, Book 2, Cent. 17, Part 2, chap. 2.

That Boniface III. was ambitious and unscrupulous, is shown in his flattery of Phocas. His unbounded arrogance led him to attach much more to the title, probably, than had his predecessors. And no honor conferred upon or claimed by the bishop of Rome was ever relinquished. But we have searched diligently, and in vain, to find anything granted by Phocas authentically established, which had not then already been conferred. Gibbon speaks the exact truth when he says that Justinian proceeded "to the full establishment of the Catholic Church."

CONSTANTINOPLE, THE NEW SEAT OF PAGANISM.

CHAPTER XII.

THE THOUSAND TWO HUNDRED AND THREESCORE DAYS.

It has been shown that a day, in prophecy, is counted for a year; and that the time and times and half a time of Dan. 7:25 are 1260 years. These were the years marked for the supremacy of the little horn, the papacy, during which it had power to wear out the saints of the Most High. The same time is marked in Revelation 12, as the period during which the dragon persecuted the woman, the Christian church, who fled into the wilderness. But the dragon may be said to do much of his work by proxy, for he gave his power and seat to the seven-headed and ten-horned beast, who also persecuted the saints, and prevailed forty and two months. Here are forty-two multiplied by thirty—the number of days in a month—making the same number of 1260 days, or years. This beast, which has all the main features of all the beasts of Daniel 7, receiving the dominion which they successively held, is identical with the little horn of that chapter. That rose up among the kingdoms that were founded on the ruins of the Roman Empire, and so did this beast. Their locality is the same; the extent of their dominion the same; their work of blasphemy and persecution the same; the period of their supremacy the same.

Rev. 13:3. "And I saw one of his heads as it were wounded to death; and his deadly wound was healed."

In the prophecy of Rev. 1:10, we must be careful to guard against an error into which many fall in the interpretation of prophecy,—we must not imbibe the idea that events are always recorded in the order of their fulfillment. Notice the

(147)

case of the two-horned beast in verses 11-17 of this chapter. 1. In verse 4, the climax is reached—speaking like a dragon —at once, before the history is given. But in tracing its history, we shall find that it is fulfilled near the close of the prophecy. 2. In regard to the wonders, verses 13, 14, the climax, fire coming down from Heaven, is the first thing mentioned; after that the general facts are given. 3. In verses 15-17, another climax is recorded at the very beginning of the account of its persecutions; the decree to put the saints to death is mentioned before that concerning buying and selling, while in the fulfillment it must come after. This order is very common in the prophecies.

And so in verses 1-10. Verse 2 mentions the beast receiving power from the dragon; verse 3 mentions its receiving a deadly wound, and the healing of the wound. And then follows its general history, including its triumphant work of 1260 years. Now, in point of fact, or in the fulfillment, verse 3 stands closely related to verse 10. It must be evident to everyone who carefully examines this prophecy, that the receiving and the healing of the deadly wound have their fulfillment near the close of its existence. Verse 4—" They worshiped the dragon which gave power unto the beast," etc.—naturally follows verse 2, where the dragon is said to give him that power. This was fulfilled when the dragon gave his power to the beast, at least fulfilled in part. Religious reverence was paid to the emperors—called Christian emperors—who built up the papacy. This work was begun by Constantine, who received the same adulations from the bishops that the popes received in the full tide of their prosperity. And that the Roman emperors were actually worshiped, we learn from different authors. Thus, Sir Isaac Newton said, in regard to the crowning of Charlemagne:—

"The pope crowned him, and anointed him with holy oil, and worshiped him on his knees, after the manner of adoring the old Roman emperors." On the Prophecies, Part 1, p. 82.

Cormenin also, in his "History of the Popes," says:—

"Then Leo prostrated himself before the new sovereign, and adored him, according to the usage of the ancient Cæsars, recognizing him as his legitimate sovereign, and the defender of the faith." P. 309.

The order above noticed, of reaching the climax and then going back to the general history, has often been overlooked in studying this chapter, for which reason some have greatly erred in giving expositions of this prophecy. In "Thoughts on the Revelation," p. 538, edition 1885, this order is noticed as follows:—

"This wounding is the same as going into captivity, Rev. 13:10. It was inflicted when the pope was taken prisoner by Berthier, the French general, and the papal government was for a time abolished."

In the exposition of this chapter it is very important that we have the dates for the giving of the power, and of giving the deadly wound, correctly fixed. These two events mark the beginning and ending of the period of 1260 years. Some have affirmed, and apparently with great confidence, that it is not possible to fix these dates with certainty; that those taken are chosen arbitrarily and without sufficient reason. But if the facts are carefully considered there will be no room for doubt that the correct dates are A. D. 538 and 1798: within these is a period of 1260 years.

It has already been noticed that Justinian's letter to the pope, dated A. D. 533, could have no effect while the Arians ruled in Italy. The Roman pontiff could not be "the effectual corrector of heretics" in the sense in which that expression was always construed, while he himself was the subject of an Arian or heretical king. Justinian's letter was written to John II. Less than ten years before that time John I. was sent as an ambassador by the king of Italy, to mediate in behalf of the heretics in the East. And the same power ruled over Rome when the famous letter of Justinian was written. Thus plainly is it seen that if the same power had continued to rule over Italy and over the pope, the letter of Justinian would have remained but an empty sound. The Ostrogoths were driven from Rome by Belisarius in 538. At that time the order of the emperor could first take effect, the pope then being free from Arian rule. Let it be remembered that the very object of

Justinian in sending Belisarius on this expedition against the Arians in Africa and Italy, was to destroy heresy and to establish the orthodox faith and the Catholic Church.

It has been noticed that we cannot look to 606, where some writers have gone, for the time of the establishing of the papacy. They who adopted that date looked to the year 1866 for some great event in connection with the papacy, as the 1260 years would end there, counting from A. D. 606. But the great event did not appear, for the good reason that they had adopted a wrong starting-point. Counting from the time of the subduing of the Ostrogoths in 538, which was the plucking up of the third horn referred to in Dan. 7:8, did any event occur just 1260 years from that time which marks the fulfillment of the prophecy?—There did. In that year Pope Pius VI. was taken prisoner, his chair was forcibly vacated, and he was taken to France, where he died in exile.

But here comes an objection, which may seem to have some force in the estimation of those who offer it, namely, that Pius VI. was not the only pope who was forcibly ejected from his chair,—not the only one who died in exile or in prison. Why, then, select his case as the one in which this prophecy was fulfilled?

It is always allowable to look to both ends of a prophetic period in order to locate it by the events. Thus, various dates have been assigned for the beginning of the twenty-three hundred days of Dan. 8:14. But the seventy weeks of Daniel 9 are the first part of those days, and we locate those weeks to a certainty by their termination. They are located by the cross of Messiah the Prince. So of the twelve hundred and sixty years. We find no certain time for their beginning but A. D. 538, when Justinian took the fourth and last step in the establishing of the papacy. From that point, twelve hundred and sixty years end in 1798—the only place where an event is found that completely fulfilled the prophecy.

Now in regard to the objection. The cases of John I. and John XXIII. have been presented as examples, and we will examine them, and see if they are in anywise parallel to that of Pius VI. in 1798.

When John I. was sent by the Arian king to Constantinople, to endeavor to induce the Emperor Justin to revoke his decree for the persecution of their Arians in the East, he was instructed by Theodoric on two points: 1. To have the persecution stopped, and the churches restored to the Arians which had been forcibly taken from them. 2. To have permission granted to those who had been compelled to renounce Arianism, to return to the faith of their choice. At first the pope refused to go if the second point was insisted on, saying that the emperor would never permit any to renounce the orthodox faith and return to Arianism. Evidently the pope did not wish that any such permission should be granted. The king ordered that he should be put on a ship and conveyed away; but the pope submitted, and went to the court of Justin. He went under a threat from the king, in case he did not succeed in his mission. But he did not procure the last-mentioned privilege, and the king did not believe that he asked for it. And some affirm (and why should we doubt it?) that the pope entered into a conspiracy with the emperor to overthrow the government of Theodoric. For one of these reasons, and perhaps for both, the king seized the pope on his return, and shut him up in prison, from which he was released only by death.

But here notice, that while Theodoric did this to protect the Arians, he gave the same protection to the Catholics in his dominions. He never did anything to lessen the dignity of the papacy, as a system. He preserved order at the election of the popes: in the case of a contest of claims, he appointed a commission to decide which was the legally elected pope. Not a single right or privilege that was ever claimed for that see was invaded by Theodoric. Had the popes ruled as leniently over their opponents as Theodoric did towards the papacy, they would have been much more worthy of the praise they exacted.

After the death of Pope John I., Theodoric interfered in the election, because the irregularities and strifes at the elections of popes endangered the peace of the city and the country. As a compromise between the quarreling factions, he designated

Felix, the third of that name, to be the successor of John. Both Bower and Cormenin record that the king paid high respect to this pope, granting certain judicial privileges, of which Bower says:—

"This privilege the king granted to the Roman clergy only in honor of the apostolic see, as he declared in his edict." Vol. 1, under Felix III.

And thus we find that Theodoric, who imprisoned Pope John I., so far from trying to inflict any injury upon the papacy, actually helped to build it up. He conferred privileges and dignity upon that see not before possessed by it.

Turn to the case of John XXIII. At the time of the Council of Constance, convened in 1414, there were three claimants to the papal chair, who respectively took the titles of John XXIII., Gregory XII., and Benedict XIII. As each had his adherents, the peace of the church was, for the time, destroyed, and the pontificate was greatly scandalized. The first-named was recognized by the council as pope, so that what was done in the cases of the others does not call for notice. But, as each had received the obedience of influential parties, it was necessary that their claims should be destroyed.

The council having acknowledged John as pope, proceeded to depose him for his crimes. This was proof that the popes were never acknowledged to be above the judgment of a council. The sentence of deposition was pronounced against him May 29, 1415. Long they endeavored to induce Benedict to resign his claims, but in vain. The act of deposition was passed against him, July 26, 1417. The see was then declared vacant. But as John was recognized as the pope, and as there cannot legally be two popes at the same time, the see was actually vacant from the day of his deposition, May 29, 1415.

Martin V. was elected November 8, 1417, after an actual vacancy of two years, five months, and ten days, but of only three months and thirteen days from the time that the vacancy was declared.

In this case the pope was deposed; and the interval from the deposition to the election of a successor was a little longer than that between the deposition of Pius VI. and the election of Pius VII. What, then, is there so special about the deposition of Pius VI., and the interval from 1798 and 1800?

We have been thus particular in the case of John XXIII., as well as of John I., because they have been presented as instances of the forcible vacation of the papal chair, and of equal importance with the ejection of Pius VI. Now we will notice the bearing on the standing of the papacy of the deposition of John XXIII:—

1. John was deposed for his crimes. Had he been a pious, or even an ordinarily moral man, there is no probability that he would have been deposed after having been acknowledged as the rightful claimant to the chair. And it is by no means certain that he would have been deposed, notwithstanding the enormity of his crimes, had it not been necessary to establish the right of succession, there being three claimants to the see. The council deposed John on *minor* charges, which were of a scandalous character, because the numerous *major* charges were altogether too scandalous for public consideration. And these charges were attended with abundance of proofs. Yet, according to papal ethics, while he legally occupied the chair of St. Peter, he was infallible.

2. It must not be forgotten that it was a duly convened Catholic council that deposed him—the same council that condemned and burned the writings of Wickliffe; the same that burned both Huss and Jerome of Prague. This of itself is a sufficient proof that it was a truly Catholic council. The deposing of John XXIII. was, therefore, a matter and action of the church itself.

So far from this council making any attack upon the papacy, it removed a great trouble and reproach from the papal chair, confirmed doctrines, condemned both writings and men for heresy, healed a dangerous schism, elected another pope, thus leaving the papacy stronger than it was before.

Now let us see what was done in 1798, and note the effect and bearing of these events.

Pius VI. was wicked enough to have been deposed by the church itself, as was John XXIII. But had wickedness alone been considered a sufficient cause for the church to depose a pope, the chair would have been often vacated. Pius was not deposed as a criminal, except as one against the peace and welfare of the people. The reasons for his being deposed were of a political nature.

Croly, who wrote some excellent things on this subject, fell into the mistake of beginning the 1260 years with the date of the letter of Justinian to Pope John II., A. D. 533. It has been shown that that letter would forever have remained a dead letter if the Arians had not been driven from Rome. And it is a fact that nothing occurred 1260 years from A. D. 533 to mark the termination of that period. Mr. Croly's comments on that termination are as follows:—

"A. D. 1793. The Bible had passed out of the hands of the people, in all the dominions of popery from the time of the supremacy. The doctrines had perished, and left their place to human reveries. The converts were martyred. At length the full triumph of the old spirit of corruption and persecution terribly arrived. In the year 1793, twelve hundred and sixty years from the letter of Justinian declaring the pope 'universal bishop,' the gospel was, by a solemn act of the legislature and the people, abolished in France. The indignities offered to the actual copies of the Bible were unimportant after this; their life is in their doctrines, and the extinction of their doctrines is the extinction of the Bible. By the decree of the French Government declaring that the nation acknowledged no God, the Old and New Testaments were slain throughout the limits of republican France." The Apocalypse, by Croly, pp. 176, 177, second edition, London, 1828.

But not a sentence in the above, nor in the remarks following, in the comments of Mr. Croly, furnishes any justification of his view of the ending of that period. It was the gospel—not the papacy—that was abolished in France in 1793. And Mr. Croly himself has furnished full and sufficient evidence in disproof of that position, and in proof that 1798 is the correct date for the ending of the 1260 years. Thus again he speaks:—

"The death of Christianity was local and limited; no nation of Europe joined in the desperate guilt of the French republic." *Ib.*, p. 427.

Mark, it was the death of Christianity, not of the papacy, of which he speaks. Of course it affected the welfare of the papal church, for it was an onslaught against all religion. But it was confined to France, as Croly says. But immediately following these words, he further says:—

"And within three years and a half, the predicted time, it was called up from the grave to a liberty which it had never before enjoyed; the church in France was proclaimed free." *Ib.*

Thus Christianity was restored; the church was free; all religions were tolerated; and here really began an era of triumph for the truth of God. But notice what Mr. Croly next says:—

"Simultaneous with this restoration, the Popedom received a wound, the sure precursor of its ruin." *Ib.*

It was not in connection with the abolition of the gospel, and the death of Christianity, that the papacy received its wound, but "simultaneous with its restoration." Thus plainly it is seen that 1793 cannot be the terminating point of the 1260 years.

But what follows? or when was the wound given to the papacy? Of the events of 1798, Mr. Croly testifies thus:—

"On the 9th of February, the French corps commanded by Berthier encamped in front of the Porta del Popolo. On the next day the castle of St. Angelo surrendered; the city gates were seized; and the pope and the cardinals, excepting three, were made prisoners.

"On the 15th, Berthier made his triumphant entry, delivered a harangue at the foot of the capital, invoking the 'shades of Cato, Pompey, Brutus, Cicero, and Hortensius, to receive the homage of free Frenchmen, on the soil of liberty,' proclaimed Rome a republic, and, declaring a suspension of every office of the old government, planted the tree of liberty.

"Ten days after, the pope was sent away under an escort of French cavalry, and was finally carried into France, where he died in captivity." *Ib.*, p. 429.

What better testimony could be given? Berthier proclaimed Rome a republic, declaring a suspension of every office of the old government. Here, then, the old government ceased. The pope and his cardinals were prisoners, and not a single office of that government was filled,—not a single function of that government was left in operation. This was not merely a deposition of the pope; it was an abolition of the papal system. How different this from the cases of John II.

and John XXIII., or of any other time or event from the rise of the papacy to that time.

The testimony of Ranke is not less explicit and forcible:—

"For a moment the revolutionary government seemed to recollect themselves—a compact was struck even without these concessions—but it was only for a moment. From contemplating an entire separation from the pope, they proceeded to entertain the idea of annihilating him. The directory found the regimen of the priests in Italy incompatible with its own. On the first occasion that offered, that of a casual commotion among the people, Rome was invaded and the Vatican occupied. Pius VI. besought his enemies to allow him to die likewise there, being where he had lived, he being already over eighty years of age. He was told in reply that he could die anywhere; the room he usually occupied was plundered before his eyes; even his smallest necessaries were taken from him; the ring he wore was taken from his finger; and at last he was removed to France, where he departed this life in August, 1799." History of the Papacy, Vol. 2, pp. 310, 311.

The death of Pius VI. took place one year and five months after his imprisonment. And here another objection may be noticed. It has been urged that the absence of the pope does not affect the standing of the papacy, inasmuch as the power of the succession, and therefore virtually the power of the popedom, rests in the cardinals. But this statement as an objection does not hold in this case. The government itself was abolished, and the cardinals were among the prisoners. As already shown, every office of the old government was suspended. The outlook of those times is thus given by Ranke:—

"In fact it might seem as if the papal government had come to its final close. Those tendencies of ecclesiastical opposition which we have seen commence and rise into vigor, had now prospered to such a point as to venture to entertain the idea of aiming at such a result."

By the facts which have been here presented, the papacy is clearly identified as the subject of this prophecy in Rev. 13:1-10. The church receiving by gift the great power and authority of the empire; the persecution of which it should be guilty; the time during which the saints of the Most High were given into its hand; and the infliction of a deadly wound just at the end of the specified period,—all prove the identity of this beast. No other power ever wore out the saints of the Most

High as the papacy has done; no other power ever held dominion long enough to fulfill this part of the prophecy. But another point follows which greatly strengthens the proof:—

"And his deadly wound was healed." Rev. 13:3.

It has been noticed that the great strength of the papacy was in its spiritual authority. The popes never presumed to dictate to the nations, or to bring kings to bow at their feet, by reason of the vastness of their civil power, for such they never possessed. Their civil power was never great. Solely by virtue of the primacy in the church, or of a pretended gift to St. Peter, and as being vicars of the Son of God and sovereigns in his kingdom, they assumed to exercise their great authority. And this spiritual authority was as extensive as the bounds of the hierarchy, which was co-extensive with the empire. This was the extent of the power conferred by the primacy, and the declaration of Justinian that the pope was the head of all the churches. The extent of their power is also indicated by this beast possessing the main features of all the beasts of Daniel 7. Now, counting from the days of Nebuchadnezzar to this present year of grace, what great power, what dominion or government, was abolished or destroyed, and again restored? Every power or kingdom that was destroyed was succeeded by another, which remained until it in turn was overthrown. This is true of every power except one, that is, the papacy. No greater, no more arbitrary, no more relentless power ever existed, than the papal. No power or government was ever more completely prostrated or abolished than was the papal in 1798. And it seems quite superfluous to ask if it was restored. Everybody knows that it was.

But the question is raised, Has it been so restored as to fulfill the prophecy? Verse 14 says it had a deadly wound by a sword, and did live. Its wound was unto death; and it must be brought from death if it did live after the wound was inflicted. But was the bringing it to life the healing of the wound? or does the healing remain to be accomplished?

This question is not difficult to settle. If the deadly wound was given in 1798, and surely that cannot be denied, for then the papal government was entirely abolished, then whenever it is restored to the position that it occupied before and up to 1798, its deadly wound must be healed. Until the year 1798 the power of the popes was twofold, spiritual and civil. They held supreme authority over the church, and kingly authority over a small territory. The popes were "sovereign pontiffs," which has reference to their "spiritual supremacy," which is the only supremacy they ever held. Their prestige, their influence over the nations and over kings, greatly differed at different times. The haughty, overbearing conduct of Pope Symmachus toward the Emperor Anastasius was before the popes claimed any independent civil authority even in Rome. The influence of many popes before the times of Pepin and Charlemagne was greater than that which Pius VI. ever possessed. Yet Pius VI. did possess both spiritual and civil power. He ruled a king over the papal States, and he was supreme in the church; but since the Reformation the influence of the popes had been waning. If the wound was given in 1798, in the pontificate of Pius VI., then all that was necessary to the healing of the wound was to place his successor, Pius VII., at the restoration of the papacy and the papal government, in the same position that Pius VI. occupied when the wound was given. This proposition is so evident that it cannot require any argument to impress it upon the mind. Restoring the papacy to just that position that it occupied when the wound was given must be the healing of the wound. Then the question arises, Was the papal government re-established? and was all the power restored to Pius VII. that was taken away from Pius VI.?

Very strange combinations are often formed among nations for the accomplishment of their purposes. The action of the French directory was looked upon with jealous eyes by the powers of Europe. And this brought help to the prostrate papacy from an unexpected quarter. Thus again Ranke speaks:—

"The chief result of the hostility which the pope experienced at the hands of the revolutionary government was, that the rest of Europe, whatever even may have been its sentiments otherwise [that is, though these nations were Protestants], took him under its protection. The death of Pius VI. happened at the very time in which the coalition once more was triumphant, and *thus it became possible for the cardinals to meet* at St. George's at Venice, *and proceed to the election of a pope*, Pius VII., March 13, 1800." Vol. 2, p. 311.

The cardinals have no power to act except in conclave, and they could not elect a successor to Pius VI. until they had permission to meet.* The coalition above referred to rendered it possible for them to meet, as Ranke says: "This election in Venice was two years and one month after the papal government was abolished." Ranke further says: "It is true that the revolutionary power triumphed soon after, and won for itself a decided preponderance, even in Italy." But the appearing of Napoleon on the field, ambitious to concentrate the power of Europe, changed the scene. He found it politic to avail himself of every possible force, and therefore opened negotiations with the pope, for the re-establishment of the government of the church. Of the motives for the action of the several powers Ranke says:—

"The constituent assembly had endeavored to cast off its connection with the pope; the directory had wished to annihilate him; Bonaparte's idea was to preserve him, but at the same time to keep him in a state of subjection, and to make him the mere instrument of his omnipotence." P. 314.

But whatever the motive, the restoration of the papacy was accomplished. McClintock & Strong's Cyclopedia, of Pius VI., says:—

"A concordat concluded with Napoleon Bonaparte in 1801, restored to the pope his ecclesiastical and temporal power."

Napoleon made constant efforts to turn the pope's influence and power to his own advantage. But the pope was well aware of his designs, and resisted him to the utmost. A work entitled "Lives of the Popes," first published by the London Religious

---

*It will be noticed that during the halcyon days of the papacy she *dictated* terms in matters of religion, and often of State, but at the partial restoration of 1800 she asked *permission* of earthly powers. The temporal power was restored, but the spiritual supremacy was gone. Rome was no longer acknowledged as "head over all the churches."

Tract Society, well states the circumstances, and the decision of the pope:—

"Pliable as he had shown himself in merely spiritual matters, Pius VII. began to grow resolute when his temporal possessions were touched. Napoleon required that a league should be formed between France and the papacy, in the war which he was then waging with England. Pius saw in this demand, not only a disgraceful submission to France, but certain and absolute ruin to his power, whichever should be the victor." Carlton & Porter, New York, 1856, p. 546.

All this proves that his temporal possessions were restored to the pope, and he very foolishly esteemed them his most precious treasures. But Napoleon would not suffer refusal. Dr. George Weber, in his "Church History," says:—

"When the pope refused to lay an embargo upon the English ships in the ports of the States of the Church, and to enter into an offensive and defensive alliance with France, Napoleon inflicted upon him a succession of injuries, and united some portions of the ecclesiastical States to the kingdom of Italy." P. 542.

And as long as he held the power he continued to embarrass the pope, and finally despoiled him of all his territory. Thus the New American Encyclopedia, Art. Papal States, says:—

"In May, 1809, Napoleon declared the remainder of the Roman States annexed to the French Empire; and soon afterward the pope was carried prisoner to France, and did not return to his capital until after the emperor's abdication, 1814. The Congress of Vienne restored to him all the territories of the church, and he devoted the rest of his life to reforming the administration, after so many years of disorder."

But note this fact, that while Napoleon harassed the pope, despoiled him of his possessions, and carried him away a prisoner, he did not by any means abolish the papal government. He had restored the church in the French Empire, and his actions against the pope were the result of personal ill-will toward him because he would not become the pliant tool he wished to make him. Among the many changes and misfortunes of the papacy, we find in one place alone, the abolition of the papal government, both in its temporal and spiritual features, and that was in 1798, when Rome was declared a republic, and "every office of the old government was suspended." Though Napoleon for a time took from the pope his temporal possessions, they were all restored to him by the Congress of Vienne; and he continued to hold them in part until 1870, when they were united to the new kingdom of Italy, erected by Victor Immanuel.

And now, to show that the declaration is correct, that the papacy does not depend upon the possession of civil authority, and that its life and strength is in its spiritual authority, we may cite the present position of the papacy, 1889. While some predicted that with the taking away of the temporal power, in 1870, the papacy would decline and lose all its prestige and influence, the facts have all turned in the other direction. An influential London paper in 1887 said that with the loss of his temporal power, there had been a steady advance of his spiritual power and influence among all nations. With the loss of his territory and kingship, all jealousy toward him as a king was effectually removed, sympathy for the pope was created, and Leo XIII., who has shown himself a most skillful diplomatist, has, in the words of a recent writer, "achieved successes that may well have flattered his pride, showing, as they have, that he has imparted a new luster to the holy see." These words spring from the events that have occurred, and show how far have failed all predictions that the papacy is speedily declining.

Whether the pope has lost prestige with the loss of his civil power, may well be judged by the results of the late jubilee of Leo XIII. It is impossible to give any extended notice of it, but a few words from the *Catholic Times,* of January 6, 1888, will give an idea of the direction in which things are tending. The *Times* denominated the jubilee as a "festival of Christendom" (while in fact its extent was not bounded by Christendom), in which all nations sought to do honor to the "skillful statesmanship, the incomparable diplomatic ability," of Leo XIII. The *Times* says:—

"Within the Vatican are treasured letters and gifts from all the sovereigns of the world except the king of Italy. The queen of this country [England], the emperor of Germany, the emperor of Austria, the queen regent of Spain, the president of the United States, the president of France, the king of Belgium, the king of Greece, the emperor of Brazil, the sultan of Turkey, the mikado of Japan, and the shah of Persia, have, amongst others, sent to the holy father their tributes of esteem and their hearty congratulations. These and the other innumerable testimonies of good-will and affection received by Leo XIII., must, while bringing joy to the heart of his holiness, prove of immense advantage to the church. They must awaken throughout Christendom a due sense of the power of the papacy and the unity of the church."

As a comment on Rev. 13:2, 3, in regard to giving the power of the empire to the beast, we have found that the last step in the full establishing of the Catholic Church was taken by Justinian in subjecting to the pope all the churches of the East, and extending the civil powers of the Roman see. The act of Justinian became effective to accomplish its purpose in A. D. 538; and the deadly wound was given in 1798, by the entire overthrow of the papacy under the pontificate of Pius VI. Although the civil power was again taken away in 1870, the papacy was not interfered with, the freedom of the pope had not been infringed upon, notwithstanding reports circulated for the purpose of exciting sympathy. The Italian government protects him and will protect him in the exercise of the functions of his office as head of the Catholic Church throughout the world. The present pope, Leo XIII., has brought the empires of Prussia and Great Britain under obligation to him for services rendered, that they thought that no other power could render. And this is but the beginning of the honor that will be accorded to him, in the midst of the troubles that are coming upon the nations. All the world still wonder after the beast, and their wonder is destined to increase, for all will worship him whose names are not found written in the Lamb's book of life. Rev. 13:8.

CHAPTER XIII.

THE BEAST WITH TWO HORNS.

FOLLOWING the description of the beast with seven heads and ten horns, in Rev. 13:1-10, is that of a beast with two horns, which we must now examine, inasmuch as they are closely related in the fulfillment as they are in the record.

We have seen that in the description of the third beast, the locality and extent of its dominion are perfectly identified. Some have said that the power of the papacy was great in degree, but quite limited in extent. Already in 325, when the church was organized according to the provinces of the whole empire, the primacy was given to the bishop of Rome. In 538 all the churches of the whole East were subjected to him; and even before this he was the central power of the western churches, being considered the representative of orthodoxy, and its constant defender. According to the prophecy, the dragon gave him his power, and his seat, and great authority. And so great was his authority that it was asked, Who is able to make war with him? If any yet doubt of the extent of his dominion, let them point to the king or the nation who dared to resist the authority of the popes during the middle ages of the Christian era. The mightiest kings led his horse, held his stirrup when he mounted, or prostrated themselves at his feet. Was there any other ruler on the face of the earth so nobly served, and so highly honored? All know that there was not.

The description of this beast indicates that he was the heir to the monarchies represented by the lion, the bear, the leopard, and the dreadful and terrible beast of Daniel 7. And this was the case. Was not the dominion of Rome as extensive as that of the preceding kingdoms? And did not the spiritual authority of the popes extend to the full extent of the empire? And did they not, in their spiritual authority, rule over the kings of the earth? Not the shadow of a reason can be given for denying the great extent of the rule of the papacy.

And, therefore, if we have another beast, not having any of the features of the beast of Daniel 7, we must conclude that it comes up outside of the limits of their dominion. But they ruled over the whole earth. Daniel said to Nebuchadnezzar that the God of Heaven had given him a kingdom and dominion wheresoever the children of men dwell. From Eastern or Central Asia to Africa and to the Atlantic, the dominions of those beasts extended. As their dominion was worldwide, how can it be that another beast should rise up, but not within the bounds of their dominions? It could be possible only by this beast coming up in some part of the earth not included in the world as known to the ancients. If it came up on the territory of any of the four beasts of Daniel 7, we should expect that it would present some of the features of those beasts, somewhat after the fashion of the first beast; but it does not. Its description is as follows:—

Rev. 13:11. "And I beheld another beast coming up out of the earth; and he had two horns like a lamb, and he spake as a dragon."

The beasts of Daniel 7 all rose out of the sea; and so did the first beast of Revelation 13. Waters, according to Rev. 17:15, represent "peoples, and multitudes, and nations, and tongues." They were kingdoms that arose among the multitudes of people, and such kingdoms generally rise by means of revolutions and strifes. This was indicated in Daniel 7 by the striving of the winds upon the sea, whence the four beasts came up. But John saw this beast coming up out of the earth. It was coming up at the time that the other beast went into captivity, namely, in 1798. It was coming out of the earth, as a plant grows, and not by the striving of the people. These and other facts point unmistakably to the power which was then growing up on the newly-discovered continent of

THE BEAST WITH TWO HORNS.

America—the United States. It did not arise by overturning other governments, but by improving wild forests, by conquering the wilderness. History does not record the rise and growth and actions of any nation or government that perfectly fulfills the prophetic description of this beast, except the United States.

It had two horns like a lamb, and the horns had no crowns upon them, as was the case with the ten horns of the first beast—quite different in appearance from the other. The horns of a lamb express both youthfulness and innocence. We have learned by Daniel 7 that a horn may represent a church power. The following remarks on this point are copied from "Thoughts on the Revelation," chap. 13, p. 567:—

"One of these horns may therefore represent the civil republican power of this government, and the other the Protestant ecclesiastical. This application is warranted by the facts already set forth respecting the horns of the other powers. For, (1) the two horns may belong to one beast, and denote a union instead of division, as in the case of the ram in Daniel 8; (2) a horn may denote a purely ecclesiastical element, as the little horn of Daniel's fourth beast; and (3) a horn may denote the civil power alone, as in the case of the first horn of the Grecian goat. On the basis of these facts, we have these two elements, Republicanism and Protestantism, here united in one government, and represented by two horns like the horns of a lamb. And these are nowhere else to be found; nor have they appeared since the time when we could consistently look for the rise of the two-horned beast, in any nation upon the face of the earth, except our own. This nation must therefore be the power in question."

And yet it will be seen in the end that it has the same nature, in some respects, as the other beast, for "it speaks as a dragon." This is the climax, reached before the history is given, according to what was pointed out as of frequent occurrence in prophecy.

Verse 12. "And he exerciseth all the power of the first beast before him, and causeth the earth and them which dwell therein to worship the first beast, whose deadly wound was healed."

He exercises the power of the first beast—the same in kind, both civil and religious—and in his sight, as the original means, and as verse 14 reads. He causes the earth and them that dwell therein to worship the first beast, whose deadly wound was healed.

This last sentence gives the chronology of this beast to a certainty; at least it brings us down to the present century. The deadly wound was given to the first beast in 1798. The wound was healed when the papal government was restored, and another head created to the Catholic Church, as has been shown. Pius VII. was elected in 1800. When the deadly wound was given, the second beast was seen coming up from the earth. And all the work described in the life of this beast, comes down this side of 1800 A. D.

One of the most interesting declarations of this prophecy is found in the words—"and causeth the earth and them that dwell therein to worship the first beast." And it is one of the most easily identified. Not only them that dwell in the earth, but the earth itself, is caused to worship the first beast. The expression is so unusual that there can be no mistaking the fulfillment when it is once pointed out. But we shall pass by the interpretation of this point until we come to another branch of the subject.

Verse 13. "And he doeth great wonders, so that he maketh fire come down from heaven on the earth in the sight of men."

Verse 14. "And deceiveth them that dwell on the earth by the means of those miracles which he had power to do in the sight of the beast; saying to them that dwell on the earth, that they should make an image to the beast, which had the wound by a sword, and did live."

It has been assumed, with little consideration, that these wonders are manifested in the wonderful inventions and improvements in these last days. That these are times of great improvements and inventions, none can deny. Let the reader imagine that the world were suddenly placed exactly where it was threescore years ago, and how could people live? Limited steam navigation, no railroads, no telegraphs, no telephones, not even the common friction match, and hundreds of other common necessaries of life, which were not known a hundred years ago. The middle-aged of the present generation have not the remotest idea how people plodded along at the beginning of this century. If they were suddenly transported to the likeness of a hundred years ago, they would behold a world that they could neither recognize nor understand. But all this has nothing to do with this prophecy. The prophecy presents miracles designed to deceive, and the deception has for its object false worship. Nothing which is mechanical or scientific can be called a miracle. Others have applied this prophecy to the papacy itself, and said that the priests have always maintained their ascendency over the people by pretending to work miracles, and thus deceiving them. But the prophecy does not admit of such an interpretation; it does not say that the beast deceived them that dwell upon the earth by pretending to work miracles, but he deceived them by means of those miracles *which he had power to do.* They are workings with power, intended to deceive, and to turn people away from the true worship of God. As it is said again in this book of Revelation, "For they are the spirits of demons, working miracles." Rev. 16:15. The Saviour prophesied of the same, when, speaking of the days when his second coming is near, he said:—

"For there shall arise false Christs, and false prophets, and shall show great signs and wonders; insomuch that, if it were possible, they shall deceive the very elect." Matt. 24:24.

These wonder-workings are not strange in these days. Spirit communications, or spirit manifestations, as they have been called, are well known throughout the world, in this century, and especially for the last forty years, during which time they have become prevalent everywhere. Such things have always existed, but they have shown themselves with unusual prominence at certain times. When God was about to deliver his people from the bondage of Egypt, the magicians came forward with their enchantments to resist the message of the Lord to the king, and to counterfeit the miracles wrought through Moses and Aaron. See Ex. 7:10-12, etc. Again, when the Son of God appeared on this earth, the spirits of demons were busily working, possessing the minds of the people, and opposing the truth. The Saviour gave his disciples power over unclean spirits, and told them to cast out demons; and they reported that the spirits were subject to them in this name. Matt. 10:1-8; Luke 10:17-20. And Paul said that in the last days there would be deceivers resisting the truth as Jannes and Jambres withstood Moses. 2 Tim. 3:1-9. And again, in discoursing of the second coming of Christ, he said:—

"Whose coming is after the working of Satan with all power and signs and lying wonders, and with all deceivableness of unrighteousness in them that perish." 2 Thess. 2:9, 10.

It is a fact that these modern wonders, these spirit manifestations, first revealed themselves in the United States, in the western part of the State of New York. And it has been through American mediums that they have gone to every quarter of the globe. There are some who yet insist that there is no reality in these professed manifestations; that they are mere deceptions. That they are deceitful and deceiving, we have no doubt; neither have we any doubt that there is reality in them. And they who deny their reality, who deny that there is power and intelligence in them above that of the mediums, cannot have examined the subject with much care. Some of the most painstaking students, men of the highest scientific attainments, have spent months and even years putting them to the severest tests, and have declared, as the result of their inquiries, that they were not produced by any means within human control. In other words, they confess that they are superhuman, supernatural, or truly miraculous.

At the first, Spiritualism appeared, as it is in fact, an antichristian system, commending itself solely by its physical manifestations. By this means it attracted attention, and though it reviled the Bible and Christianity, and blasphemed the name of God and of Christ, it convinced the multitude that there was power in it, and thousands were turned away from the truth of God to accept its silly fables. That the world was ripe for the deception is proved by the fact that, in a few years, its believers and adherents were numbered by millions.

It has been remarked that these miracles are deceitful, and were intended to lead the people to embrace a false system of worship. But the question would constantly arise in many minds, How can that lead to a false system of worship which is so openly irreligious; which reviles all that is esteemed sacred by religious people? To some, and for a time, this seemed a problem too difficult to be solved. But the advocates of Spiritualism have themselves given the solution. They determined that their course was impolitic; that, instead of trying to destroy the Bible and Christianity, it would prove to their advantage to uphold them, and to turn their testimony to the benefit of their system. The foundation of Spiritualism is the doctrine of the immortality of the soul. And as nearly all professed Christians regard that as one of the leading doctrines of Revelation, and inasmuch as they had no direct proof for it in the Scriptures, and Spiritualism proposed to demonstrate that it is true, it was easy to foresee that a compromise between the parties would not be difficult to effect. And the consequence is just what was anticipated. Tens and hundreds of thousands of members of all the leading denominations, who would yet be unwilling to be known as Spiritualists, are following it. Many hold social circles, where neighbors meet to converse with their supposed friends, and where mediums are developed. These parties suppose that their conduct is innocent; but they do not consult the word of God in regard to the nature of Spiritualism. They take it for granted that it is the spirits of their lost friends with whom they hold converse, and are unwilling to be aroused from their delusion. If they would turn to the Bible they would learn better.

This work is well characterized by the prophet of God, in these words:—

"And when they shall say unto you, Seek unto them that have familiar spirits, and unto wizards that peep, and that mutter; should not a people seek unto their God? for the living to the dead? To the law and to the testimony; if they speak not according to this word, it is because there is no light in them." Isa. 8: 19, 20.

Shall men turn away from the word of God, to seek knowledge of the dead? Shall a living man go to inquire of the dead? That is done in these days, but the Scriptures utterly condemn the practice. Thus the Lord said to the children of Israel:—

"There shall not be found among you anyone that maketh his son or his daughter to pass through the fire, or that useth divination, or an observer of times, or an enchanter, or a witch, or a charmer, or a consulter with familiar spirits, or a wizard, or a necromancer." Deut. 18:10, 11.

A necromancer, literally, and as the original plainly reads, is one who inquires of the dead. The Lord said to his people that they should not learn to do after the abominations of the nations that dwell in the land of Canaan. He then enumerated the prohibited works, as here quoted, and added:—

"For all that do these things are an abomination unto the Lord; and because of these abominations the Lord thy God doth drive them out from before thee." Verse 12.

The Lord declares that inquiring of the dead is an abomination in his sight; but this practice is the very life and front of Spiritualism. But it has been argued that this law was for Israel, and for no other people, and cannot bind us. But mark this: The Lord did not say that these things were the abominations of Israel. They were the abominable practices of the nations in Canaan, whom the Lord drove out before Israel. And he said it was because of these wicked practices that he destroyed them out of the land. "For," said he, "all that do these things are an abomination to the Lord." And the folly as well as the wickedness of this practice is shown in the Bible, which plainly declares that "the dead know not anything." Eccl. 9:5.

But one replies: If the dead know not anything, as, indeed, the Bible plainly says, what can be the harm of inquiring of them, seeing they cannot hear or know what is said? But the facts of Spiritualism abundantly prove that *somebody* or *something* hears and answers the inquiries. The scripture under investigation (Rev. 13:13, 14) says that these miracles are wrought to deceive; and one part of the deception is this, that the spirits consulted profess to be our dead friends, when they are not. God has stored the treasures of knowledge in his word—in the law and in the testimony. They who neglect this word, and seek knowledge from forbidden sources, must expect to be deceived. Jesus, speaking of the last days, the days preceding his second coming, says:—

"There shall arise false Christs, and false prophets, and shall show great signs and wonders; insomuch that, if it were possible, they shall deceive the very elect." Matt. 24:24.

They profess to be Christs, sent of God; but they are not. They profess to be prophets, commissioned of God to speak to the world, and to instruct mankind concerning the future, but they are not. They are living spirits, the angels of the adversary, Satan. Compare Matt. 25:41; 2 Peter 2:4; Jude 6.

But again it is asked, How can we be deceived? We have heard the familiar tones of the voices of our friends, and some have beheld their very faces. They must be what they profess to be.

But this reasoning is not good. All Spiritualists confess that spirits have not material forms nor visible faces. They say that these are materialized for the occasion. And if they have power to assume forms which do not properly belong to the nature of a spirit, they can certainly assume one form as readily as another, and can personate whom they will. And that they do so we are well assured. The apostle says that Satan is transformed into an angel of light. And if he can assume the form and appearance of an angel of light, it is no marvel that his ministers profess to be the ministers of righteousness; that his angels assume to be Christs and prophets. 2 Cor. 11:14, 15.

Now it is a fact clearly taught by Jesus and his holy apostles, that wicked spirits, professing to be sent of God to enlighten the world, will work signs and wonders to deceive. They profess to be the spirits of the dead, but the Bible says that the dead know not anything, and therefore they cannot communicate with us. What, then, are these spirits in fact? On this the divine word informs us:—

"For they are the spirits of devils [Greek, demons], working miracles, which go forth unto the kings of the earth and of the whole world, to gather them to the battle of that great day of God Almighty." Rev. 16:14.

And just at this time Jesus says: "Behold, I come as a thief. Blessed is he that watcheth." Verse 15.

Spiritualism is built upon the assumption that man is immortal in his nature, which is contrary to the Scriptures.

In Rom. 2 : 7 we are told that if we would have immortality we must seek for it; and 2 Tim. 1 : 10 informs us that Jesus Christ our Saviour has brought life and immortality to light through the gospel. In 1 Cor. 15:51–54, we learn that immortality will be put on by the saints in the resurrection. In this present state man is mortal, corruptible. Rom. 1 : 23. The Scriptures do not say, in any manner, that man is immortal in his present state; they do not speak of the finally wicked, the lost, as ever becoming immortal, because they fail to seek for immortality where it can only be found,—in the gospel of Christ. In the resurrection the righteous put on immortality; but again the apostle writes:—

"He that soweth to his flesh shall of the flesh reap corruption; but he that soweth to the Spirit shall of the Spirit reap life everlasting." Gal. 6: 8.

In the beginning, as we have before noticed, when man was created, he was placed on probation. Life and death were set before him, and he was a probationer for life. But he sinned, and was shut away from the tree of life, lest he should eat and live forever in sin. Gen. 3 : 22–24. But God had regard to the work of his own hands, and would not leave him to perish utterly. He provided a way, through the seed of the woman, to recover man from the ruin that he had brought upon himself. "God so loved the world, that he gave his only begotten Son, that whosoever believeth in him should not perish, but have everlasting life." John 3 : 16. Jesus, our only Redeemer, said : "My sheep hear my voice, and I know them, and they follow me; and I give unto them eternal life; and they shall never perish, neither shall any man pluck them out of my hand." John 10 : 27, 28.

Jesus brought life and immortality to light through the gospel, because he is the only Saviour from sin. Matt. 1 : 21. "The wages of sin is death; but the gift of God is eternal life through Jesus Christ our Lord." Rom. 6 : 23. Wherever sin prevails, there death must follow. The only way to escape the penalty of sin, which is death, is to be saved from sin; and as Jesus alone can save from sin, he is the only way of eternal life. Hence he is called our life. Col. 3 : 4. And of this the Father bears most emphatic witness as follows:—

"He that believeth not God hath made him a liar; because he believeth not the record that God gave of his Son. And this is the record, that God hath given to us eternal life, and this life is in his Son." 1 John 5:10, 11.

Eternal life is not in our nature. Adam did not bequeath it to his posterity. By his sin he was shut away from the tree of life, and returned unto the ground out of which he was taken. And in Adam all die. 1 Cor. 15:22. Death has passed upon all men. Rom. 5:12. The seed of the woman, the second Adam, came to seek and to save the lost. He came to bring life and immortality to light in the gospel, and to give life to as many as will believe and follow him. John 6:40. But we must turn to him with all our hearts, for Christ hath no concord with Belial; he will not divide honors with his great enemy. To say that we have immortality without his gospel, is to rob him of the highest glory of his mission. To submit to the deceptions of Satan and his angels, is to reject the Saviour.

The result of these wonder-workings is just what would be expected from such a deception as this has proved to be. Satan has always shown a greater desire to pervert worship than to destroy it. Man has a natural inclination to worship; he has also a natural aversion to purity of heart—to humility and self-denial. Therefore an effort of Satan to destroy worship would meet with the opposition of even the carnal heart, for only the lowest tribes of earth have no system of worship. But perversion of worship is pleasing to the carnal mind. False worship satisfies the hardened conscience, and lulls the sinner to sleep. It is the most fatal of all delusions.

Rev. 13:14 says that the object of these deceitful miracles is to induce them that dwell upon the earth to make an image to the beast, which had a wound by a sword and did live. We have seen that it was the papacy that was wounded to death, and had its deadly wound healed. The papal church system was a worldly church, a State or national church, a base perversion of Christianity.

We have also seen that the beast with two horns, where these modern miracles took their rise, is the United States of

America. Within the dominion of this beast, an image or likeness will be made to the first or papal beast. That is, the government will be turned into a State church government—a likeness of the religious system established by Constantine and his successors in the throne of the Roman Empire. So plainly is this fact indicated by this prophecy that there have been those who have preached and published, for the last forty years, that Church and State would be united in this government. Nay, they even pointed out the very religious questions that would be put forward to bring about such a result. But as there has always been a strong aversion to the very name of Church and State in this nation, these expositors of the prophecy were laughed to scorn for preaching that such a state of things would ever be in America. But now what do we behold? —Some years since, an organization was formed called the "National Reform Association," the object of which is to nationalize Christianity, or what they may call Christianity; for, as a matter of fact, there can be no national Christianity in any nation in a wicked world. Christianity is a matter of conscience. The moment it is put under restraint of civil law it becomes a worldly religion, and ceases to be Christianity. We do not mean that there can be no Christians under legalized religion; for individual Christians can live under unfavorable conditions. But just as far as an individual's religion is governed and moulded by civil law, just so far it is worldly, and not heavenly—not the religion of Christ. Over the conscience no government can hold rightful control. The worst usurpation is that of exercising power over the consciences of men, for it is usurping the place of God; it is setting aside the authority of the Most High.

This so-called National Reform Association has become very strong and influential; and it has secured the interest of the Woman's Christian Temperance Union,—an organization as widespread as the nation, which has pledged its influence towards securing a religious amendment to the national Constitution, by means of which such Christianity as the dominant party may happen to favor, may be enforced by law. Whenever this object is accomplished, and the prospects are favorable to its speedy accomplishment, then the United States Government will have become a perfect image of the first beast, which had the wound by the sword and did live.

Verse 15. "And he had power to give life unto the image of the beast, that the image of the beast should both speak, and cause that as many as would not worship the image of the beast should be killed."

Here the climax is reached. Here is where this beast speaks like a dragon. But there are preliminary steps taken before this bitterness of persecution is shown. Verses 16, 17 say:—

"And he causeth all, both small and great, rich and poor, free and bond, to receive a mark in their right hand, or in their foreheads; and that no man might buy or sell, save he that had the mark, or the name of the beast, or the number of his name."

It is a notable truth that any government, however mild and just it may have been before, becomes oppressive and persecuting as soon as it unites the religious to the civil power. Or, in other words, all religion becomes oppressive and persecuting when the sword of power is put into its hands. If the people do not feel the oppression, it is because they have suffered their religious convictions to fall to the low level of mere formalism. And lifeless formality is the natural product of enforced religion. And, true to the spirit of national religion, the leaders of the movement above referred to, already boast that when they have changed the form of the American Government, none will be considered *bona fide* citizens, none will be eligible to offices of trust, except those who subscribe to the national faith. When the rights of conscience are denied, the rights of citizenship are of little worth; and when these are denied, then will this scripture be fulfilled,—no man may buy or sell save he that worships the image of the beast and receives his mark.

The Scriptures reveal this fact that the conscientious and God-fearing are the very ones against whom this persecution will be directed. And so it has always been when the church has held control of the sword of power. Heresy is considered the highest crime. The martyrs of the papal power were considered the greatest criminals of the realm. None were so sure to be burned alive as the heretics. What a burning shame that in this enlightened age, with the force of historical facts to warn us, men should seek to repeat, in the name of Christ, such a history by clothing religious bigots with the power to punish those who will not subscribe to their particular creeds.

We need not think that all the persecution will fall on the devoted ones in this land. Already the wheels of the Reformation inaugurated by such men as Huss, Luther, Melancthon, Zwingle, Calvin, and other valiant men, for the truth of God, are turned backward. The pope of Rome is recovering the favor he lost in the fifteenth and sixteenth centuries, and there are none who dare stand up, as did Huss and Luther, in defense of the Bible as the only rule of religious rights.

But God, who points out the trials through which his people have to pass, does not leave them cast down with such a dark prospect. Immediately after this revelation of the working of iniquity, and the bitter persecution of the saints, the prophet beholds the Lamb standing on Mount Zion, and with him a glorified company, who have gotten the victory, and are singing the song of their redemption. Rev. 14:1-5. This is not the whole assembly of those who shall be redeemed of Adam's race; it includes only those who have passed through the persecution just described. They are not redeemed from the graves. They are redeemed from among men,—out from the generations of the living; they are they who are alive and remain unto the coming of the Lord (1 Thess. 4:15-17), as will be further shown.

Nor does God in his wisdom leave the vision here. He does not reveal the wickedness of the wicked without pointing out the sad consequences of their actions. He not only shows us the triumph of the faithful, who refuse to worship the beast and his image, but he also forewarns of the destiny of the persecutors and of those who are willingly deceived by their wiles. In Rev. 14:9-11, are the following terrible words concerning the very things we have been considering:—

"If any man worship the beast and his image, and receive his mark in his forehead, or in his hand, the same shall drink of the wine of the wrath of God, which is poured out without mixture into the cup of his indignation; and he shall be tormented with fire and brimstone in the presence of the holy angels, and in the presence of the Lamb; and the smoke of their torment ascendeth up for ever and ever; and they have no rest day nor night, who worship the beast and his image, and whosoever receiveth the mark of his name."

Attention is called to the connection of these awfully solemn words.

1. The verse following says: "Here is the patience of the saints; here are they that keep the commandments of God, and the faith of Jesus." This shows that the commandments of God, and the faith of Jesus, separate between the saints and those who worship the beast and receive his mark. And this furnishes a clue to the understanding of the message, what it is to worship the beast, and to receive his mark.

2. By verse 14 and onward, we learn that the Son of man comes on a white cloud to reap the harvest of the earth, immediately after this solemn warning is given. The Lord said the harvest is the end of the world, and that the Son of man will send forth his angels to gather his elect, and they will also gather them that do iniquity to destroy them. Matt. 13: 39-43; 24: 30, 31. As we have passed by the great tribulation under papal Rome; have passed the wounding of that power in 1798; and as we are in the time of the wonder-working of the second beast, when the elements are in motion to bring the world under further deception, even to the making of an image to the beast, and receiving of his mark, now is the time to heed this warning, for now we are in the last days, when the Son of man is near to come to reap the harvest of the earth.

3. By verse 9 we learn that the solemn warning message, quoted above, is given by "the third angel." Two angels precede this one, the first one (verses 6, 7) declaring that the hour of God's judgment is come. These important truths must be noticed, that we may understand our relation to the perils of the last days, and that we may perfectly understand the solemn warning that God in mercy has sent to this generation.

CHAPTER XIV.

THE HOUR OF JUDGMENT.

In his sermon at Athens, the apostle Paul said that God "hath appointed a day, in the which he will judge the world in righteousness by that man whom he hath ordained." Acts 17:31. According to this, there was a time appointed for the judgment,—a definite day when it would come. In Rev. 14:6, 7, the hour of judgment is announced by an angel, of whom the prophet thus speaks:—

"And I saw another angel fly in the midst of heaven, having the everlasting gospel to preach unto them that dwell on the earth, and to every nation, and kindred, and tongue, and people, saying with a loud voice, Fear God, and give glory to him; for the hour of his judgment is come; and worship him that made heaven, and earth, and the sea, and the fountains of waters."

In regard to this, we notice:—

1. The importance of the message. It is called the everlasting gospel. Being a part of the gospel, whenever it is given it must be heeded. But it has been asked, How can a proclamation of the judgment be any part of the gospel? To this we offer two answers: 1. Every dispensation of God is gracious toward his people. But that which is gracious to the righteous may be everlasting ruin to the wicked. The Scripture says that when Noah and his family went into the ark, "the Lord shut him in." Gen. 7:16. This assured the perfect safety of Noah; but when the Lord shut him in, by the same act he shut all the others out. The psalmist praised him who "overthrew Pharoah and his host in the Red Sea; for his mercy endureth forever." Ps. 136:15. It was no mercy to Pharaoh and his host; they had forfeited the mercy of God. But it was mercy to the Lord's people; it was necessary to rescue them, if

their enemies were destroyed. And so, without the judgment, God's people would never receive their reward. 2. The question is more fully answered by showing the order and nature of the judgment. It is in truth a part of the gospel—necessary to the perfect fulfillment of the purposes and promises of God. The gospel is revealed in Isa. 61:1, 2. These verses read as follows:—

"The Spirit of the Lord God is upon me; because the Lord hath anointed me to preach good tidings unto the meek; he hath sent me to bind up the broken-hearted, to proclaim liberty to the captives, and the opening of the prison to them that are bound; to proclaim the acceptable year of the Lord, and the day of vengeance of our God; to comfort all that mourn."

In Luke 4:16-21, we read that Jesus came to Nazareth, "and as his custom was, he went into the synagogue on the Sabbath-day, and stood up for to read." Opening the book of Isaiah, he began to read chapter 61, as quoted above, and read as far as to this sentence, "to proclaim the acceptable year of the Lord," and there abruptly stopped. Had he read the next sentence,—"and the day of vengeance of our God,"—he could not have said, as he did in verse 21. "This day is this scripture fulfilled in your ears," because the time had not yet come to proclaim the judgment. But by this we learn that the proclamation of the judgment is a part of the gospel—but a part that was not yet fulfilled in the time of our Saviour's preaching. The apostles of the Lord took up the proclamation just as he gave it at Nazareth. Paul said, "Behold, now is the accepted time; behold, now is the day of salvation." 2 Cor. 6:2. But to Felix he reasoned of righteousness, temperance, and judgment *to come*—not *is come*. Acts 24:25. The preaching of the hour of judgment *is come*, was necessarily reserved to the last days, when the coming of Christ is near.

It has been seen, by the prophecy of the beast with two horns (Rev. 13:11-18),that we are in the last days, and that the last message, given just before Christ comes to reap the harvest of the earth, is based on the facts that are now transpiring. The question then naturally arises, Has the first message, of Rev. 14:6, 7, been given? Has a proclamation been made to the world of the nature of this judgment-hour cry. It surely has; a message in this very language was proclaimed to all the world between the years 1836 and 1844. It was very extensively preached in Europe and America, and also in Asia. Publications were sent to every missionary station on the globe. Those who preached it fully believed that it was a precursor of the coming of the Lord, as it really was. Yet they did not understand the nature of the messages connected with it, and immediately following it.

This message of Rev. 14:6, 7 is a message *of time*. It was preached as a message of time by those who proclaimed it. It is true, they overlooked the connection, and were therefore mistaken in the events that should succeed their work. But that mistake was altogether owing to the fact that they had wrong views of the nature of the judgment itself—the very same views that are even now held by the great majority of Bible readers. It is generally believed that the judgment does not take place until the Lord comes. But a reading of this chapter must convince everyone that that idea is not correct. Four events are presented in this chapter, which stand in this order: 1. The declaration that the judgment is come. 2. The cry that Babylon is fallen. 3. The warning against the worship of the beast and his image, called the Third Angel's Message. 4. The coming of the Lord to reap the harvest of the earth. This shows that the judgment comes while men are yet here on probation, and that the proclamation of its coming must be made before time closes, that men may prepare for the time when Jesus shall close his priestly work of intercession. The common view that the judgment cannot begin until after Christ comes is certainly incorrect.

In 1 Cor. 15: 42-54, it is shown that the righteous are immortalized in the resurrection. They are raised incorruptible, glorified. In the very event of the resurrection, at the sounding of the trump of God, the change from mortal to immortal takes place, in a moment, in the twinkling of an eye. This refers to the righteous, for they alone have part in the first resurrection. Rev. 20: 4-6 says the blessed and holy have part in the first resurrection; but the rest of the dead will not live again for the space of a thousand years. Now, inasmuch as the gift of God through Christ is eternal life, and Jesus brought immortality to light through the gospel, it is absurd to suppose that these blessings will be conferred before the judgment. It is surely absurd to suppose that the great boon of immortality and eternal life would be conferred on the saints of God, and that afterward they should stand to be judged. Again, Christ is specially the advocate of his people, and it is unreasonable to suppose that he would cease his work as an advocate, an intercessor, a priest, before the decision of the judgment was rendered, and leave them to pass through the ordeal of that awful event without a priest, without an advocate. Revelation 14 proves clearly that the judgment precedes the coming of Christ and the resurrection; and the resurrection of the righteous to glory and immortality is proof that the judgment has been fully decided in their favor, while the fact that the rest of the dead remain in their graves during the one thousand years, the fact that they are not raised when the righteous are, is sufficient proof that their cases have been decided against them. They have already been counted unworthy of eternal life, and will be raised to the resurrection of damnation to suffer the second death.

This again is strongly confirmed by Rev. 22: 11, 12. At a certain time the Saviour will proclaim:—

"He that is unjust, let him be unjust still; and he which is filthy, let him be filthy still; and he that is righteous, let him be righteous still; and he that is holy, let him be holy still. And, behold, I come quickly; and my reward is with me, to give every man according as his work shall be."

This gives the same order; every case is decided and fixed before the Lord Jesus comes to reward everyone according to his work. As far as the righteous are concerned, the judgment is fully completed before the Lord comes. But not so with the wicked; they are rejected as being unworthy of eternal life; but what shall be the measure of the punishment of each individual—whether with few or many stripes—will be decided by Christ and the saints, during the thousand years in which the unrighteous remain in the graves. Compare Rev. 20:2-6; 1 Cor. 4:5; 6:1-3.

2. The nature of the judgment shows that it is a part of the work of the gospel. In approaching this subject, we shall have to examine the question of the time on which the proclamation rests. This is a matter of prophecy in Daniel 8. It has been shown that chapters 2 and 3 of this prophecy are specially given to the outlines of the world, as presented under four great kingdoms, Babylon, Medo-Persia, Greece, and Rome. Of the fourth or Roman Kingdom chapter 2:40 says:—

"And the fourth kingdom shall be strong as iron; forasmuch as iron breaketh in pieces and subdueth all things; and as iron that breaketh all these, shall it break in pieces and bruise."

In chapter 7:7 the same power is thus described:—

"Behold a fourth beast, dreadful and terrible, and strong exceedingly; and it had great iron teeth; it devoured and brake in pieces, and stamped the residue with the feet of it."

As before remarked, the first, Babylon, was the most glorious, and the fourth, Rome, was the strongest, even strong exceedingly. In chapter 8 is another vision of the kingdoms, beginning with the Medes and Persians. This kingdom has the symbol of a ram, while the Grecian is represented by a goat, which had a notable horn between his eyes, which was the first king—Alexander. The prophecy says:—

"When he was strong, the great horn was broken; and for it came up four notable ones toward the four winds of heaven. And out of one of them came forth a little horn, which waxed exceeding great." Verses 8, 9.

In the interpretation it is said:—

"The ram which thou sawest having two horns are the kings of Media and Persia. And the rough goat is the king of Grecia; and the great horn that is between his eyes is the first king. Now that being broken, whereas four stood up for it, four kingdoms shall stand up out of the nation, but not in his power." Verses 20-22.

Out of that kingdom stood up these four kingdoms: Egypt, Syria, Asia Minor, and Greece or Macedon. The prophecy says that out of one of them came forth a little horn that waxed exceeding great. Out of the last-named of the above four, the Macedonian division, arose the Roman Kingdom, small in its beginning, not counted among the divisions of the empire, but it became exceeding great, just as was said of it in chapters 2 and 7. No other kingdom but the Roman could possibly fulfill this prophecy. But there is this difference between the little horn of chapter 7 and the little horn of chapter 8. The former represented papal Rome, while the latter was Rome in its entire history, in both the pagan and papal forms. This power magnified itself, not only against the host of Heaven, but against the Prince of the host. It cast down the truth to the ground, and practised, and prospered. Verses 10-12. The prophet heard a holy one ask another how long should be the vision, to give the sanctuary and the host to be trodden under foot. The answer was returned to Daniel, thus:—

"And he said unto me, Unto two thousand and three hundred days; then shall the sanctuary be cleansed." Dan. 8:14.

The truth concerning the cleansing of the sanctuary is the solution of this whole matter. This we find fully explained in the books of Exodus and Leviticus. To make this clear to the reader, we shall have to refer again to the work of the sanctuary. In Exodus 25 the Lord commanded Moses to take an offering of the children of Israel: "And let them make me a sanctuary; that I may dwell among them." Verse 8. It is not necessary that a full description of the sanctuary be here given. It was a tabernacle of two rooms; the first had in it the seven golden candlesticks, the table of show-bread, and the golden altar of incense. In this room called the holy, the priests ministered daily. In the inner apartment, called the most holy, was the ark containing the two tables of stone, on which were written the ten commandments. The covering of the ark was called the mercy-seat, upon which were the golden cherubim. The Lord commanded Moses, saying:—

"And thou shalt put the mercy-seat above upon the ark; and in the ark thou shalt put the testimony that I shall give thee. And there I will meet with thee, and I will commune with thee from above the mercy-seat, from between the two cherubim which are upon the ark of the testimony, of all things which I will give thee in commandment unto the children of Israel." Ex. 25:21, 22.

Of the priestly work in the most holy, we have full description in Leviticus 16. After making an offering for himself, the high priest was required to take a goat for a sin-offering for the people. The order was then as follows:—

"Then shall he kill the goat of the sin-offering, that is for the people, and bring his blood within the vail, and do with that blood as he did with the blood of the bullock, and sprinkle it upon the mercy-seat, and before the mercy-seat; and he shall make an atonement for the holy place, because of the uncleanness of the children of Israel, and because of their transgressions in all their sins; and so shall he do for the tabernacle of the congregation, that remaineth among them in the midst of their uncleanness." Verses 15, 16.

Why was an atonement to be made for the holy place? It could commit no wrong. The answer is in the order; it was because of the uncleanness of the people; because of their transgressions. But how came the sanctuary to be defiled with the sins of the people, seeing that the people were forbidden under the penalty of death to approach unto it? See Num. 3:10. *Answer*—The high priest represented the people; the Lord said that the high priest should bear their judgment. Ex. 28:30. The wages of sin is death, and the law demands the life of the transgressor; therefore the Lord said that the blood was given to make an atonement, because the life is in the blood. Lev. 17:11. The blood that was sprinkled on the mercy-seat, in the immediate presence of God, represented the life of the transgressors; in it was borne the sins of the people. Thus the entering of the high priest with the blood of the sin-offering, caused him to bear their judgment, and the most holy was defiled. As he did in the most holy, so was he required to do in the holy: he was to anoint the altar of incense, " and he shall sprinkle of the blood upon it with his finger seven times, and cleanse it, and hallow it from the uncleanness of the children of Israel." Lev. 16:18, 19.

All this was to take place on the tenth day of the seventh month, which was the day of atonement. Lev. 16:20–31; 23:27. Making the atonement, blotting out the sins from the presence of the Lawgiver, was called cleansing the sanctuary. See Eze. 43:20–22.

This completed the yearly service of the sanctuary; and the service of each year represented the complete priestly work of the Saviour. The nature of the sanctuary service in the law of Moses, is shown in Hebrews 8 and 9. After discoursing of the priesthood of Christ, after the order of Melchizedek, a kingly priest, the writer says:—

"Now of the things which we have spoken this is the sum: We have such an high priest, who is set on the right hand of the throne of the Majesty in the Heavens; a minister of the sanctuary, and of the true tabernacle, which the Lord pitched, and not man. For every high priest is ordained to offer gifts and sacrifices; wherefore it is of necessity that this man have somewhat also to offer. For if he were on earth, he should not be a priest, seeing that there are priests that offer gifts according to the law; who serve unto the example and shadow of heavenly things, as Moses was admonished of God when he was about to make the tabernacle; for, See saith he, that thou make all things according to the pattern showed to thee in the mount." Heb. 8:1-5.

Here we learn: 1. That the sanctuary, and the priestly work of the earthly priests, were examples and shadows of things in Heaven. 2. That Christ could not be a priest on earth, for the earthly priests were types of him. 3. That his is a kingly priesthood on the throne of his Father. 4. That there is a true sanctuary or tabernacle in Heaven, of which that on earth was a figure. In this book we learn also that Christ is a Mediator, not only for sinners under the new covenant, but also for those under the first covenant. Chapter 9:15. This proves that Jesus is a Mediator before the same law that God spoke to Israel on Mount Sinai, and wrote on the tables of stone. That law stands against their transgressions, until Jesus blots them out with his own precious blood.

But a question of great interest and importance will here arise: Does the heavenly sanctuary need to be cleansed from the sins of the people, even as the pattern and example did? To this we have a clear and decided answer in Heb. 9:23, 24. After speaking of the efficacy of the blood of Christ, in contrast with the blood of bulls and goats, which was offered under the old covenant, and of the necessity of shedding blood in order to remission, the writer says:—

"It was therefore necessary that the patterns of things in the Heavens should be purified with these; but the heavenly things themselves with better sacrifices than these. For Christ is not entered into the holy places made with hands, which are the figures of the true; but into Heaven itself, now to appear in the presence of God for us."

And why should not this be so? Is not our High Priest in the sanctuary in Heaven? Does he not bear our judgment? Does he not present our sins in the presence of God? Does he not present his own blood, the better sacrifice, in that sanctuary? It is for this reason that the heavenly things need to be purified. If they did not, there would have been no necessity for the patterns—the shadow and example; they would have been without meaning.

That there are indeed two holy places in the sanctuary above, we learn not only in Heb. 9: 23, 24, but also in the book of Revelation. In chapter 4: 1–5, John had a vision of the open temple in Heaven, and of the throne, and he said "there were seven lamps of fire burning before the throne." The seven lamps were in the holy place. But in a vision of the heavenly things very near to the close of the dispensation, under the seventh trumpet, when the time to judge the dead had come (Rev. 11: 15–19), the prophet said: "And the temple of God was opened in Heaven, and there was seen in his temple the ark of his testament." The ark of the testament was in the most holy place, which was opened only on the day of atonement, when the sanctuary was to be cleansed from the sins of the people. This is the last part of the priestly service. It is the judgment. At the time when this part of the sanctuary is opened it is declared that the time of the dead, when they should be judged, has come. Verse 18. This coincides with the time of the first message of Revelation 14, verses 6, 7: "The hour of his judgment is come." Then the time is come when the sanctuary in Heaven shall be cleansed.

And this clearly shows that the proclamation of the judgment is gospel preaching; for the beginning of the judgment is the work of the priest in the most holy place in the sanctuary in Heaven,—the blotting out of the sins of the saints. To the people of God it is a most important part of the gospel work. To the impenitent it is the time of deciding that they shall never see eternal life; the time to determine when he that is unrighteous shall remain unrighteous still.

But time does not close with that announcement. Another message of warning is going forth to the world, while our High Priest is engaged in judging the dead. Still there is opportunity to make our calling and election sure. But we must not presume on the mercies of the Lord. Remember his own warning: " Watch therefore; for ye know not what hour your Lord doth come." Matt. 24: 42. To all those who do not watch, that day will come as a thief. But to the waiting ones, the Scripture says, " But ye, brethren, are not in darkness, that that day should overtake you as a thief." 1 Thess. 5: 4.

CHAPTER XV.

BABYLON IS FALLEN.

FOLLOWING the first message of Revelation 14 (verses 6, 7) is another, containing a simple brief statement. It is not framed like a warning; it declares no particular duty. It is only the statement of a fact, but important to be considered, as are all the declarations of the word of God. It is as follows:—

> "And there followed another angel, saying, Babylon is fallen, is fallen, that great city, because she made all nations drink of the wine of the wrath of her fornication." Rev. 14: 8.

There are two things that are often taken for granted, both of which must be noticed, namely: 1. That Babylon is the Catholic, or Roman, Church and that only. 2. That her fall means her overthrow, or destruction. The first of these propositions is not altogether true, as will be seen in due time; the last is altogether wrong. Nobody supposes that Babylon, whatever it means, will be entirely destroyed and the world move on as it did before. That will be a grand catastrophe which will affect the whole world, as may be seen in Revelation 18. In that chapter is another announcement of the fall of Babylon, showing its connection with other facts and events, as follows: 1. An angel announces that Babylon is fallen, the same as Rev. 14: 8. 2. He announces also that she has become the habitation of demons, and the hold of foul spirits, and a cage of every unclean and hateful bird. This is additional to the statement of Rev. 14: 8. 3. Another voice says: "Come out of her, my people, that ye be not partakers of her sins, and that ye receive not of her plagues." 4. It is said that in one day shall her plagues come—death, and mourning, and famine—and she shall be utterly burned with fire. Reversing these events, we find that when this announcement is made Babylon is yet to be destroyed. And before her destruction, God's people are called out of her. And before they are called out of her, she becomes the habitation of demons. And before she becomes the habitation of demons, her fall takes place. Thus it is positively shown that her fall is before her destruction; doubtless it leads to her destruction finally. We are therefore forced to the conclusion that the fall referred to in Rev. 14:8, is a moral fall; it has reference to a change of condition in the sight of Heaven.

For the immediate cause of her fall we are left to draw our conclusion from the context. Her connection with the world is stated; also that, instead of being the light of the world, she has been guilty of misleading the world. Through her the world has been led to lightly regard its responsibility to God, and to indulge a false hope. But, doubtless, that which has led to this fatal state was the rejection of the proclamation of the everlasting gospel, as made known in the preaching of the hour of judgment come. This message being the gospel, to reject it must bring the frown of God, as certainly as did the rejection of the gospel in the days of Christ. Or if not, why not? Is not that always of importance which the word of God calls the everlasting gospel?

But the question may be raised, This message being founded on time could the people surely know that the time had arrived when it should be given? To answer this we must return to the prophecy of Daniel, where the time is revealed.

Between the years of 1832 and 1840, the minds of many Bible students, in different countries, mainly in Europe and America, became deeply impressed with the prophecy of Daniel, as furnishing the evidence that we are in the last days, and that the coming of the Lord is drawing near. Their attention was directed to the declaration of Dan. 8:14, that the sanctuary was to be cleansed after two thousand three hundred days, or years. In chapter 8 there is no explanation of this time—no starting-point from which to count; but there is in chapter 9. In chapter 8:16, Gabriel was ordered to make Daniel understand the vision. This he proceeded to do, as far as the beasts and kingdoms were concerned; but of the time he said nothing, and Daniel said (verse 27) that it was not understood.

In chapter 9, Daniel makes a most earnest confession and prayer for his people, and in behalf of the city of Jerusalem, then in ruins. While he was praying Gabriel appeared unto him again, and told him to consider the vision, for he had come to give him understanding. And as he had explained all but the time in chapter 8, he spoke of nothing but the time in chapter 9. Gabriel said to him (verses 24, 25), that seventy weeks were determined (literally, cut off) upon his people, and that from the going forth of the commandment to restore and build Jerusalem unto Messiah the Prince, should be seven weeks and threescore and two weeks; that is, sixty-nine of the seventy weeks should reach to Messiah the Prince. We reckon this to the time when he was made known to Israel as the Messiah, by John the Baptist, which was in A. D. 27.

It is universally agreed that these weeks are weeks of years—seven years to a week. In sixty-nine sevens are four hundred and eighty-three years; counting from the time when John announced Jesus as the Lamb of God, we find that A. D. 26 taken from 483, leaves 457 B. C., which was the year in which the commandment went forth to restore and build Jerusalem—which was the beginning of the two thousand three hundred years of Dan. 8:14. In Ezra 7:11–26, is found the decree of Artaxerxes the king of Persia for the restoration of the temple and its service, and for the complete government of Jerusalem according to the ordinances of God. This decree was given to Ezra 457 years before Christ. Both Cyrus and Darius had given decrees of like import before this, but the work was not completed until the time of Artaxerxes. And in Ezra 6:14, it is said that the work of restoration was done under the decree (singular) of Cyrus, Darius, and Artaxerxes. Thus what these three kings did was counted but one and the same decree, which was not completed until the days of Artaxerxes. And this date, 457 B. C., is the only one that agrees with the manifestation of Messiah the Prince. The Messiah came to establish the new covenant, and Dan. 9:27 says that he shall confirm the covenant with many of Daniel's people (see verse 24) for one week, that is, the last of the seventy. In the midst of the week, or in the middle of the last week of years, he should cause the sacrifice and oblation to cease, which he did when he was cut off, for then all the sacrifices of the Levitical law met their antitype, and were of no further use. It is wonderful how accurately every item of this prophecy was fulfilled. The ministry of Christ was just three and a half years—half a prophetic week, or week of years. After his resurrection, he told his apostles still to begin their work at Jerusalem, for the seventy weeks in which the covenant was to be confirmed to Judah and Israel were not yet ended.

Now it is always counted great hardness of heart on the part of the Jews to deny that Jesus was the Messiah, when the very time of his crucifixion was so definitely foretold by one of their own prophets. But the prophecies were for all times and all peoples, and let us see that we do not bring ourselves under the same censure that falls upon them. The same period—the seventy weeks—that fixes the time of the crucifixion, fixes the date of the two thousand three hundred years, the time for the cleansing of the sanctuary, the closing work of our High Priest for the judgment of his people. The seventy weeks point out the time when our Messiah should make his sacrifice and begin his priestly work. The two thousand three hundred years point out the time when he should enter upon the closing work of his priesthood. When Jesus began his ministry he said, "The time is fulfilled." Mark 1:14, 15. In like manner it is shown by the prophecy that it must be proclaimed to the world, "The hour of his judgment is come." Rev. 14:6, 7. The explanation of the seventy weeks is the explanation of the vision of the time given in Daniel 8. And this time reaches to the beginning of the judgment.

Beginning the two thousand three hundred years with the decree of Artaxerxes, we can readily see where they end. This decree was B. C. 457. Subtracting 457 B. C. from 2300 leaves A. D. 1843—the very time when this message of Rev.

14: 6, 7 was being so extensively preached to the nations of the earth. If this time were not made sure, how could the message of the judgment ever be given? How could men declare the hour is come unless the time were fixed by prophecy? Every word of the Scriptures must be fulfilled. As the seventy weeks prove that Jesus was the Messiah, so do they fix the two thousand three hundred years, beginning at the same point, and clearly show us the time for the cleansing of the sanctuary above, where our great High Priest is presenting his precious blood for us.

Here it is necessary to say a few words in regard to the numbering of the year at which the two thousand three hundred years end. At the time when the prophecy was written, they did not begin the year in midwinter, as is now generally done, but in the spring. Therefore while the figures in the above computation always bring A. D. 1843 as the result, the years really ended in 1844 of our year, as theirs began and ended about three months later than ours. But that is a point of little consequence in the settlement of the main fact.

Now we see, not only the importance of the message, as being the gospel, but the certainty of the time of its fulfillment. And we cannot discover any possible reason why professed Christians, with all the light of Bible truth we have in these days, should not incur the displeasure of God if they reject or neglect this gospel proclamation, even as they did who rejected the gospel in the days of the apostles. The Jews as a nation became a fallen people when they rejected Jesus as the Messiah. They did not fall so that they could not find salvation, for thousands of them repented and accepted the Saviour, and that is their privilege to this day. But they fell from the high position of being the special people of God.

Now it is our solemn conviction that a change equally great has taken place with the religious bodies of this day, who have rejected the gospel proclamation of the judgment come, and who slight the message of the near coming of our blessed Lord. This change is plainly to be seen among the churches of both continents. In America there is a very visible decline of vital piety, and a great increase of those things which indicate an unhallowed alliance with the world—a leaning towards worldliness in all their methods. For the support of the church an appeal is made to the passions and the love of folly of all classes. They who are not acquainted with the facts cannot imagine to what an extent these things are, not so much eating out the vitality and spirituality of the churches, as proving that vital piety does not exist. Church buildings are fitted up with kitchens, where suppers are served, where plays are enacted, and even petty gambling is resorted to, in the form of raffles and lotteries, to raise money for the cause of Christ. This state of things is often lamented by the few who realize the nature and the tendency of such practices; but they confess that the tide is so strong in the direction of folly in the churches, that it cannot be turned.

To show that we do not overestimate the evil which is afflicting the churches in that direction, we notice a few facts.

A few years since the grand jury in an important city of America, notified the churches of that city that their methods of raising money for religious uses were in violation of the statutes against gambling, and that they would be presented in court if they did not desist. The jury did not make any presentment, because the evil was so general that they did not like to present one to the exclusion of the others.

In two States of the American Union, the governors called the attention of the legislatures to this subject. One of them said that, while the existing laws against gambling were quite sufficient for general purposes, special legislation would be in place to suppress certain practices prevalent in the churches, which were clearly of the nature of gambling. A minister, writing for a certain religious paper, said:—

"I hide my face in shame, when I hear of a governor of a State being compelled to call upon the law-making department of his State to pass laws to counteract the swindling carried on under the auspices of the church, under the name of church fairs, festivals, and other forms of 'pious' church gambling."

This is only one direction in which the popular tendency

is manifested. The extent of the demoralization produced by these things is thus pictured by another religious paper:—

"The selling of indulgences was no more misleading, no more a perversion of the gospel, than are Protestant church fairs, where petty gambling is carried on under the wicked pretense of supporting the religion of Christ."

It must not be supposed, from this reference to "Protestant church fairs," that such things are done only in the Protestant churches, as some of the very worst that have ever been carried on in America were under the auspices of high dignitaries of the Catholic Church.

Crossing the Atlantic, what state of things is found in Europe? An important commemoration meeting was held in Manchester, England, in the latter part of the year 1888. Of the present and prospective condition of religion in England, let the speakers of that meeting inform us. The published report says that, in moving a resolution, Lord Montague made the following remarks:—

"He was afraid they saw a great deal of popery, or a great want of Protestantism, in the upper classes of this country. . . . Ritualism was the Trojan horse of popery. The pope had built up the system of ritualism, and he had put inside of it a number of Jesuits, armed to the teeth. They had dragged this great horse of ritualism inside their church, and these Jesuits, armed to the teeth with their theology, had sprung out, and now the Church and State were in the greatest danger."

Another well-known minister said that—

"The revolution of 1688 placed Protestantism on the throne of this country. It had been on the throne two hundred years, and they asked if it now was what it was two hundred years ago. They must answer that it is not. A change had come over it, and a crisis was impending. The Protestantism of England was seriously menaced and undermined. Three thousand ritualistic clergymen were now laboring night and day in the English church, to restore to this country the false doctrines and superstitions abolished by the Reformation."

The words of these speakers fail to give us a just idea of the extent of the defection from the faith that is taking place in England. We cannot realize what three thousand ritualistic ministers may accomplish in the Established-Church, working without rebuke from those who are set up to guard the interests of religion in the State. The emblems of popery are

SOME OF THE REFORMERS.
CALVIN. LUTHER. FAREL.
MELANCHTHON. FREDERICK OF SAXONY.

erected in the first churches in England, and the protests of those who still have regard for the Protestant faith are not heeded. Had not the principles of the Reformation lost their value in the eyes and the hearts of the people, it would not be possible for the Jesuits to control the professed Protestant church as they do. And a state of things equally deplorable exists in the Independent or Nonconformist churches. Men of high standing openly deny the inspiration of the Scriptures, and declare that its histories are fables. Others, by preaching a future probation, rob the judgment of its terrors.

The following will show to what extent folly has taken hold of the churches in England, and to what professed Christians in that land will resort to unite the church and the world. The first notice is copied from the *Sword and Trowel*, a paper which, however, does not approve of such unseemly doings:—

"Another specimen of the doings of worldly religion is from a handbill bearing the name of Howard, Stanford: 'A dance and entertainment will be held in the school-room, Collyweston, on Friday, November 16, 1888. Dancing to commence at 7:30 P. M. A good quadrille band will be in attendance. Refreshments will be provided. Tickets may be obtained from the rectory, Miss Ridlington, and Mr. R. H. Close. Price, 6d. each. The proceeds for new church lamps."

A minister, speaking of the prevalence of such things, well says:—

"Entertainments, concerts, tableaux, and such like, are playing havoc with the work of God. In the name of religion our children are being trained for the theater, and under the shadow of the name of Christ young people are being introduced to the 'world.'"

A party of High Church clergymen at Croyden made an exhibition of their own folly in what they called an exhibition of "The Conversion of England." It is thus announced by a secular paper:—

"CLERGYMEN ON THE STAGE AT CROYDEN. 'THE CONVERSION OF ENGLAND.'

"What, clergymen of the Church of England acting in a veritable drama on the stage, with bare feet. and painted faces, wigs, and theatrical paraphernalia? Yes, indeed, all this was to be seen at Croyden on Saturday afternoon and evening, and will be again this evening. One of our reporters went down and witnessed the play, and talked with some of the performers. The large public hall, George Street, Croydon, is within a few minutes' walk of the East and New Croyden railway stations. There is a capital stage in the hall, admirably adapted for amateur and even more ambitious performances. But it may well be doubted whether amateurs were ever more ambitious than the clerical party from Vauxhall, who on Saturday enacted the historical drama in the ten tableaux of 'The Conversion of England.'"

But the real conversion of England may be considered postponed indefinitely under the ministrations of such clergymen as the church furnishes, of which these giddy theatrical imitators are too nearly a sample.

How is it on the Continent, in the home of the Reformation? Are the children of the Reformers holding fast those principles of religious liberty bequeathed to them? They certainly are not. While the Catholic Church does not fail to revile the name and work of Luther in Germany, Protestant ministers are not permitted to speak in disrespectful terms of the pope and his church and its institutions. There is not a minister to-day in Germany, who, if he has regard for his own personal safety, would dare to nail to a church door such theses as Luther nailed to the church door in Wittemburg, three centuries ago. Should any minister at this time attempt to restore to Germany the Reformation as it was given to her by Luther, Melancthon, and their noble co-workers, he would not find a "Christian prince" in all the wide domain who would rise up to defend him from the general indignation that his actions would raise. It is a truth that cannot be denied, that the religion of the established churches on the Continent is a religion of worldliness and formality, destitute of that power that attended the preaching of the word of God three centuries ago.

The misfortune attending Protestantism in Europe was, that almost as soon as it was born it was *nationalized*. It was adopted by certain powers and converted into a State system, the heads of these governments determining what should and what should not be considered Christian faith and practice in those kingdoms. But as a national religion, it made all its conquests in the century in which it arose; it has not taken a single advance step in that direction in the three centuries that have followed.

BABYLON IS FALLEN.   197

Chambers' Cyclopedia gives the following truthful view of the real object of the Reformation, and of the mistake that was made in nationalizing Protestantism:—

"The symbols or confessions of the Protestant churches were not intended as rules of faith for all time, but as expressions of what was then believed to be the sense of Scripture. When, at a later time, it was sought to erect them into unchangeable standards of true doctrine, this was a renunciation of the first principle of Protestantism, and a return to the Catholic principle; for, in making the sense put upon Scripture by the Reformers the standard of truth, all further investigation of the Scripture is arrested, the authority of the Reformers is set above that of the Bible, and a new tradition of dogmas and interpretation is erected, which differs from the Catholic only in beginning with Luther and Calvin, instead of with the apostolic Fathers." Article Reformation.

When Jesus said, "My kingdom is not of this world" (John 18:36), he effectually shut out his gospel from becoming the authoritative religion of the kingdoms of this world. It was never intended that the things of God should be placed in the hands and under the power of Cæsar (Matt. 22:21), or that the fear of God should be taught by the precept of men. Isa. 29:13,14. The object of the Reformation was hid, and its power was neutralized by religion being made subject to human authority, and the fear of God is taught, not by what the Scriptures teach, but by what a king or parliament may decide that they teach; and too often, by what they would be pleased to have them teach.

The error of setting up Protestantism as a national religion —of modeling it after the Church of Rome as organized by Constantine—has borne its fruit, as might have been expected. It has tried to live on its nationality, and has failed. In 1842, Alexander Vinet gave the following view of its condition:—

"Three centuries of external life should not deceive Protestantism. It is now living on the first and vigorous impulse which it received in the sixteenth century. It lives on its political antecedents. *It lives on the elements of nationality.* But this impulse is exhausted. The beams of the frame-work are disjoined. The edifice is creaking on all sides. The accessory and auxiliary forces are leaving it. Protestantism remains alone and disorganized. No institution can exist in a disorganized state; no institution can long suffer an organization foreign to its principles. Protestants there are, but Protestantism is no more."

Arresting the investigation of Scripture by making religion subject to government control, binding the consciences of Christians by civil law, could not fail to turn it into a lifeless system of formalism. When Constantine took it upon him to reorganize the Christian church, he acted simply as a politician, anxious to preserve and strengthen the unity of his empire. Accordingly he took the general supervision of the church into his own hands. The Council of Nice was called by him to unite the various parties which were growing up among the churches, created by the efforts which were made to amalgamate the discordant philosophy of the heathen with the doctrines of Christianity. The decisions of the council became of authority only by the approval of the emperor. For centuries the emperor was considered the actual head of the church. The bishop of Rome, the chief in dignity of all the bishops, was elected under his direct notice, and was not ordained without his consent. The Council of Chalcedon was called by the Emperor Maurice, and its decisions were for a time much disputed, which caused the emperor to make the following proclamation:—

"He does injury to the judgment of the holy synod, who shall discuss or dispute the articles which were there rightly judged and disposed of; since those matters appointed by the bishops assembled at Chalcedon, concerning the Christian faith, were ordained by us, or were decided by our commandment; and those who despise this law shall be punished."

Thus it appears that the will and commandment of the emperor became the law of Christian faith in all the realm. The Christian conscience became subject to the State. Nothing could be more foreign to the will of the divine Head of the church, as laid down in the Holy Scriptures. But such of necessity is the nature, and such are the results, of *national religion;* and Protestantism was wrecked by following this example.

The true object and foundation of the Reformation is thus stated by the cyclopedia in the article from which we quoted:—

"That the authority of the Bible is supreme, and above that of councils and bishops; that the Bible is not to be interpreted and used according to tradition, or use and wont, but to be explained by means of itself—its own language and connection; . . . the doctrine that the Bible, explained independently of all external tradition, is the sole authority in all matters of faith and discipline, is really the foundation-stone of the Reformation."

The real, the only triumph of Protestantism was in giving the Bible to the people as the inspired word of God; as the sole and supreme authority in all matters of faith and life. But it is a fact to which we cannot close our eyes, that this foundation-stone has been removed. At this time, in the schools, in the ministry, in the religious journals, the idea of inspiration of the Bible is rejected and openly opposed. The following is the testimony of Edward Stapfer, author of a new French translation of the New Testament, and Professor of Theology in the Protestant College of Paris:—

"It has been said for a long time, and is perhaps said still, that the Reformation of the sixteenth century rested on two principles: justification by faith, and the authority of the Holy Scriptures. We think that justification by faith should alone be mentioned now. . . . We must acknowledge in all frankness—the belief in a direct inspiration of Revelation, making it of authority, has passed its time, and is no more held."

But what power can faith have, when the inspiration of the Scriptures is denied? Dr. Felix Kuhn, Lutheran minister, author of a "Life of Luther," for many years editor of the French Lutheran organ, *Le Temoignage*, said:—

"During the hundred years that we have been struggling with Rationalism, trying to mould the old gospel to the fashion of the day, we have, alas! succeeded in diminishing all things, curtailing everything. The old ideas do not correspond to the claims of our science, the new ones are as soon dead as born, and we stand to-day in the painful position of a large spiritual body which has only contradictory answers to give to a world seeking salvation."

Dr. Zahn, of Germany, wrote a book (which it has not been our privilege to see) which called forth the following words from Mr. C. Appia, a Lutheran pastor, in a review:—

"If, after surveying, with the author, the realms of politics, of theology, and of Christian life among the Protestants of our time, we again ask ourselves the question, 'What is the Protestantism of to-day lacking?' the answer, distinct and cutting, like the book itself, and which seems to arise from its perusal, is, that Protestantism is lacking everything. It has particularly shaken the faith in the word of God, and abandoned the true doctrine of justification by faith, without being able to substitute anything for the two solid foundations which it has tried to demolish."

On the occasion of the 350th anniversary of the Reformation, November 5, 1882, M. Chautre, a minister in Geneva, made the following remarks:—

"By an irresistible current the doctrines which our spiritual ancestors proclaimed in the sixteenth century as the truth, the absolute truth, the divine truth, are leaving us to-day. . . . The fact is general. Everywhere with more or less frankness, with more or less distinctness, the great doctrines of the Reformation are abandoned among the Protestant churches. . . . While the minority in the Protestant world, in England, in Germany, and elsewhere, is in many respects drawing near to the Catholic principles, the great majority of the Reformed Christians (both orthodox and liberal), modify, transform, abandon, and even oppose, the old faith of Protestant orthodoxy."

We know that on anniversary occasions people are not apt to make the cause with which they are allied, worse than it really is. Mr. E. Faucher, member of the Consistory of Marseilles, and of the synods of 1872 and 1879, in a pamphlet published in 1889, the object of which was "to awaken the most serious attention of our churches of all denominations," to the present danger to the truth and to Christian life, says:—

"But to-day, strange to say, it is no more against the adversaries of Christ that we have to defend our old Bible; it is against those who confess with us his divine personality, and who accept, as we do, his work of salvation. And, more strange still, this Bible, to which they confess themselves to be indebted for all their knowledge of Christ and his work, and which is still, in their opinion, the 'sovereign' document of Christian faith, 'above which we cannot put our own thoughts when in the presence of Christ,'—it is this Bible of which they endeavor—while our old adversaries shout with joy and applause—to spread out in the full light of day, the stains, the imperfections, the errors, both material and moral."

This calls to mind the saying of Count Gasparin, that "pious rationalism makes ravages that impious rationalism has never made."

An influential religious weekly, while expressing regret for the publication of this pamphlet, because of the influence it must have throughout the land, yet justifies that which the author condemns, declaring that the ministers have gradually repudiated—with almost all the new theological generation of all Protestant countries of both the Old World and the New— the old traditional ideas of the mode of revelation, which means that they have repudiated the ideas of the inspiration of the Scriptures, and the receiving them as of complete authority, for the paper itself openly opposes those ideas.

The testimonies here given are from representative sources, and to these we might add largely, but one more must suffice. It is from the celebrated historian of the Reformation, Merle D'Aubigne. In the preface to the English edition of the "History of the Reformation," he says:—

"But modern Protestantism, like old Catholicism, is, in itself, a thing from which nothing can be hoped, a thing quite powerless. Something very different is necessary to restore to men of our day the energy that saves. A something is requisite which is not of man, but of God."

Such is the Protestantism of Europe to-day. If it were a change from the faith of the Reformers in the understanding of the teachings of the sacred word, no one could complain, for the Reformers had not a perfect understanding of the Bible. If, with diligent study of the Bible, new and larger views of its teachings were presented, new truths were unfolded with the fulfilling of the prophetic word, it would be cause for rejoicing. But it is not this; it is nothing less than an effort to entirely destroy the authority of the Bible, by a general denial of its inspiration. And it is not confined to the State churches. The free churches are moving in the same direction. In England there is a sharp controversy in the nonconformist churches on the subject of the inspiration of the Bible, with an evident majority with those who deny.

And the present deplorable state of things has not come without warning. From time to time faithful men have risen up and sounded the alarm, but their words have not been heeded. In 1860, Count Gasparin said that Protestantism would collapse if it did not change its course in regard to the Bible. Referring to the claims that Protestantism is doing evangelical work in the world, he said:—

"We have prayer-meetings, but we are not concerned about the assaults made against the Bible; we count with joy the numbers of the orthodox party, but we do not ask ourselves what the word orthodoxy is coming to mean. . . . Under our progress, under our orthodoxy, under our works of piety, under our missions, under our evangelization, under our revivals, an abyss is enlarging, and everything will fall into it, and that shortly, if we leave this subterranean work to go on which is undermining the faith in the Scriptures."

Under existing circumstances, one thing is very suggestive. With the almost universal denial of the inspiration of the Bible, there is a quite universal movement in favor of more rigid laws for the observance of Sunday! This is quite in keeping; as the authority of the Bible is denied, the favorite child of tradition, "the venerable day of the sun," is fast rising in public favor. This is the case all over the world—both in Europe and America. Observance of Sunday, in some form, is coming to be regarded as the highest type of Christian character, sufficient to atone for all other short-comings.

In the United States, among the leading Protestant churches, there is also an extensive and very decided leaning towards Romanism. The Catholics make no advances; all the overtures for union are on the part of the Protestants. And so in England. The Catholics remain as intensely Romanist as they are in any part of Italy. All the ground that is yielded is yielded by professed Protestants. And so in Germany. While it is officially declared that with the passing of three centuries, or since the time of Luther, great changes have been wrought in public sentiment and public feeling, all the change is with the Protestants; Catholicism has not yielded a particle in its principles or its professions.

About the time of the Papal Jubilee, a certain writer of Switzerland made the following striking remark: "Protestants there are, but Protestantism is dead." This is only too true. In view of all these things it cannot be difficult to locate the message of Rev. 14:8, "Babylon is fallen." The name Babylon signifies "confusion." This is found in the discordant fables which pass for religious truth in the churches of this day. In Rev. 17:1-6, is shown a woman—a woman being the symbol of a church—who has a name written: "Mystery, Babylon the great, the mother of harlots and abominations of the earth." Now the Reformers and many commentators have strongly insisted that this referred to the Romish Church; but if they were correct, then it is very evident that she has daughters, who must also bear the name of Babylon. And is it not a fact that the great body of Protestants have allied themselves to the kings of the earth as closely as the Romish Church ever did? Constantine corrupted Christianity by binding it to his throne, and from that day to this, the leading bodies of professed Christians, Protestants and Catholics alike, have fled for their refuge to the kings of this world. By this means their religion has become worldly. And if we are asked to point to a church or to churches that have become fallen in the present age, churches which have lost their first love, and have declined from the purity of Bible godliness, we could not point to the Romish Church, for surely she has not suffered a moral decline for centuries past. She fell too long ago to be a fulfillment of this prophecy. We should be compelled to point to the Protestant churches, which are sleeping on the eve of mightier events than have ever transpired since the foundation of the world. The Lord has sent solemn messages to this generation, but their ears are closed to his words. He has had it proclaimed to the world that "the hour of his judgment is come," and that soon will his priestly work be ended, and he will come again to redeem his faithful ones, and to cut off the idle, the slothful, the unfaithful, but they refuse to listen to the warnings written by his prophets. Instead of being the light of the world, they lull the world to the sleep of carnal security when destruction is impending. 1 Thess. 5: 1-3.

But a scene still more sad will open to our views. Another mighty cry will be heard: "Babylon the great is fallen, is fallen, and is become the habitation of demons, and the hold of every foul spirit." We have examined Revelation 13, where the works of Spiritualism are described, and Rev. 16: 15, which says these wonders are wrought by the spirits of devils working miracles, by which the kings of the earth are gathered to the battle of the great day of the Lord. These wonder-workings are being accepted by the people of all countries, high and low, from the monarch to the peasant. Whole churches are believers, and when these fallen churches have fully indorsed these spirits, then will this final cry be sounded. Then will be proclaimed, "Come out of her, my people, that ye be not partakers of her sins, and that ye receive not of her plagues." There is but one way to escape the destruction that is coming on the earth, and that is to heed all the words of the Scriptures, for the Lord has promised to look to him that trembleth at his word. Isa. 66: 1, 2.

CHAPTER XVI.

THE COMMANDMENTS AND THE FAITH.

The Third Angel's Message, of Revelation 14, verses 9-12, is given in words full of terror. Its closing sentences serve as a key to the interpretation of some of its other terms, therefore those will be examined first. Verse 12 reads: "Here is the patience of the saints; here are they that keep the commandments of God, and the faith of Jesus." In Rom. 5:1-3, we are told that tribulation works patience. The connection of this message, Revelation 13, shows that there will be a season of bitter persecution of the saints, to compel them to renounce the commandments of God for the institutions of the church which have no divine authority. This will require patience on the part of those who cling to the word of God. In this scripture, verse 12, the commandments of God are united with the faith of Jesus. The law of the Father is shown to be in harmony with the faith of the Son.

It is often claimed that the gospel has taken the place of the law; that the law was for the Jews, and the gospel is for Christians. But that is a very serious error. It has been shown in the first chapters of this book that great and important truths were given to Adam, to Abraham, and to others long in the past, which come down through all dispensations. The promises on which rests the hope of all Christians, were given to the patriarchs. But the blessings promised were for the obedient. Adam lost all by transgression; and the Lord gave the promises to Isaac because his father Abraham kept his commandments. Gen. 26:1-5. There is no truth of greater importance than the law of Jehovah—the law by which man must form his character in the sight of his Maker;

the law by which every work will be brought into judgment. There will be but one judgment-day; all will be judged by Jesus Christ whom God hath appointed. Acts 17:31. All will be judged by one rule of righteousness. Jesus is mediator for those who sinned under the first covenant, as has been already noticed. Heb. 9:15. The law did not save the patriarchs and prophets without faith in the coming Son of God, the Messiah. And faith will not save us now without obedience. James says, "Faith without works is dead." James 2:17, 20, 26. And Jesus said: "Not everyone that saith unto me, Lord, Lord, shall enter into the kingdom of Heaven; but he that doeth the will of my Father which is in Heaven." Matt. 7:21. Paul says that the will of God is known by his law. See Rom. 2:17-23. And he says, "Do we then make void the law through faith? God forbid; yea, we establish the law." Rom. 3:31. Thus we find that Christ and faith in him establish the law, instead of releasing us from obedience to it.

There is a prophecy of the Saviour in Isa. 42:21, which reads thus: "He will magnify the law, and make it honorable." This does not mean that the law was in any way dishonorable, or that it was lacking in any element of dignity or purity. It means that the law had been dishonored by disobedience, and he would honor it and rescue it from the reproach that had been put upon it: that he would elevate it in the eyes of those who had even lost sight of its holiness and its authority. He could not do this if he set it aside, or if he set man free from the observance of it, in the least particular. The psalmist said, "The law of the Lord is perfect." Ps. 19:7. But if the Saviour changed it in any respect, or set aside any part of it, that would have been equivalent to a declaration that it was imperfect—that it needed amending. Speaking himself, through prophecy, of the law of his Father, he said, "I delight to do thy will, O my God; yea, thy law is within my heart." Ps. 40:8. After such expressions as these, we are prepared to hear him declare, in his celebrated sermon on the mount, that he came not to destroy the law, and that not a jot or tittle should pass from it till heaven and earth should pass away. Not the smallest fragment should perish, not the least item be changed, through any word of his. And when one asked him what he should do to inherit eternal life, he replied, "If thou wilt enter into life, keep the commandments." Matt. 19:16, 17. This is in harmony with his message to the churches: "Blessed are they that do his commandments, that they may have right to the tree of life, and may enter in through the gates into the city." Rev. 22:14. This he spoke of his Father's commandments, which are given as the rule of life, but not as the means of justification to a sinner. Only the faith of Christ can cleanse from sin; but obedience to the law prevents sin.

"By the law is the knowledge of sin." Rom. 3:20. The law is that which points out sin, and condemns sin, and by which sin is made to appear exceeding sinful. Rom. 7:7, 13. Of Jesus the angel said, "He shall save his people from their sins." Matt. 1:21. He shall save them from transgressing the law of his Father, for sin is the transgression of the law. 1 John 3:4. If he set his people free from obedience to the law, then he would be a minister of sin, instead of a minister of righteousness. Gal. 2:17. Again it is said that he came to put away sins. Heb. 9:26. If he saves his people from their sins, he must enable them to put away their sins, and to walk in obedience to his Father's will.

But the most striking testimony that he gives, is that in which he rebukes those who make void the commandment of God by their tradition. Matt. 5:1-9. It appears that in his time there were some who thought it a mark of peculiar piety to professedly consecrate all that they had to the service of God, and thereby deprive their aged parents of the honor and care that were due unto them. But the law of God required that parents should receive the honor that was their due, and nothing but rendering this would meet the divine precept and secure the divine favor. So Saul thought that he would show great piety in saving for sacrifices that which God had told him to utterly destroy. 1 Sam. 15:1-3, 13-23. There have always been those who thought they could improve the divine requirements, and offer better service than God had ordained. But the Lord has forbidden the adding to or taking from that which he has commanded. He knows best what is fitting, and what is acceptable to him. Man tries to improve the way of God, because in so doing he flatters himself that he is worshiping God, and this pleases his conscience, and at the same time he is having his own way—something that is very dear to the carnal mind.

By the law of God we mean that law which God himself spoke on Mount Sinai, and wrote with his own finger on tables of stone. These were above all others the commandments of God, separated from all other laws, put into the ark, over which the priest made an atonement in the most holy place of the sanctuary. They do not relate to types and ceremonies, but are altogether moral, growing out of the will of God alone. Laws regarding types were made necessary by sin, and they would never have existed had not sin existed. But not one of the ten commandments was thus originated.

To one part of the law we now call special attention, because it is so generally disregarded. When it is said, "Here are they that keep the commandments of God," it means, all the commandments, for no one can be called a keeper of the law who keeps only a part of the law. If he breaks any part of the law he is a law breaker. The first institution of which we read in Paradise, is the Sabbath of the seventh day. In Gen. 2:3 it is written:—

"And God blessed the seventh day, and sanctified it; because that in it he had rested from all his work which God created and made."

To sanctify means, "to set apart to a sacred use." Jesus said, "The Sabbath was made for man." Mark 2:27. Therefore it was blessed, it was consecrated, or set apart to be sacredly used by man. But it could not be set apart for man's use without giving man instruction to use it for sacred purposes. It was a hallowed day from the beginning. When God laid the foundation of the earth he laid the foundation of the Sabbath. When he had created the heavens and the earth, he first separated the light from the darkness, and employed six successive days in his work, and rested the seventh day; and there he established the week of seven days, the seventh of which was his rest, or Sabbath—the only rest-day of the week which he ever made.

That this was the origin of the Sabbath, and that the rest from the work of creation was the only reason for the sanctification of the Sabbath, is proved positively by the words of Jehovah himself, in the fourth commandment. It reads thus:—

"Remember the Sabbath-day, to keep it holy. Six days shalt thou labor, and do all thy work; but the seventh day is the Sabbath of the Lord thy God; in it thou shalt not do any work, thou, nor thy son, nor thy daughter, thy man-servant, nor thy maid-servant, nor thy cattle, nor thy stranger that is within thy gates; for in six days the Lord made heaven and earth, the sea, and all that in them is, and rested the seventh day; wherefore the Lord blessed the Sabbath-day, and hallowed it." Ex. 20:8-11.

The readers of the Bible will notice that the Lord always called the seventh day his Sabbath. "The seventh day is the Sabbath of the Lord thy God." "Verily my Sabbaths ye shall keep. . . . The seventh is the Sabbath of rest, holy to the Lord." "If thou turn away thy foot from the Sabbath, from doing thy pleasure on my holy day." Ex. 20:10; 31:13-17; Isa. 58:13. The word "sabbath" means rest. The seventh day is the Lord's Sabbath, because the Lord himself rested on that day from the work of creation. It commemorates creation, and no other work, and therefore belongs to the Creator alone.

But some have so far departed from the Scriptures of truth as to call the seventh day the Sabbath of the Jews. Surely the rest-day of the Creator cannot be a Jewish institution. True, he commanded the Jews to keep it, and so he did all the precepts of his moral law. He gave the commandment to the Jews which guards the sacredness of the marriage institution; is marriage, therefore, a Jewish institution? We find both marriage and the sanctified rest-day in the second chapter of Genesis. Both come to us from Paradise; and it is no more just to call the seventh day, the rest-day of the Creator, a Jewish Sabbath, than it would be to call marriage a Jewish rite, and to set it aside as belonging only to the Jews.

14

Let us contrast the Sabbath, and the honor that God put upon it, with the substitute, that the Church Fathers have given to us,—the Sunday. God rested the seventh day from the work of creation. He blessed and hallowed the seventh day. He commanded that the seventh day be kept holy. With his own hand he wrote on the tables of stone, "The seventh day is the Sabbath of the Lord thy God." He threatened severe punishments upon those who did work upon the seventh day. He promised great blessings to those who sacredly keep the seventh day. When he led the people of Israel, to whom he showed his wonders and his goodness, he gave them manna six days, and withheld it on the seventh day. The manna gathered on the sixth day remained pure and good over the seventh day. If kept over any other day it corrupted and became loathsome. For the space of forty years he wrought these miracles every week to put honor upon the seventh day. No other institution has ever received so much honor at the hands of the Lord as the seventh-day Sabbath. And no other institution has been so much abused and despised by men.

On the other hand, every reader of the Bible knows that the Lord never blessed the first day, now called Sunday. He never set it apart for any reason nor to any use. He never claimed it as his own, but gave it to man as a working-day. He never commanded anybody to keep it. He never uttered any threats against those who do not keep it; he never made any promises to those who do keep it. It is a day of man's choosing, and not a day that God required at his hands. The first honor conferred upon the Sunday was by the pagans, who consecrated it to the honor of the sun, and gave it the name it still bears—*dies solis*, the day of the sun.

Melanchthon, in his "Apology of the Confession," article 15, treating on the human ordinances of the church, classes the Sunday with them. Coleman, a historian, in the *Bibliotheca Sacra*, gives testimony as follows:—

"The Augsburg Confession classes the Lord's day under the same category as Easter, Whitsunday, and the like; merely human ordinances." Vol. 3, p. 538.

Gieseler, in his "Church History," Vol. 3, p. 399, says that "Luther considered the keeping of Sunday merely as a human ordinance."

The German theologian, Beyschlag of Halle, in his work, "Der Altcatholocismus," page 53, mentions Sunday and other holidays, infant baptism, and confirmation, and says: "These we have not from the New Testament, but from the tradition of the church." And in this testimony there is complete agreement.

The London *Telegraph*, an able and influential paper, recently noticed the efforts that are being made to give Sunday a better legal standing, and said:—

"Everybody knows that the seventh—not the first—day was ordained as a day of rest, and that the seventh is Saturday. The change to Sunday was made by man, and there is all the difference between the two that there must be between a divine and a merely human ordinance. . . . In comparatively modern times the Puritans transferred to the first day the obligations imposed on the seventh. The early change from one day to the other, however, and the application to the Sunday of Sabbatarian restrictions, were of purely human origin, and have no divine authority over the souls or consciences of men."

Any amount of testimony like this can be produced, but it does not seem necessary, where there is not a line of proof against it. The Catholic Church has always claimed that she is the sole authority for the keeping of the Sunday as the Lord's day, though Constantine had decreed that there should be partial rest on that day in A. D. 321. His law was for judges and towns-people, not forbidding country people to labor in their fields and vineyards.

The catechism of P. J. J. Scheffmacher will show you what the Catholic Church has to say about the change from Sabbath to Sunday:—

"*Question*—How do you further prove that the church has the right to institute holidays?

"*Answer*—Had the church not this right, she would not have ordained that Sunday be kept instead of the Sabbath.

"*Q.*—How else can you answer our opponents that they may feel still more the injustice that they do us when they scoff at us for such things?

"*A.*—We may ask them why they observe Sunday and do not refrain from flesh meats on Friday and Saturday.

"*Q.*—But cannot our opponents say that the observance of Sunday is commanded in the Bible, which is not the case with the Friday and Saturday fasts?

"*A.*—The Holy Scriptures mention nothing whatever of the observance of Sunday, but indeed of the Sabbath; and there is no command in the Holy Scriptures for the observance of Sunday."

In an appeal to all Bible Christians, a Catholic author says:—

"We blame you, not for making Sunday your weekly holiday, instead of the Sabbath, but for rejecting tradition, which is the only safe and clear rule by which this observance can be justified."

It is even so, that church tradition is the only basis for Sunday-keeping; but the words of the Saviour stand as strong to-day as in the day when he reproved the Jews for making void the commandment of God by their tradition. And it is indeed true, as the Catholics claim, that when Protestants keep Sunday without any authority but that of the church, to the neglect of a plain commandment of God, they are doing the highest homage to the principles and power of that church.

It has been clearly shown that God has pointed out that power as one that has done great injury to the truth and to the saints, and has most solemnly warned us against worshiping it, or following its ways. In Rev. 13:11-17, is a very striking prophecy of the action of the beast with two horns, which has been described, especially in the expression of verse 12. It says:—

"And he exerciseth all the power of the first beast before him, and causeth the earth and them which dwell therein to worship the first beast, whose deadly wound was healed."

It is very clearly true that we worship any power when we observe the institutions of that power in preference to those of the Scripture, and especially when they make void the precept of the Most High. Here we have a prophecy that the very earth, as well as those who dwell upon it, shall be caused to worship the first beast, the papacy. There is only one institution in which the earth is made to do homage to that power, and that is the Sunday. God commanded that in seed-time and harvest the earth should rest on the Sabbath. But that church has commanded that all kinds of labor be done on the Sabbath of the Lord, and that no work shall be done on the Sunday. The earth must not be plowed nor reaped on the Sunday, but rest, and thus do homage to the authority of that power. Shall we, too, continue to honor that power, to the neglect of the commandments of God? This is the very sin that is so fearfully denounced in the last message of Rev. 14: 9–12.

CHAPTER XVII.

THE SEAL AND THE MARK.

The Third Angel's Message, in Rev. 14:9-12, is the last that will be given to this world. When this closes, the Son of man will come to reap the harvest of the earth. Because probation closes with this message, therefore it is given in the most terrible language that the Bible contains. It is as follows:

"And the third angel followed them, saying with a loud voice, If any man worship the beast and his image, and receive his mark in his forehead, or in his hand, the same shall drink of the wine of the wrath of God, which is poured out without mixture into the cup of his indignation; and he shall be tormented with fire and brimstone in the presence of the holy angels, and in the presence of the Lamb; and the smoke of their torment ascendeth up forever and ever; and they have no rest day nor night, who worship the beast and his image, and whosoever receiveth the mark of his name. Here is the patience of the saints; here are they that keep the commandments of God, and the faith of Jesus."

It has been seen that the beast of this prophecy represents the papacy; that the image is made by the beast with two horns, that is, the United States of America. The message is not confined to any one country. Though the work of the image may be somewhat local, the warning is against the worship of the beast, whose power and influence are recognized everywhere. It also warns against receiving the mark of the beast in the forehead or in the hand. It now remains to point out what is the mark of the beast. When this is done, the message is understood in all its particulars.

To explain this message we must examine other texts which refer to the same time. Rev. 6:12-17 contains a vision of the opening of the sixth seal, giving the signs of the Lord's coming, and introducing the terrors of the last day. In chapter 7:

1–3, are seen four angels holding four winds, until the servants of God are sealed in their foreheads. In Dan. 7: 2, 3, the striving of the four winds was said to bring up four great beasts, which represented the four great kingdoms which ruled over the whole earth. These kings arose by successive wars, in which one kingdom was thrown down, and another arose in its place. In Revelation 7, the four winds indicate wars and strife in the four quarters of the earth. These are the same as the battle of the great day of God Almighty, just as the Lord comes. Rev. 16 : 14, 15. Before that day of terror comes, a special work must be done for the servants of God, who have to stand complete when the Lord Jesus closes his work of intercession in Heaven. It is an awful hour that is coming, and a thorough preparation is needed to stand in the battle of the day of the Lord. Eze. 13 : 5.

The same time and circumstances are presented in Ezekiel 9. They are represented under a vision of Jerusalem, and an angel is directed to set a mark upon the foreheads of the men that sigh and cry for the abominations that are done in the midst thereof. And other angels are told to go after him and smite and slay utterly; neither to spare nor to pity, but to destroy all upon whom the mark was not set. Verses 4–6. There is a time of utter destruction impending, when the priesthood of Jesus is ended, and probation is closed. That is the time of this prophecy, the same as Rev. 7 : 1–3.

Again, after the persecution of Revelation 13 is described, there is given a view of the triumph of the persecuted saints standing on the Mount Zion with the Lamb, having his Father's name written in their foreheads. This is after the Son of man has come to redeem them. Now we have three similar views of the saints of God,—one, where a seal is put in their foreheads, before the winds of war blow on the earth; a second, where a mark is set on their foreheads, before the sword of utter destruction is sent forth; the third, where they have passed through the time of trouble, having the Father's name in their foreheads. But all these refer to the same thing; the seal and the mark are the same as having the Father's name in their foreheads. In Rom. 4:11, also, we learn that sign and seal mean the same thing, both being in this text referred to circumcision. Both indicate a mark whereby a person or thing may be identified.

Now we have the two classes, both marked, the servants of God in their foreheads. and the worshipers of the beast in their foreheads or in their hands. But we do not suppose, in either case, that a literal mark or stamp is put upon them, but that something attaches to them by which they may be known, respectively, as the servants of God, or the worshipers of the beast. In the Third Angel's Message these two classes are represented—one, as worshiping the beast and receiving his mark; the other, as keeping the commandments of God, and the faith of Jesus. But inasmuch as the mark in the foreheads of the servants of God is said to contain the Father's name, we must look for this sign in the commandments of God, rather than in the faith of Jesus. In searching out this matter our first inquiry will be—

WHAT IS THE SIGN OR SEAL OF GOD?

As this is a subject of unusual importance, we will examine the testimony of the Scriptures in regard to the Father's name, or the evidence and title of his authority. In the opening words of the Bible, God reveals himself to us as Creator: "In the beginning God created the heaven and the earth." Gen. 1:1. To create, to bring into existence, and to give life to inanimate objects, is the very highest manifestation of power, far beyond the comprehension of finite minds. In all the Scriptures God presents his power to create, and his work as Creator, as that which distinguishes him from false gods or idols. After declaring the vanity of false gods, he directed his servant to point out the difference between the true and the false, in the following manner:—

"Thus shall ye say unto them, The gods that have not made the heavens and the earth. even they shall perish from the earth, and from under these heavens. He hath made the earth by his power, he hath established the world by his wisdom, and hath stretched out the heavens by his discretion." Jer. 10:11, 12.

And so, again, when Paul would turn away the Athenians from their idols to the worship of the true God, he said:—

"Whom therefore ye ignorantly worship, him declare I unto you. God that made the world and all things therein, seeing that he is Lord of heaven and earth, dwelleth not in temples made with hands." Acts 17:23, 24.

And so in many other texts of Scripture.

At first thought it seems strange that any nation should ever forget God, the Creator, whose wonderful works are ever before their eyes. Ps. 19:1. But the reason is found in the fallen nature of man, in the perverseness of the human heart. The apostle thus explains the matter; he says, "They did not like to retain God in their knowledge." Rom. 1:28. The knowledge of God keeps alive in man some sense of responsibility; it causes him to look forward to the judgment. To put away the knowledge of God gives a sense of carnal security; it leaves the conscience without restraint.

Man loves to honor and to exalt himself. The pride of life is one of the deadly evils of the world. 1 John 2:16. Inspiration has pointed out the process by which man sunk so far below the position for which his Maker designed him. The word speaks thus:—

"When they knew God, they glorified him not as God, neither were thankful; but became vain in their imaginations, and their foolish heart was darkened. Professing themselves to be wise, they became fools, and changed the glory of the uncorruptible God into an image made like to corruptible man, and to birds, and fourfooted beasts, and creeping things." Rom. 1:21-23.

And thus it is proved that it is altogether of man's own perverseness that he is sunken so low, and is so far from God. And even in his low estate he has nothing to plead in excuse for his condition. For the apostle, speaking of the same class who had so far degraded themselves, says:—

"Because that which may be known of God is manifest to them; for God hath showed it unto them. For the invisible things of him from the creation of the world are clearly seen, being understood by the things that are made, even his eternal power and Godhead; so that they are without excuse." Rom. 1:19, 20.

These have shut their eyes against the evidences of the

deity of God,—evidences shown in his work of creation. For truly, " the heavens declare the glory of God; and the firmament showeth his handiwork." Ps. 19: 1.

Thus it is clear, as God's word is true, that the eternal power and Godhead of the Supreme One may be " understood by the things that are made." Had not man perverted his way, and "worshiped and served the creature more than the Creator," he would forever have lived happy in the love of his heavenly Father. And this was the intention of the Creator. He made the best and wisest provision for keeping the children of his creation near to himself.

It is written in the Scriptures that " he hath made his wonderful works to be remembered." Ps. 111: 4. And when he made the world he instituted a memorial to keep his work in remembrance. It has already been noticed that the Lord claimed the seventh day, the Sabbath, as his own, because he rested upon it from his wonderful work of creation. He blessed it, he sanctified it, that it might be separated from all other days. He wrought thousands of miracles before his people to put honor upon this holy day. Of this institution the Lord said to Moses: " It is a sign between me and the children of Israel forever." Of what is it a sign? The words following explain this: "For in six days the Lord made heaven and earth, and on the seventh day he rested, and was refreshed." Ex. 31: 17. It was not a type, or anything peculiar to " Israel after the flesh," but it is a sign of a work in which all nations have an equal interest; a sign of the creation of that " first dominion" which shall be given to all "the Israel of God" (Gal. 6: 16), the true children of Abraham. And thus the words of the Lord himself declare that the seventh-day Sabbath is a sign of the creation of the heavens and the earth.

If his eternal power and Godhead may be understood by the things which he has made, as the Scriptures teach; and if he has given his power to create, and his work of creation, as that which specially distinguishes him from false gods, how necessary that this work should ever be borne in mind. They who forget the work of creation, forget the Creator. The nations who know not God have lost all idea of any work of creation. How could they retain an idea of creation, and of a Creator, and yet worship the work of their own hands?

This presents the Sabbath institution as having a far higher object than that of affording merely physical rest to mankind. Man needs periods of rest; he needs a period of rest in every twenty-four hours. And God wisely and beneficently provided for it by giving alternate periods of light and darkness. But the Sabbath had another and more important office to fill. It is the Creator's memorial; it is intended to keep alive in the minds of men the great and all-important truth that there is a God of almighty power, the Creator of heaven and earth, and that "they be no gods, which are made with hands." Acts 19:26.

We have seen that the words sign and seal refer to the same thing. God himself declared that the Sabbath is his sign, imparting the knowledge that he is God, the Creator of all things. Thus he spoke:—

"I am the Lord your God; walk in my statutes, and keep my judgments, and do them; and hallow my Sabbaths; and they shall be a sign between me and you, that ye may know that I am the Lord your God." Eze. 20:19, 20. Also verse 12; Ex. 31:13.

The Sabbath is the sign of God—the seal of his law. It is the evidence of his authority; it is that mark by which they that keep all his commandments may be known from all the world besides. This is the testimony of Jehovah himself; it is his own claim,—his sign to the highest title of authority,— the Creator.

Now another question must be examined. It is this:—

WHAT IS THE MARK OF THE BEAST?

In regard to the sign or seal of God we have given the Lord's own testimony from the Scriptures. So, on the other hand, we shall let the papacy speak for itself as to what it offers as the peculiar evidence, or sign, or mark, of its authority and power. As the Sabbath is the sign that God is Creator of all things, the very highest claim of power would be to assume to set aside that sign, and substitute one of its own. And the evidence would be strengthened if that other sign were in direct opposition to the sign of God. And such we find to be the case in regard to the sign of the beast. The Catholic Church claims that it has the right to make that sinful which God has expressly permitted, and to make that a virtue and a Christian duty which God has expressly prohibited. What higher power can there be in Heaven or on earth than the power to annul the laws of the Most High—to sit in judgment upon the precepts of the Almighty. That these things are so is known to all the world.

When Leo III. was accused of harboring evil designs against the rights of the people, Charlemagne summoned a court to hear the charges, but they unanimously declared that they dared not judge the apostolical see, the head of all the churches of God. They considered Leo as high priest appointed to judge all, and himself to be judged of no man. The pope then saluted Charles as emperor of Rome. Robinson's "Ecclesiastical Researches," recording these transactions (pp. 172, 173), says:—

"Charles was complimented with the name, but the pope had the thing. The title of emperor is a shadow; to be above law is the substance."

This is a correct estimate of the relative positions occupied by emperors and popes for many centuries. But to be above human law and above the judgment of man, was far beneath the ambition of the occupants of the papal chair. They must be superior to all law, human and divine. This might well be considered a harsh judgment did they not openly make the claim, and boast of it as their right?

In the Council of Trent, the question came up as to how the Church of Rome should meet the Protestants on the subject of tradition and the Scriptures. Holtzman's "Canon and Tradition" (p. 163) says:—

"The archbishop of Rhegio declared in a speech, January 18, 1562, at the Council of Trent, openly, that tradition stood higher than the Scriptures. The authority of the church could not be [already was not] bound to the authority of the Scriptures, because the church had, not on the authority of

Christ, but on its own, changed the Sabbath into Sunday." Le Plat, I, 309-314, Council of Trent.

It is recorded that in Eck's disputations with the Reformers, he said:—

"Finally, the power of the church over the Scriptures holds good from this fact, that the church, resting on the fullness of power granted to it, has made changes with certain precepts of the Scriptures. For, notwithstanding the Sabbath commandment, Sunday has taken the place of the Sabbath." Eck's Loci, I, 15.

Thus it appears that whenever Catholic authorities wish to give ample proof of the great power of the church, they refer to the act of changing the Sabbath into Sunday, contrary to the plain commandment of God. And their testimony is even more direct than that which is here given. In a Catholic work entitled, "Abridgment of Christian Doctrine," the institution of Sunday is set forth as the evidence of the great power of the church, and as that ordinance in which the Protestants do homage to her power, in spite of their professions. It speaks thus:—

"*Question*—How prove you that the church hath power to command feasts and holy days?

"*Answer*—By the very act of changing the Sabbath into Sunday, which Protestants allow of; and therefore they fondly contradict themselves, by keeping Sunday strictly, and breaking most other feasts commanded by the same church.

"*Q.*—How prove you that?

"*A.*—Because by keeping Sunday they acknowledge the church's power to ordain feasts, and to command them under sin; and by not keeping the rest by her commanded, they again deny, in fact, the same power."

Here the Sunday is given as the sufficient evidence that the church has power to make a sin of that which the Lord has not spoken; nay, more, to make it a sin, and worthy of a curse, to do that which the Lord has expressly commanded. The Lord commanded to keep the Sabbath-day; but the Council of Laodicea declared that they who kept the Sabbath in preference to the Sunday, should be accursed from Christ. And thus have we found, in the precepts of that church, an institution the very opposite of the sign of God, set forth as the sign of her power. If this is not that mark of the beast, what could be? And if any act of presumption could call for vengeance from Heaven, why should not this? If we follow her in this presumption against the commandment of God, how shall we meet it at the last day? Let the Third Angel's Message, of Revelation 14, be our warning in this matter.

It has been shown in the prophecy of Daniel that this same power should think to change times and laws. Dan. 7:25. And here we behold the fulfillment in that church affirming its power to change the highest laws of the Infinite One. It is this, more than all else, that identifies that power as the "man of sin" spoken of in 2 Thess. 2:3,—that man of lawlessness, that man against all law, setting himself to be above all law. In this he has truly exalted himself above God, as having authority to annul the statutes of God. He is not only a sinful man; there are multitudes of such in the world. He is what the Scripture says, the man of sin. He makes merchandise of sin; he pretends to make wrong right, and to make right wrong; for surely there can be no higher standard of right and wrong than the law of God, and this he essays to reverse. Thus in his hands sin loses its sinfulness, and under his touch virtue is no longer beautiful. Every word of this strong indictment is fully justified by the high claims put forth by that church to be above the Scriptures, and above all law.

CHAPTER XVIII.

SIGNS OF THE SECOND COMING OF CHRIST.

It is quite generally believed that we cannot know anything about the time of the second advent of our Lord, until it takes place; that he will come the second time without warning. But no greater mistake could be made. We firmly believe that the great majority do not want to know or hear anything about it, because the thought is unpleasant to them. They realize that it will be a day of terror to those who are not prepared for his coming, and they seem to realize, to some extent, that such an extraordinary event will require extraordinary preparation. Our Saviour said it will be as the days of Noah; and we know that Noah had to make special preparation for the flood—he had to do something entirely different from all that was required of his fathers.

But that day will also be a day of great joy and glory. To the saints who have heeded the warnings given in the prophecies, who are looking for him (Heb. 9:28), who love his appearing (2 Tim. 4:1-8), who have kept the commandments of God when persecution raged on every side (Rev. 13 and 14), it will be a day of joyful triumph. The prophet, describing that day, says the saints will exclaim, " Lo, this is our God; we have waited for him, and he will save us; this is the Lord; we have waited for him, we will be glad and rejoice in his salvation." Isa. 25:9. In order to wait for him, they must make the special preparation needed; and in order to make that special preparation, they must understand the warning and instructions of the Scriptures on that subject.

Noah went into the ark seven days before the flood came upon the earth. Gen. 7:1-6. During those seven days he waited for the flood; he surely did not wait while he was building the ark. When our characters are completely formed in the sight of God—when Jesus has blotted out all our sins, and probation has closed, and the time of trouble comes—then the saints will anxiously wait for the Lord.

The prophet Joel wrote thus:—

"Blow ye the trumpet in Zion, and sound an alarm in my holy mountain; let all the inhabitants of the land tremble; for the day of the Lord cometh, for it is nigh at hand." Joel 2:1.

The day of the Lord is a long period of time which will immediately succeed the "day of salvation," which has now continued many centuries. Writing to the Thessalonians, Paul connected the coming of Christ, the resurrection of the dead, etc., with the coming of the day of the Lord. 1 Thess. 4:13-18; 5:1-4. And Peter said the perdition of ungodly men, the melting of the earth, and the burning up of all the works of men, will take place in the day of the Lord. That is the day of which the prophet Joel spoke.

Now every word spoken by the mouth of the holy prophets, must be fulfilled; and before the day of the Lord comes an alarm must be sounded. This alarm, as we have seen, is the solemn warning of the three angels' messages (Revelation 14), given just before the coming of Christ. And this proves that the students of prophecy will know when that day of the Lord is near; otherwise they could not sound the alarm.

Paul, in Heb. 9:28, says that Christ will come the second time without sin unto salvation to them that look for him. In chapter 10:25 he exhorts them to faithfulness, especially when they see the day approaching. He has spoken of no other day than that of the coming of Christ. The saints will see it approaching; they will heed the warning; they will love his appearing; they will anxiously wait for him.

This is not a matter of conjecture, but of the most certain knowledge. Jesus made it as sure as the heavens and the earth, in his instruction to his disciples. When he had spoken to them of the destruction of the temple, and the city of Jerusalem, they anxiously besought him, saying:—

"Tell us, when shall these things be, and what shall be the sign of thy coming, and of the end of the world?" Matt. 24:3.

Two questions are here asked: 1. When shall these things be? that is, when shall the temple and the city be destroyed? 2. What shall be the sign of thy coming, and of the end of the world? In the first of these questions we have now no interest; therefore we will attend to only those parts of the chapter which have a clear reference to the second, enough to ascertain the certainty with which we may know when the coming of the Lord is near.

Verses 4-8 speak of wars and rumors of wars, kingdom rising against kingdom, and nation against nation, and pestilences and famines in divers places, which are the beginning of sorrows: the end is not yet. These verses clearly refer to the last days, and the end spoken of is the end of the world, or of the gospel age; for it is not true that these things took place after Jesus spoke these words, and before the destruction of the temple, which was in A. D. 70. Verses 9-14 also refer to the end of the world, showing that the last days will be marked by a declension of piety, love growing cold, and the necessity of endurance on the part of the faithful. For a similar testimony, see 2 Tim. 3:1-5.

Also the great tribulation, verses 21, 22, has reference to the long persecution of the church under the Roman power, specially under papal Rome. Twelve hundred and sixty years were marked off for the triumph of the papacy, and in that time the saints of the Most High were given into his hand. But the days were shortened for the elect's sake, lest the church of God should be utterly cut off. That is, the persecution did not continue the entire time of the twelve hundred and sixty years.

The false Christs and false prophets of verses 23, 24, also belong to the last days. They are the same as the wonder-workers of Rev. 13:13, 14, and 16:13, 14. These signs and wonders, false and deceitful miracles, will increase unto the end.

In verses 26, 27 is given very important information—a

sure defense against the deceptions of the last days in regard to the Lord's coming. In many parts of the world the church is fast departing from the faith of the gospel; many are denying that the Lord will ever come to this world again personally. All such will readily be deceived by false Christs and false prophets and false miracles. But Jesus says that as the lightning shines from one end of heaven to the other, so will his coming be. "Every eye shall see him." Paul says, "The Lord himself shall descend from heaven with a shout, with the voice of the archangel, and with the trump of God, and the dead in Christ shall rise." 1 Thess. 4:13-18. They who confidently rely upon these scriptures cannot be deceived on this subject, for nobody can counterfeit the lightning's flash—much less the coming of Christ with his myriads of holy angels, the resurrection of the dead, etc.

Verse 29 contains the signs of the Saviour's coming, as follows:—

"Immediately after the tribulation of those days shall the sun be darkened, and the moon shall not give her light, and the stars shall fall from heaven."

Some have thought that other signs follow these, because other things are there mentioned. But among the things mentioned are the coming of the Lord, and his sending his angels to gather his elect. The signs cannot include his coming, for they are signs of his coming. The shaking of the powers of the heavens takes place at his coming, under the sixth plague of Revelation 16; it is not a sign.

In Mark 13:24 the signs are thus spoken of: "But in those days, after that tribulation, the sun shall be darkened," etc. The days of papal triumph, twelve hundred and sixty years, ended in 1798, as has been seen, but the tribulation—the persecution of the church unto death—ceased before that time. The Reformation did not deprive the papacy of its power to persecute; but the opposition raised against papal errors and practice made it inexpedient for the popes to try to exercise that power. Nor did it convert them to a different disposition, for the papacy never changes. In the "Syllabus of Errors," published by Pius IX., the doctrine is condemned that different religions may be tolerated where the power exists to suppress them.

FIRST SIGN, "THE SUN SHALL BE DARKENED."—It is a well-known fact that on the 19th of May, 1780, after the persecution had ceased, but before the days had ended, the sun was darkened in a most remarkable manner, and to a remarkable extent. The darkening was principally on the American continent, just where the miracles of these last days took their rise, and where the Lord in his providence caused the Third Angel's Message to first go forth. The darkening was so extensive and of so long continuance that it fulfilled the prophecy in a striking manner. A few testimonies of the many that might be given will suffice to make the fulfillment apparent.

Noah Webster, LL.D., in his large English Dictionary, gives the following information concerning it:—

"Dark Day, The. May 19, 1780;—so called on account of a remarkable darkness on that day extending over all New England. In some places, persons could not see to read common print in the open air for several hours together. Birds sang their evening song, disappeared, and became silent; fowls went to roost; cattle sought the barn-yard; and candles were lighted in the houses. The obscuration began about ten o'clock in the morning, and continued till the middle of the next night. . . . The true cause of this remarkable phenomenon is not known."

In a valuable work, entitled, "Guide to Knowledge," is the following:—

"On the 19th of May, 1780, an uncommon darkness took place all over New England, and extended to Canada. It continued about fourteen hours, or from ten o'clock in the morning till midnight. The darkness was so great that people were unable to read common print, or to tell the time of day by their watches, or to dine, or to transact their ordinary business, without the light of candles. They became dull and gloomy, and some were excessively frightened. The fowls went to roost. Objects could not be distinguished but at a very little distance, and everything bore the appearance of gloom and night."

The American Tract Society publish the "Life of Edward Lee," an eminent minister of the gospel, in which is the following testimony. Particular attention is called to its expressions:—

"In the month of May, 1780, there was a very terrific dark day in New

England, when 'all faces seemed to gather blackness,' and the people were filled with fear. There was great distress in the village where Edward Lee lived, 'men's hearts failing them for fear' that the judgment-day was at hand; and the neighbors all flocked around the holy man; for his lamp was trimmed and shining brighter, amidst the unnatural darkness. Happy and joyful in God, he pointed them to their only refuge from the wrath to come, and spent the gloomy hours in earnest prayer for the distressed multitude."

These writers speak of the sun being darkened till the following midnight; how could this be known? It is easily explained by what follows.

SECOND SIGN, "THE MOON SHALL NOT GIVE HER LIGHT."— Matthew Henry, a commentator on the Bible, well remarked on this text:—

"The moon shines with a borrowed light, and therefore if the sun, from whom she borrows her light, is turned into darkness, she must fail, of course, and become bankrupt."

An eye-witness of these scenes, speaking of the dark day, said:—

"The darkness of the following evening was probably as gross as has ever been observed since the Almighty first gave birth to light. I could not help conceiving at the time, that if every luminous body in the universe had been shrouded in impenetrable darkness, or struck out of existence, the darkness could not have been more complete. A sheet of white paper held within a few inches of the eyes was equally invisible with the blackest velvet."

Another writer said:—

"Almost everyone who happened to be out in the evening, got lost in going home. The darkness was as uncommon in the night as it was in the day, as the moon had fulled the day before."

In regard to the continuance of the darkening of the sun, it is to be judged from the continued darkening of the moon, which was at the full, when her clearest light was to be expected. Another writer said:—

"About midnight the clouds were dispersed, and the moon and stars appeared with unimpaired brilliancy."

This shows that the sun gave no light to the moon till midnight, and the darkness continuing from ten in the morning till midnight, shows that darkness was on the earth fourteen-twenty-fourths of the entire surface, from east to west. A remarkable darkness indeed!

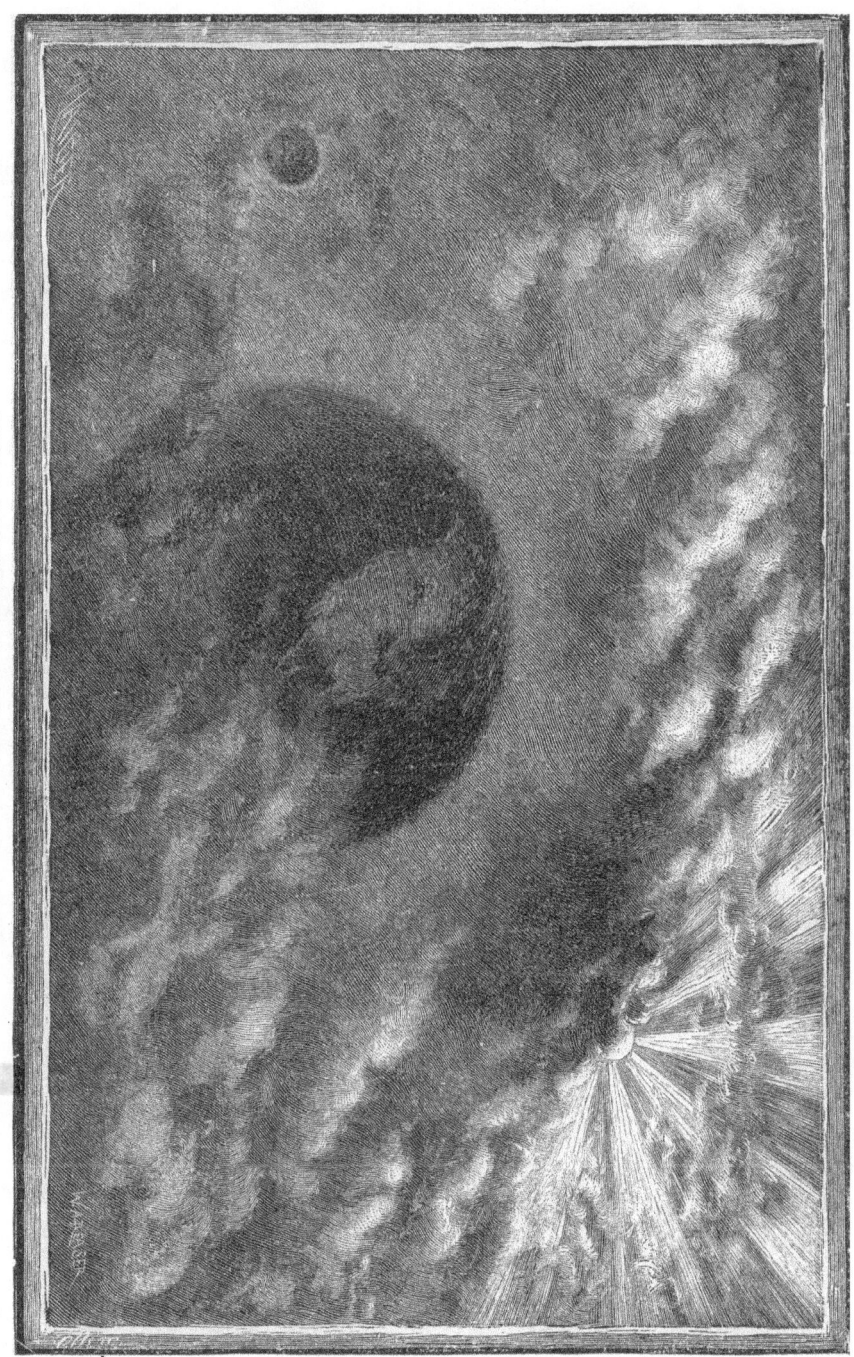

THE DARKENING OF THE SUN AND MOON.

THIRD SIGN, "THE STARS SHALL FALL FROM HEAVEN."—
This is the last of the three signs given by our Saviour, and was altogether the most glorious and magnificent in its fulfillment, which was November 13, 1833. Rev. Henry Dana Ward, of New York City, thus described the appearance of the falling stars:—

"At the cry, 'Look out of the window,' I sprang from a deep sleep, and with wonder saw the east lighted up with the dawn and meteors. The zenith, the north, and the west also, showed the falling stars in the very image of one thing, and only one, I ever heard of. I called to my wife to behold; and while robing, she exclaimed, 'See how the stars fall.' I replied, 'That is the wonder;' and we felt in our hearts that it was a sign of the last days. For, truly, 'the stars of heaven fell unto the earth, even as a fig-tree casteth her untimely figs, when she is shaken of a mighty wind." Rev. 6:13. This language of the prophet has always been received as metaphorical. Yesterday, it was literally fulfilled. The ancients understood by aster, in Greek, and stella, in Latin, the smaller lights of heaven. The refinement of modern astronomy has made the distinction between stars of heaven and meteors of heaven. Therefore the idea of the prophet, as it is expressed in the original Greek, was literally fulfilled in the phenomenon of yesterday."

In regard to the extent and nature of this heavenly display, Professor Olmstead, of Yale College, speaks as follows:—

"The extent of the shower of 1833 was such as to cover no inconsiderable part of the earth's surface, from the middle of the Atlantic on the east, to the Pacific on the West; and from the northern coast of South America, to undefined regions among the British Possessions on the north, the exhibition was visible, and everywhere presented nearly the same appearance. The meteors did not fly at random over all parts of the sky, but appeared to emanate from a point in the constellation Leo, near a star called Gamma Leonis, in the bend of the sickle."

This shows that they were not mere atmospheric phenomena, but came from the regions far beyond our atmosphere. It was the privilege of the writer of these pages to behold this scene, and it was one never to be forgotten. They began to fall about an hour before midnight, increasing in frequency until, in a few hours, they became a perfect shower. They could no more be counted than one can count the fast-falling flakes of snow in a hard storm. They continued to fall without any diminution of numbers until the dawn of day obscured them. And when the approaching light of the sun paled them in the east, they still colored the western sky. And when the spreading light obscured them in every direction, occasionally one of great brilliancy would leave its trace in the west, showing that they were still falling.

After giving these signs, the Saviour spoke a parable, in application of his instruction. He said:—

"Now learn a parable of the fig-tree; when his branch is yet tender, and putteth forth leaves, ye know that summer is nigh. So likewise ye, when ye shall see all these things, know that it is near, even at the doors." Matt. 24:32, 33.

In Luke 21:29, 30 it reads, "Behold the fig-tree, and all the trees; when they now shoot forth, ye see and know of your own selves that summer is now nigh at hand." Even so; we do not doubt it; we do not need that any should offer us proof; we know it. And thus, says the Saviour, shall we know when his coming and the end of the world is near, even at the doors. It is true that he says that of that day and hour knoweth no man. This we firmly believe; but that is not all the truth. He gives signs by which we may positively know when it is near; he commanded us to know, and gave the days of Noah as an example of the danger of not knowing. We may know, and it is our duty to know; and if we would not be neglectful of our Saviour's words, we shall search diligently to know all the truth of his sacred word. By so doing, we may be the children of the light, and that day shall not overtake us as a thief. 1 Thess. 5:4.

THE FALLING OF THE STARS.

CHAPTER XIX.

THE RESURRECTION OF THE DEAD.

The coming of Christ will bring joy and glory, not only to the living, waiting saints, but to those who are sleeping in the dust of the earth. Paul said to the church of Thessalonica, but the words are really spoken to us of the last generation, that when the Lord comes the dead will be raised and the living caught up with them to meet the Lord in the air. 1 Thess. 4:13-17. The dead in Christ may have been sleeping thousands of years, but they will lose nothing, as they will be glorified at the same time as the living. Nor will they have any preëminence over the living, for the Scriptures say that all the faithful of ancient times died in faith, not having received the promise, God having reserved some better thing for us, that they without us should not be made perfect. Heb. 11: 39, 40. Both classes will be caught up together to meet their coming Lord in glory.

It has been noticed that the great primary truths of the government of God over men, are common to all dispensations. The gospel was revealed when Adam was expelled from Eden. The plan was developed in the covenant with Abraham; and the prophets declared in advance the complete fulfillment of the work of redemption through Jesus, the Son of God, the Son of Abraham, the Son of David, the Seed of the woman who alone can triumph over the serpent.

The penalty announced to Adam for sin, was death; and this penalty was executed by causing man to return unto the ground out of which he was taken. Gen. 2:16, 17; 3:17-19; 5:5. To rob man of life was the great triumph of the serpent —the enemy of God and man. As has been noticed. the seed of the woman must restore all that was lost by sin; otherwise the triumph of the serpent would be permanent. Man must be restored from death; he must be brought back from the dust of the ground.

In view of this evident and necessary truth, it is surprising that Bible readers should deny—as many do—that a future life and immortality were revealed and promised to the patriarchs, the prophets, and to all the Israel of God. Had we no further proof than is afforded by the many appeals in the Old Testament Scriptures to the future judgment, we should even then confidently deny their position. But the proof to the contrary of their assertion is both abundant and explicit. It is true that there is no revelation made of the Platonic doctrine of the immortality of the soul, nor is there in the New Testament. The promise of eternal life is through the resurrection of the dead; here only it may be found in the Bible.

It has been noticed that the trial of Abraham in his being commanded to offer Isaac as a sacrifice, was much more than a trial of his love for an only son; it was a trial of his faith in the promise of God, who had said to him, " In Isaac shall thy seed be called." Gen. 21:12. Why did not Abraham plead to be excused from offering his son, on the ground that if Isaac were slain the promise of God must fail? The reason is given in Hebrews 11, that remarkable chapter on the power of faith. There we read:—

"By faith Abraham, when he was tried, offered up Isaac; and he that had received the promises offered up his only begotten son, of whom it was said, That in Isaac shall thy seed be called; accounting that God was able to raise him up, even from the dead; from whence also he received him in a figure." Heb. 11:17-19.

Here is the evidence that the faith of Abraham embraced the resurrection of the dead. And inasmuch as Abraham, in these promises, saw the day of Christ and rejoiced in it (John 8:56), he understood that the Messiah was the true seed through whom the promises were to be fulfilled. In the sacrifice of the son of promise he saw and believed in the sacrifice of the true Seed, the Son of God, and in his resurrection.

But further; it is said of Abraham and others to whom the promises were given: "By faith he sojourned in the land of promise, as in a strange country," receiving no inheritance in it, but "confessed that they were strangers and pilgrims on the earth." Verses 8–13. And this certainly proves that they looked to a future life for the fulfillment of the promises embraced in the covenant.

But the evidence is yet more direct. After reciting the cases of patriarchs, prophets, and others, and referring to the host of believers whom he had not time to name, the writer says that they endured great persecutions, not accepting deliverance when they might have obtained it by a denial of their faith, "that they might obtain a better resurrection." Heb. 11:35. This is decisive; it shows how entirely at fault are those professed teachers of the Bible who deny that the faith of the ancients embraced the future life. They saw it through the resurrection of the dead.

Besides this, we have specific declarations of individuals. Job distinctly referred to the resurrection in chapter 14:13–15, and yet more plainly in the following:—

"For I know that my Redeemer liveth, and that he shall stand at the latter day upon the earth; and though after my skin worms destroy this body, yet in my flesh shall I see God. Whom I shall see for myself, and mine eyes shall behold, and not another; though my reins be consumed within me." Job 19:25-27.

David showed his faith in speaking of the resurrection of Christ:—

"Therefore my heart is glad, and my glory rejoiceth; my flesh also shall rest in hope. For thou wilt not leave my soul in sheol; neither wilt thou suffer thine Holy One to see corruption." Ps. 16:9, 10; compare Acts 2:25-32.

And David gave his own hope in the same event, saying, "As for me, I will behold thy face in righteousness; I shall be satisfied, when I awake, with thy likeness." Ps. 17:15 ;see also Ps. 49:15.

The prophet Isaiah is most decisive in his testimony. He says:—

"Thy dead men shall live, together with my dead body shall they arise.

Awake and sing, ye that dwell in dust; for thy dew is as the dew of herbs and the earth shall cast out the dead." Isa. 26:19.

In Matt. 2:16-18, we learn that Jeremiah prophesied of the destruction of the children in Bethlehem, by Herod. The prophecy we find in chapter 31:15-17. In verses 16, 17, the weeping mothers are comforted with hope from the word of the Lord:—

"Thus saith the Lord: Refrain thy voice from weeping, and thine eyes from tears; for thy work shall be rewarded, saith the Lord; and they shall come again from the land of the enemy. And there is hope in thine end, saith the Lord, that thy children shall come again to their own border."

There is hope that they shall come again from the land of the enemy. Their children were dead; and Paul says the last enemy is death. 1 Cor 15:26. This refers unmistakably to a resurrection from the dead.

Ezekiel is equally strong and explicit in his testimony. He saw in vision a valley of dry bones, and by the word of the Lord they were caused to live. Then the Lord thus explained the vision:—

"Then he said unto me, Son of man, these bones are the whole house of Israel; behold, they say, Our bones are dried, and our hope is lost, we are cut off for our parts. Therefore prophesy and say unto them, Thus saith the Lord God: Behold, O my people, I will open your graves, and cause you to come up out of your graves, and bring you into the land of Israel. And ye shall know that I am the Lord, when I have opened your graves, O my people, and brought you up out of your graves, and shall put my Spirit in you, and ye shall live, and I shall place you in your own land." Eze. 37:11-14.

And Daniel adds his testimony in language equally strong. When Michael the Prince stands up, or reigns, the time comes for the deliverance of the people of God. And at that time—

"Many of them that sleep in the dust of the earth shall awake, some to everlasting life, and some to shame and everlasting contempt." Dan. 12:2.

Hosea also gives the word of the Lord on the same subject:

"I will ransom them from the power of the grave; I will redeem them from death; O death, I will be thy plagues; O grave, I will be thy destruction." Hosea 13:14.

This is some of the testimony of the Old Testament in regard to a future life—to a life beyond the grave. And what more could be asked to make it sure? They who overlook, or lightly esteem, the resurrection, find no evidence of a future life in the Hebrew Scriptures. Immortality, as they teach it, inherent in the nature of man, they fail to find in that book. Of that the word of God is silent. Now that the Jews believed these scriptures concerning a future life is proved in the New Testament by the many references to the resurrection as a well-known article of faith, except with the Sadducees. When Jesus said to the sister of Lazarus, "Thy brother shall rise again," Martha replied, "I know that he shall rise again in the resurrection at the last day." John 11:23, 24. How did she know it except by faith in the word of God, wherein it was revealed? Also when Paul was unjustly accused, he created a division among his accusers, by crying out:—

"Men and brethren, I am a Pharisee, the son of a Pharisee; of the hope and resurrection of the dead I am called in question." Acts 23:6.

It requires but few words to show the great importance of the doctrine of the resurrection, or, rather, of the resurrection as a revealed truth. It is confessed that as far as the Old Testament is concerned, the resurrection presents the only hope of future life. The words of Jesus should be carefully considered. He said to one who had invited him to dine with him, that when he made a feast he should call the poor, the lame, and the blind, for this reason:—

"And thou shalt be blessed; for they cannot recompense thee; for thou shalt be recompensed at the resurrection of the just." Luke 14:14.

And this, in turn, shows the importance of the second advent of our Saviour; for the resurrection of the just will take place when he comes, and it will never take place unless he comes: therefore, should he never come, the just would never receive their recompense. Paul connects them in the following manner:—

"For the Lord himself shall descend from Heaven with a shout, with the voice of the archangel, and with the trump of God; and the dead in Christ shall rise first; then we which are alive and remain shall be caught up together with them in the clouds, to meet the Lord in the air; and so shall we ever be with the Lord." 1 Thess. 4:16, 17.

This is parallel with that important declaration which follows:—

"Behold, I show you a mystery: We shall not all sleep, but we shall all be changed, in a moment, in the twinkling of an eye, at the last trump; for the trumpet shall sound [when Christ comes], and the dead shall be raised incorruptible, and we shall be changed." 1 Cor. 15:51, 52.

In both these texts, the coming of Christ and the resurrection of the dead are presented as the hope of glory for the saints. To the latter are added these words:—

"So when this corruptible shall have put on incorruption, and this mortal shall have put on immortality, then shall be brought to pass the saying that is written, Death is swallowed up in victory." Verse 54.

Many other texts speak of the coming of Christ as bringing the reward of the saints. Jesus himself testifies: "Behold, I come quickly; and my reward is with me, to give every man according as his work shall be." Rev. 22:12. And again: "For the Son of man shall come in the glory of his Father with his angels; and then he shall reward every man according to his works." Matt. 16:27. Says Paul: "When Christ, who is our life, shall appear, then shall ye also appear with him in glory." Col. 3:4. "Looking for that blessed hope, and the glorious appearing of the great God and our Saviour Jesus Christ." Titus 2:13. Peter also says: "And when the chief Shepherd shall appear, ye shall receive a crown of glory that fadeth not away." 1 Peter 5:4.

It is justly called that blessed hope, for at the second advent of the Lord the saints will receive the fullness of their hope in endless life and glory. Who that loves the Lord Jesus, the blessed and only Saviour, would not join the beloved disciple in the prayer, "Even so, come, Lord Jesus"? Rev. 22:20.

In this chapter we have thus far only spoken of the resurrection of the just—the saints of God. But the whole argument concerning the judgment proves that there will also be a resurrection of the wicked, as Paul teaches in Acts 24:15. Our Lord and Saviour taught the same thing. After stating that the Father had given power to the Son to execute judgment, he adds:—

"Marvel not at this; for the hour is coming, in the which all that are in the graves shall hear his voice, and shall come forth; they that have done good, unto the resurrection of life; and they that have done evil, unto the resurrection of damnation." John 5:28, 29.

All mankind now return to the dust of the earth, as did Adam, because of the perishable nature inherited from him; and by the second Adam all will be brought from the ground, for thus it is written: "For as in Adam all die, even so in Christ shall all be made alive." 1 Cor. 15:22. But it is also shown that all are not of one order. They that are Christ's are raised at his coming. They will have the resurrection unto life. When the last trump sounds, this corruptible shall put on incorruption, and this mortal shall put on immortality; for it is sown in corruption, it is raised in incorruption. See 1 Cor. 15:42-53. But of the other order it is said:—

"He that soweth to his flesh shall of the flesh reap corruption; but he that soweth to the Spirit shall of the Spirit reap life everlasting." Gal. 6:8.

In the book of Revelation it is said that the second death hath no power on such as have part in the first resurrection. But when the sea gives up its dead, and death and hades deliver up the dead which are in them, all who are not found written in the book of life will be cast into the lake of fire, which is the second death. Rev. 20:6, 13-15. From the second death there is no resurrection. Beyond that, for all who shall suffer it, is only eternal gloom. To them "is reserved the blackness of darkness forever." Jude 13.

Behold, what a contrast between the just and the unjust, in the judgment, in the resurrection, and in eternity. Thus we may see how God, the Judge of all, regards the difference of their characters. When one is plunged into the abyss, into the fire of everlasting destruction, to the other is given the enjoyment of an exceeding and eternal weight of glory.

CHAPTER XX.

RESTORATION OF THE FIRST DOMINION.

Paul said that we who believe are sealed with the Holy Spirit of promise, which is the earnest, or assurance, of our inheritance until the redemption of the purchased possession. Eph. 1:13, 14. Jesus has purchased our inheritance, but it waits to be redeemed—it is still under the curse of sin. Yes, this whole creation groans under its burden of sin and woe. Rom. 8:22, 23. But it will be redeemed, for the enemy shall not triumph forever, and "the meek shall inherit the earth; and shall delight themselves in the abundance of peace." Ps. 37:11. But that can never be in the present state of the earth, for in this world they are pilgrims and strangers, and here they shall suffer tribulation. 1 Peter 2:11; John 16:33.

Peter speaks of three conditions of this world, and these are so different that he calls them three earths, or worlds. 2 Peter 3:5-7, 10, 13. He says that in the last days scoffers shall say, "Where is the promise of his coming? for since the fathers fell asleep, all things continue as they were from the beginning of the creation." Verses 3, 4. We do not look to creation to read the promise of his coming; this is found, in plain terms, in the sure word of prophecy. But they are wrong in their statement. All things do not continue as they were from the beginning of the creation. Inspiration said that the earth should wax old as a garment; and the earth shows unmistakable signs of age.

The earth was first peopled in Asia. After the flood, Asia was again first peopled. There man fell; there the wonders of God were displayed in his dealings with patriarchs and prophets; there Abraham was called, and there he offered up Isaac; and there the Son of God offered up himself; and there the gospel was first proclaimed, and thousands embraced it and were faithful unto death. But with another generation the light of the gospel began to decline in that part of the world, and it traveled westward; and westward has been its course to the present day; and now it has circled the earth. Its light is now shining on the eastern shore of the Pacific, where it has not flourished before the present generation. The Saviour foretold that the gospel of the kingdom, the message of the King coming in his glory, should "be preached in all the world for a witness unto all nations; and then shall the end come." It will not convert the nations, but it will triumph, just as it did in the days of Christ and his apostles,—it will gather out from all nations a chosen company to the glory of his name. Acts 15:14; Rev. 7:9.

Of those who scoff at the Lord's coming, Peter said they are willingly ignorant. 2 Peter 3:5. They are ignorant of the fact that all things consist by the word of God; that, not by chance, but by that "word of God the heavens were of old, and the earth standing out of the water and in the water; whereby the world that then was, being overflowed with water, perished." Verses 5, 6. When the windows of heaven were opened, and the fountains of the great deep were broken up, and the raging waters rose above the tops of the highest mountains (Genesis 7), the whole face of nature was changed; and when Noah looked from the ark upon the earth, it was a scene of desolation, utterly unlike anything he had ever seen before. Truly, the world had perished.

And Peter proceeds to speak of the heavens and earth which are now, in distinction from those which perished, which by the same word are kept in store, reserved, not to perish again by water, but reserved unto fire, against the day of judgment and perdition of ungodly men. 2 Peter 3:7. And the fire will have a still greater effect upon the earth than the water had upon the earth that existed before the flood. "The elements shall melt with fervent heat, the earth also, and the works that are therein shall be burned up." Verse 10.

And this is the day of perdition of ungodly men. When

the earth is melted, it will be literally a sea of fire, and that will be the lake of fire into which the ungodly are to be cast. Rev. 20 : 15. But Peter continues:—

"Nevertheless we, according to his promise, look for new heavens and a new earth, wherein dwelleth righteousness." Verse 13.

That new earth will be related to the earth that now is, as this is related to that which was before the flood; there will be the same material under far different conditions. The change wrought by the flood left the earth still bringing forth thorns and thistles,—still under the curse. But when the earth is melted with fervent heat, and all the works that are therein are burned up, it will come forth renovated, renewed, without a trace of sin or the curse remaining. Thus speaks the prophet:—

"For, behold, the day cometh, that shall burn as an oven; and all the proud, yea, and all that do wickedly, shall be stubble; and the day that cometh shall burn them up, saith the Lord of hosts, that it shall leave them neither root nor branch." Mal. 4 : 1.

The Scriptures say that the wicked, as well as the righteous, shall be rewarded in the earth. Prov. 11 : 31. But their rewards are so essentially different that it is impossible that they should be rewarded in the earth at or during the same time. The psalmist says:—

"But the meek shall inherit the earth; and shall delight themselves in the abundance of peace." "The Lord knoweth the days of the upright; and their inheritance shall be forever." "The righteous shall inherit the land, and dwell therein forever." Ps. 37: 11, 18, 29.

But how different is the fate of the wicked:—

"For yet a little while, and the wicked shall not be; yea, thou shalt diligently consider his place, and it shall not be." Verse 10.

The wicked will never behold the earth renewed, restored to its original state of purity, for in that new earth dwelleth righteousness; no sin nor curse will be there. Yet they will be recompensed fully, entirely, in the earth. The Scriptures say that they shall have their portion in the lake of fire; and the day that cometh shall burn them up. This present world is the place of their choice; for this they have rejected eternal life and all the joys of Paradise. But "they shall be destroyed forever" (Ps. 92:7), and their very place shall not be, for the old earth shall pass away with them. As says the prophet:—

"And I saw a new heaven and a new earth; for the first heaven and the first earth were passed away." Rev. 21:1.

The animals which God created upon the earth, over which he gave man dominion in the beginning, will be restored to their innocency; for it is written:—

"The wolf also shall dwell with the lamb, and the leopard shall lie down with the kid; and the calf and the young lion and the fatling together; and a little child shall lead them. And the cow and the bear shall feed; their young ones shall lie down together; and the lion shall eat straw like the ox. And the sucking child shall play on the hole of the asp, and the weaned child shall put his hand on the cockatrice's den. They shall not hurt nor destroy in all my holy mountain; for the earth shall be full of the knowledge of the Lord, as the waters cover the sea." Isa. 11:6-9.

And again the word of the Lord comes by the same prophet:—

"The wolf and the lamb shall feed together, and the lion shall eat straw like the bullock; and dust shall be the serpent's meat. They shall not hurt nor destroy in all my holy mountain, saith the Lord." Isa. 65:25.

When the earth was created there was no city upon it; a city was not then needed. But it is very evident that a city was intended when the earth should become peopled, and that city would have been the capital of the whole empire. The garden that the Lord planted in Eden, wherein was the tree of life, would have been the center. To this all the nations would have resorted. This would have been the permanent home of Adam, the patriarch of the race. In the comparatively brief record of God's revelations to Abraham, we find no mention of the city in the divine purpose; yet we know that it was promised to Abraham, for the apostle says of him, "For he looked for a city which hath foundations, whose builder and maker is God." Heb. 11:10. This is spoken of as a part of his faith, but if God had not promised it, his faith could not have embraced it. And we have seen that the covenant with Abraham is God's method of accomplishing his original purpose in the creation.

This city is called a woman. There is nothing incongruous in this. In Rev. 17:18, a certain power is presented, and the two terms, a woman and a city, are applied to it. Note what St. Paul says of this subject in the book of Galatians:—

"For this Agar is Mount Sinai in Arabia, and answereth to Jerusalem which now is, and is in bondage with her children. But Jerusalem which is above is free, which is the mother of us all." Gal. 4:25, 26.

In this chapter the two women, Hagar and Sarah, are made to represent the two covenants and the two Jerusalems. The old Jerusalem, rejected of God for her iniquities, is represented by Hagar; her children are in bondage. Jerusalem which is above, but which is to come down upon the earth, is free; she is represented by Sarah, whose son was the child of promise, the only heir. The followers of Jesus are her children; she is their mother. Paul says, "Now we, brethren, as Isaac was, are the children of promise." Gal. 4:28. We are the children of the heavenly city, the free woman.

It has always been customary to speak of any people as the children of their certain land or city. We find in Isaiah 54, the chapter from which Paul quotes in Galatians 4, that the two Jerusalems are called wives and mothers:—

"Sing, O barren, thou that didst not bear; break forth into singing, and cry aloud, thou that didst not travail with child; for more are the children of the desolate than the children of the married wife, saith the Lord." Isa. 54:1.

These words Paul applies to the New Jerusalem. The old city was the married wife, for God there built his temple; there he set his name, and he took her children to be his people. But she was put away for their unfaithfulness. All the true children of the promise are the children of the New Jerusalem, which has not yet been married. And why not?—Because Jesus Christ has not yet received that inheritance and that kingdom of which that city is the metropolis. But when the priesthood of our Saviour closes, then the Father shall give unto him the throne of his father David; the nations are then given to him for an inheritance; his enemies will be put under his feet; the kingdoms of this world become the kingdoms of our Lord and his Christ, and he takes possession of the city, the capital. This is the time of the fulfillment of that prophecy of Daniel:—

"And in the days of these kings shall the God of Heaven set up a kingdom, which shall never be destroyed; and the kingdom shall not be left to other people, but it shall break in pieces and consume all these kingdoms, and it shall stand forever." Dan. 2:44.

The setting up of the kingdom is the investing the Lord Jesus with the authority, and bestowing upon him the capital. This gift is made in Heaven, as is shown in Dan. 7:13, 14:—

"I saw in the night visions, and, behold, one like the Son of man came with the clouds of heaven, and came to the Ancient of Days, and they brought him near before him. And there was given him dominion, and glory, and a kingdom, that all people, nations, and languages, should serve him; his dominion is an everlasting dominion, which shall not pass away, and his kingdom that which shall not be destroyed."

The Son of man is brought before the Ancient of Days, where the throne of judgment is set (see verses 9, 10), to receive the kingdom. This scene is located in Heaven—not on the earth. And the words of Jesus show the same thing, in the following parable:—

"He said therefore, A certain nobleman went into a far country to receive for himself a kingdom, and to return. And he called his ten servants, and delivered them ten pounds, and said unto them, Occupy till I come. But his citizens hated him, and sent a message after him, saying, We will not have this man to reign over us. And it came to pass, that when he was returned, having received the kingdom, then he commanded these servants to be called unto him, to whom he had given the money, that he might know how much every man had gained by trading." Luke 19:12-15.

After the account of reckoning with his servants, he added:—

"But those mine enemies, which would not that I should reign over them, bring hither, and slay them before me." Verse 27.

Himself was the nobleman who was to receive the kingdom. The far country to which he went to receive the kingdom, is Heaven. The kingdom is this earth, for here he has given his servants their talents to improve, and here they use them or hide them. And very decisive is the statement that his citizens hated him. Here his enemies refuse to have him rule over them, and here they will be slain. It is impossible to consider that the kingdom he receives is anything but this earth, unless we admit that the inhabitants of Heaven hate him, and that he will destroy them. He does not go to the locality of the kingdom, but to a far country, to receive it, and returns to the locality having received the kingdom. This earth, the first dominion, which he has purchased with his blood, is to be his everlasting kingdom. Though it is conceded that forever and everlasting have different significations, their duration being determined by the subjects to which they are applied, there can be no question as to the eternal duration of the kingdom of Christ upon this earth, for thus the angel spoke:—

"And the Lord God shall give unto him the throne of his father David; and he shall rule over the house of Jacob forever; and of his kingdom *there shall be no end.*" Luke 1 : 32, 33.

We have noticed that Abraham was taken to Palestine to behold his inheritance, because that was the land in which was to be located the capital. But that capital is the New Jerusalem, which Paul says is above; it is in Heaven. When John was shown this city he said it was by one of the angels that had the seven last plagues. Rev. 21 : 9. By this we know that the fulfillment of this part of the vision is not before the close of the present dispensation; for these angels do not appear until this dispensation is about to close.

It may be well to remark that the book of Revelation is not to be read from the standpoint of John when the vision was given, but from the standpoints of the progressive fulfillment of its several parts. John stood as the representative of the church through all the ages. What he saw in vision in A. D. 96, the church must see in fact through all the centuries, even to the restoration of the earth, and into eternity beyond. The several lines of prophecy, as the letters to the seven churches, the opening of the seven seals, the sounding of the seven trumpets, and the history of the dragon and the two beasts of chapter 13, each covers the entire dispensation. They began in the days of John, but end in the ushering in of eternity.

But the seven last plagues do not cover the dispensation.

They are all poured out in a brief period, after the Third Angel's Message is given, as we have already seen. The seven angels receive the vials or plagues just before probation closes, as we may judge from Rev. 7 : 1–3, where the angels are restrained from opening the judgments of God upon the earth; and also from Rev. 15 : 7, 8, where the plagues are given to the angel before the temple is filled with the glory of God, which latter event indicates that there will be no priestly service during the pouring out of the plagues. Now John saw all the seals opened in his vision, but only one of them was really opened in his age. The church sees them all opened in its experience in the whole dispensation. John saw in vision a beast with two horns, which made an image to the first beast; and in vision he saw an angel give a solemn warning against the worship of the beast and his image. But it is reserved to the church in the last days to see these things in fact. John said that an angel, one of those having the seven last plagues, came to him and talked with him. This angel did not appear to John at his standpoint of A. D. 96, for that was not the date of this angel; but John was carried down in vision to the standpoint of the church at the close of the dispensation. It is here that the angel talked with him in his vision. Losing sight of this necessary order, some have been led to spiritualize this prophecy which we are now considering, as they could not locate it in the time of John, where they assumed that it belonged, and give it a literal or correct interpretation. As John said that the New Jerusalem comes down from Heaven, and Paul said it is above, we must for a moment consider what the Scriptures say on the subject of its being in Heaven:—

1. As the capital is to be in Palestine, we conclude that the New Jerusalem will be located just where the old city stood. Thus we read of the preparation of the land to receive the city :—

"And his [Jesus'] feet shall stand in that day upon the Mount of Olives, which is before Jerusalem on the east, and the Mount of Olives shall cleave in the midst thereof toward the east and toward the west, and there shall be a very great valley; and half of the mountain shall remove toward the north, and half of it toward the south. And ye shall flee to the valley of the mountains; for the valley of the mountains shall reach unto Azal; yea, ye shall flee, like as ye fled from before the earthquake in the days of Uzziah king of Judah; and the Lord my God shall come, and all the saints with thee." Zech. 14:4, 5.

Some have greatly misapprehended the teaching of this prophecy, supposing it to be a record of a consecutive series of events, because it continues to speak of what shall occur in the day of the Lord. But the day of the Lord is a period of time more than a thousand years in length, beginning when the priesthood of Christ closes, before the seven last plagues are poured out, and continuing until the final restitution of all things—the redemption of the righteous, the destruction of the wicked, and the renewing of the earth. The verses quoted above are widely separated from those which immediately precede them, in time of fulfillment. In like manner we often find the two advents of our Saviour connected in the prophecies, but they are far apart in fulfillment. The city of God comes down upon the earth, not at the beginning but near the end of that great day. The cleaving of the mountain, and the making of a very great valley, will remove every trace of the old Jerusalem, and thus a place will be prepared for the new. That sacred, honored spot will be restored to the shape and condition it had when it was first created—before the curse had marred it, or the fierceness of the flood had defaced it. The prophet continues:—

"And it shall be in that day that living waters shall go out from Jerusalem; half of them toward the eastern sea, and half of them toward the western sea." Zech 14:8, Revised Version.

And so in the book of Revelation. In the description of the city, John says: "And he showed me a pure river of water of life, clear as crystal, proceeding out of the throne of God and of the Lamb." Rev. 22:1. There must certainly take place such a change in the face of that country as that described by the prophet Zechariah, for in its present shape it would be impossible for rivers to flow in different directions, at least east and west from Jerusalem. The city will be elevated upon a mountain, even upon Mount Zion. That mountain is now in Heaven, and the holy city is upon it; the mountain upon which the city is situated will come down from Heaven with it. Let us notice what the Scriptures say:—

"But ye are come unto Mount Sion, and unto the city of the living God, the heavenly Jerusalem, and to an innumerable company of angels," etc. Heb. 12:22.

In verses 25, 26, it is said that, as the voice of God was once heard from Sinai, by which the earth was shaken, so it will once more be heard from Heaven, and that it will shake the heavens and the earth. To this the prophet Jeremiah refers in his description of the terrors of that great day when all the nations shall be overthrown:—

"The Lord shall roar from on high, and utter his voice from his holy habitation." Jer. 25:30.

And other prophets speak in like manner; thus:—

"And he said, The Lord will roar from Zion, and utter his voice from Jerusalem; and the habitations of the shepherds shall mourn, and the top of Carmel shall wither." Amos 1:2.

And very explicit are the following words:—

"The sun and the moon shall be darkened, and the stars shall withdraw their shining. The Lord also shall roar out of Zion, and utter his voice from Jerusalem; and the heavens and the earth shall shake; but the Lord will be the hope of his people, and the strength of the children of Israel." Joel 3:15, 16.

Once shall the voice of God be heard from on high, and once shall the heavens and the earth be shaken by that voice. But it will be heard from Zion, from Jerusalem. There is the city, and there is the Mount Zion upon which the city rests; there is the river of the water of life, and there is the tree of life, which was once planted on the earth, but was taken away because of the sin of Adam, and is to be restored to its place on the earth by the merits of the blood of the second Adam.

Of the view of the city shown to him by the angel, John thus speaks:—

"And there came unto me one of the seven angels which had the seven vials full of the seven last plagues, and talked with me, saying, Come hither, I will show thee the bride, the Lamb's wife. And he carried me away in the spirit to a great and high mountain, and showed me that great city, the holy Jerusalem, descending out of Heaven from God, having the glory of God; and her light was like unto a stone most precious, even like a jasper stone, clear as crystal." Rev. 21:9–11.

Here follows a description of its most transcendent glory. Its walls are high, with twelve foundations of precious stones. Its gates are of pearl. The glory of God and the Lamb are the light of it. Of it John further says:—

"And I John saw the holy city, New Jerusalem, coming down from God out of Heaven, prepared as a bride adorned for her husband." Rev. 21:2.

This city comes down from Heaven, as its maker and builder is God. It was built in Heaven, but it was intended for the metropolis of the earth. And why is this earth so honored with the city of God and the eternal kingdom of Christ? Though small among the works of God, this earth has been the scene of wondrous events. Next to the war in Heaven, by which Satan and his angels were forever shut out of that holy place, the greatest conflict that the universe has known, or will know, has been on this earth. The hosts of Heaven shouted for joy when this earth was made. But here Satan triumphed over man; here sin set its blight upon the works of God; here Christ, the Son of God, by whom he made the worlds, suffered and died for man's sake; here he triumphed over death; and here he will bruise the head of Satan, and bring him to an ignominious end. Rev. 20:7–10; Heb. 2:14. And it is fitting that when the conflict is over, the curse removed, the first dominion restored, the inheritance of Abraham and his children redeemed, here the Son of God should erect his throne, and reign to endless ages among the happy millions whom he purchased with his blood.

Two expressions in regard to this city we notice: 1. John says the city was prepared as a bride adorned for her husband. Rev. 21:2. 2. He says that the angel who called him, promised to show him the bride, the Lamb's wife; and then he showed him the city, a description of which he proceeded to give. This is much more than an intimation that the city is the bride. We have already seen that the New Jerusalem is called the mother of all the faithful children of Abraham, and that it is represented by Sarah, the wife of Abraham, the mother of the only heir. So it is not new in the book of Revelation that a city should be called a woman, or a bride, a wife. And it is no more strange that a city should be called a bride, than that she should be called a mother. Yet we all know that the New Jerusalem is called our mother. And herein we find the solution of another Scripture truth which has been regarded as a mystery. Jesus, the Son of David, is referred to in the prophecy of Isaiah, as follows :—

"For unto us a child is born, unto us a son is given; and the government shall be upon his shoulder; and his name shall be called Wonderful, Counselor, the Mighty God, the Everlasting Father, the Prince of Peace. Of the increase of his government and peace there shall be no end, upon the throne of David, and upon his kingdom, to order it, and to establish it with judgment and with justice, from henceforth even forever." Isa. 9:6,7.

The position that he is to occupy—the government that he is to hold—sufficiently identify the person here referred to as the Son of God, the Messiah. The wonder has been how he who is the Prince of Peace can be called "the everlasting Father." It cannot represent him in any relation to "the Trinity," as some have supposed, for the Father is uniformly considered "the first person," while the Prince of Peace, he who appeared as the Son of David, and Heir to his throne, is as uniformly held to be the second person. If it should be claimed that he is both Father and Son in the Trinity, then it is evident there could be no Trinity, as he would be but one person with two names. It appears evident that this prophecy has no reference to any such doctrine, but refers to him as a Father in a different sense.

Now as the New Jerusalem is called the bride, our mother, and as Jesus is the bridegroom, he must by right be called our Father. Thus the bridegroom and bride are the father and mother of all the children of the heavenly city. This is both plain and reasonable.

But these children are all faithful ones, who are constituted the seed of Abraham by faith in Christ, and who are born anew to the kingdom of God. The unfaithful—they who have rejected Christ, whether among the Jews or Gentiles—have no lot nor part in that matter. They are looking also to Jerusalem for the fulfillment of the promises of God, but it is to the old Jerusalem, the "Jerusalem which now is, and is in bondage with her children." Gal. 4:25. The New Jerusalem is not the mother of these bond children, and Jesus, the bridegroom, is not their Father. They will have no part in his work of restitution.

But of his Father, Jesus says, "My Father, which gave them me, is greater than I," and, "My Father is greater than all." John 10:29; 14:28. He is over all, the universal Father; he is even "the God and Father of our Lord Jesus Christ." 2 Cor. 11:31, etc.

But Jesus Christ himself, the royal bridegroom to the New Jerusalem, is the everlasting Father of all the redeemed, and of no others.

When the kingdom is given to Christ, he takes possession of his capital, in Heaven, and this is called in a figure the marriage. The saints are the guests who are called to the marriage supper of the Lamb. Rev. 19:6-9. And we have seen that he takes possession of the kingdom in Heaven, before his return to the earth, and he commends the faithful who shall be watching when the Lord returns from the wedding. Glorious blessing that is promised! He will take them to the mansions prepared, and make them sit down to the marriage supper, and he will come forth and serve them. His own hand shall pluck of the fruit of the tree of life, and give them to eat, and bring them water from the river of life. What a feast that will be to those who have suffered in poverty in this world for his name's sake! See Luke 12:31-37.

John said that he saw in the midst of the street of the city, and on either side of the river, the tree of life, which bare twelve manner of fruits, and yielded her fruit every month. Rev. 22:2. A monthly yield of twelve manner of fruits, would give an endless variety of fruit, and yet all from the wonderful tree of life. "And the leaves of the tree were for the service of the nations." (See the Greek.)

The question has often been asked if the redeemed saints will require access to the tree of life. Why not? The tree of life was planted in Eden, and Adam and his posterity would always have had access to it if sin had not caused its removal. That the tree of life will be one of the blessed privileges and blessings of the redeemed, is decisively proved by the promise of the Saviour in his letter to the church of Ephesus. Rev. 2: 1–7. Every individual of this church is now in the grave, waiting to have part in the " better resurrection," when this mortal shall put on immortality. Jesus says of them:—

"To him that overcometh will I give to eat of the tree of life, which is in the midst of the Paradise of God." Rev. 2: 7.

Jesus has promised that we shall partake of the tree of life after our redemption, which is sufficient evidence that it will be a privilege, a blessing, to saints redeemed. It has been suggested that the immortal saints can have no need of the tree of life. But such a supposition is altogether useless. Of the nature and condition of the immortalized children of Adam's race, we know absolutely nothing. But of some things we are informed in the Scriptures, which have a bearing on this subject. The apostle speaks thus of the triumph of Jesus over death, in his resurrection:—

"Knowing that Chirst being raised from the dead dieth no more: death hath no more dominion over him." Rom. 6: 9.

But Jesus ate and drank with his disciples after his resurrection,—after death had no more dominion over him. And he also said to his disciples at the last supper:—

"But I say unto you, I will not drink henceforth of this fruit of the vine, until that day when I drink it new with you in my Father's kingdom." Matt. 26: 29.

And yet again he said:—

"And I appoint unto you a kingdom, as my Father hath appointed unto me; that ye may eat and drink at my table in my kingdom, and sit on thrones judging the twelve tribes of Israel." Luke 22: 29, 30.

These promises of the Saviour, that they should eat and drink in his kingdom, are in exact conformity with his own example of eating and drinking after his resurrection. While some feel inclined to explain away these facts, to make the statements harmonize with their preconceived ideas of the state and nature of the redeemed, we choose to acknowledge our ignorance in matters so high, and to bring ideas and theories into harmony with the express declarations of the Scriptures.

While the leaves and fruit of the tree of life will be for the use and service of the nations, we learn in the verses preceding that "the nations of them that are saved" shall inhabit the new earth, and shall walk in the light of the holy city. Rev. 21 : 23, 24. None but the blessed and holy will ever see the earth in its beauty, in its renewed state; will ever walk in the light of the glory of the city of God. It was through sin that Adam lost the privilege of the garden, lost access to the tree of life, lost the earth in its blessed, happy state; and this should be sufficient assurance to us that sinners will never be admitted to the enjoyment of those glories. They who are the children of Abraham through faith, who have washed their robes in the blood of the Lamb, who keep the commandments of God and the faith of Jesus, will have right to the tree of life, and enter in through the gates into the city. And terrible will be their disappointment who indulge a hope to partake of these privileges and glories without those qualifications.

Of the glory and joy reserved for those that love him, we can have but very faint conceptions. Having always been associated with sin and sinful surroundings, with sickness, pain, and death, we cannot imagine what it will be to be forever set free from all such things. But the great change will be made:—

"For, behold, I create new heavens and a new earth; and the former shall not be remembered, nor come into mind." Isa. 65 : 17.

This means that it shall not be remembered as an object of desire. Many beautiful things are enjoyed in this earth, but when Jerusalem is created a rejoicing, and her people a joy, and the voice of weeping is no more heard in the land, there will not be one thought of desire for the former state. Here the saints find their everlasting rest, and shall delight themselves in the abundance of peace.

"The wilderness and the solitary place shall be glad for them; and the desert shall rejoice, and blossom as the rose. It shall blossom abundantly, and rejoice even with joy and singing. . . . Then the eyes of the blind shall be opened, and the ears of the deaf shall be unstopped. Then shall the lame man leap as an hart, and the tongue of the dumb sing; for in the wilderness shall waters break out, and streams in the desert." Isa. 35:1-6.

And again the same prophet says:—

"Therefore the redeemed of the Lord shall return, and come with singing unto Zion; and everlasting joy shall be upon their head; they shall obtain gladness and joy; and sorrow and mourning shall flee away." Isa. 51:11.

And to the prophet John the angel spoke thus:—

"And God shall wipe away all tears from their eyes; and there shall be no more death, neither sorrow, nor crying, neither shall there be any more pain; for the former things are passed away. And he that sat upon the throne said, Behold, I make all things new." Rev. 21:4, 5.

Eden is then fully restored. Here the river of the water of life flows out from the Mount Zion. Here Adam regains the tree of life, planted beside the river which parts into separate heads as in the beginning. Here again is paradise, the garden which the Lord himself planted seven thousand years before. Here Abraham inherits the earth according to the promise; here is the city for which he looked, every inhabitant of which regards him as a father. Here Moses will enter into that goodly land which he saw with the eye of a prophet. Here David will behold his throne established, nevermore to be overturned, but to endure as the sun, even as the days of Heaven. Here the prophets meet with the apostles, and together walk the streets of the city upon whose gates are inscribed the names of the twelve tribes of the children of Israel, the foundations of whose walls are named after the twelve apostles of the Lamb. Here are the martyrs, rejoicing that it was their privilege to suffer unto death that they might inherit such a far more exceeding and eternal weight of glory. Here is the chosen company of those who were redeemed from the earth at the coming of their Lord, who overcame the beast and his image and the mark of his name by strict adherence to the commandments of God and the faith of Jesus, in the perilous days when all the world was overcome with the prevailing iniquity. Coming up to the city to worship is the innumerable host who inherit the land from the river unto the end of the earth. And here is He who once trod the hills round about Jerusalem, with weary feet and pitying heart, seeking the lost sheep of the house of Israel. Here He was slain to redeem this worshiping host with His precious blood. Unto Him every eye is turned; to Him every knee bows; to Him every tongue shouts praise, for to Him they owe their life, and all this joy, this heavenly beauty, this glory.

"And every creature which is in heaven, and on the earth, and under the earth, and such as are in the sea, and all that are in them, heard I saying, Blessing, and honor, and glory, and power, be unto him that sitteth upon the throne, and unto the Lamb forever and ever." Rev. 5:13.

Thus ends the conflict of ages. The reign of sin and death is forever past. And it is sad to think that the finally impenitent will never behold the earth in its beauty, in its redeemed, glorified state. They choose "this present world" as their portion, and their portion is to perish with it, dying as they have lived, ignorant of the boundlessness of the joy that God has prepared for those who love him. But to the righteous an eternity of bliss is given, where they may contemplate the wisdom of God, and ever learn more of his goodness to his creatures.

That which has appeared dark and mysterious to our limited vision, will then be made plain. Often have the persecuted saints wondered why God permitted wrong so long to triumph. But when the far more exceeding and eternal weight of glory is opened to their view, and to their experience, they will realize that the time in which sin was permitted to exhibit its hideousness, in which Satan was permitted to give full proof of his falsity, and unreasonable wickedness, was as the rising vapor, that appeareth for a little time, and then vanisheth away, compared to the eternity which they shall be permitted to enjoy. Of this fact the reader will behold an excellent illustration on the cover of this book. When God created the world, it was very good; and in this condition it was started on the circle of eternity, to ever remain a joy to its inhabitants and to the angels in Heaven. But he who rebelled in Heaven, who lost his principality before the throne of the Most High, sought to obtain an abiding-place in this world, where the rebellious spirit of his own heart could prevail. Could he succeed in making this his own, there would be one world amid the countless orbs of God's creation where he could revel in the iniquity in which his dark soul delighted.

But God intercepted his work. He placed the earth under a curse, that Satan might not have the satisfaction of reveling in the delightful scenes of Paradise. He took away the tree of life from man, that he might not "eat and live forever" in an eternity of sin and misery. Thus by the introduction of sin, by the rebellion of man, the earth was thrown out of the course which its Maker designed it to follow. This is shown by the ellipse which it followed in its temporary condition under the darkness of sin.

Then the Son of God, the Son of man, appeared, and triumphed over sin and Satan for man's sake; he redeems by his precious blood both man and his dominion. He came to destroy the works of the devil, and through him all things are made new. Man is immortalized, restored to Paradise and the tree of life. The world is restored to that position for which the Creator designed it in the beginning. The circle of eternity is its own; its state of glory shall be as endless as the throne of its Maker.

Our closing text (Rev. 5:13) is a prophecy of the time when every creature in Heaven, and earth, and under the earth, are heard ascribing praise to God and the Lamb. God will cleanse the universe from sin, and eternity shall not be burdened with the wails and curses of the lost. All the ungodly shall perish, and they only will be immortal who have sought for eternal life through Jesus Christ our Lord. David foresaw this time when he said:—

"Praise ye the Lord. . . . Praise ye him, all his angels; praise ye him, all his host. Praise ye him, sun and moon; praise him, all ye stars of light." "Let everything that hath breath praise the Lord." Ps. 148:1-3; 150:6.

INDEX OF SCRIPTURES QUOTED.

GENESIS.

Text.	Page.
1:1	216, 15
1:26	15, 16, 67, 86
1:28	86
2:3	46, 208
2:7	108
2:16, 17	231
3:1–6, 17	17
3:13	33
3:15	18, 26, 27, 31, 68
3	65
3:17–19	231
3:22–24	172
4:7, 10–12	44
5:5	231
6:5	39
7	239
7:1	39
7:1–6	223
7:11	126
7:16	178
7:24	129
8:4	126
9:21–25	44
12:1–3	21
12:7	21, 31
13:13	39
13:14–17	22
15:6	34
15:7, 10	22
15:13–16	47
17:6	67
17:11	25
17:14	25
20:4–9	44
21:12	232
24:7	23
26:1–5	205
26:2–5	23
26:3–5	38
28:3, 4, 13–15	24
31:19, 30, 32, 39	44
35:2, 3	44
35:11	67
35:11–12	24
39:7–9	44
44:4–9	44
48:34	24

EXODUS.

7:10–12	167
16:4	45
16:22, 23	45
16:28	45
17:8–14	68
19:5–8	48
19:6	67
20:8–11	209
20:10	46, 209
20:11	45

Text.	Page.
24:1–8	50
24:6–8	54
25:8	183, 51
25:10–22	51
25:21, 22	183
28:30	184
29:42, 43	51
30:1–8	52
31:13	219
31:13–17	209
31:15	46
31:17	218

LEVITICUS.

16:1–4	53
16:2	52
16:11–14	52
16:15, 16	52, 184
16:18, 19	184
16:19	52
16:20–31	184
16:29	52
17:1–6	58
17:11	184
18:3, 21–25	45
23:27, 28	52
23:27	184
23:27–32	53

NUMBERS.

3:10	184

DEUTERONOMY.

4:12, 13	41, 48
5:3	47
10:16	25
18:10, 11	170
18:12	170
18:15	29
25:17–19	68
30:6	26

1 SAMUEL.

2:30	65
8:19, 20	67
15:1–3, 13–23	207
15:22	36

1 KINGS.

8:9	51

2 KINGS.

1:7	69
17:24–41	56
20:16–18	70
25:4–10	70

1 CHRONICLES.

Text.	Page.
16 : 15-18	40
17 : 11, 12	27
17 : 11-14	68

2 CHRONICLES.

36 : 5-8	89
36 : 14-20	70

EZRA.

1 : 1-4	59
2 : 36-39	61
2 : 70	61
3 : 1	61
6 : 14	92, 190
6 : 16, 17	61
7 : 13	60
7 : 11-26	190
8 : 35	61

NEHEMIAH.

7 : 73	61

ESTHER.

1 : 1	60
9 : 17	60

JOB.

14 : 13-15	233
19 : 25-27	233
38 : 4-7	32

PSALMS.

2 : 7-9	95
14 : 3	49
16 : 9, 10	233
17 : 15	233
19 : 1	15, 217, 218
19 : 7	206
37 : 10	240
37 : 11	30, 238
37 : 11, 18, 29	240
40 : 8	206
49 : 15	233
89 : 3, 4, 29, 36	69
92 : 7	241
110 : 1	95, 103
111 : 4	218
115 : 16	16, 67
119 : 45	14
136 : 15	178
148 : 1-3	256
150 : 6	256

PROVERBS.

21 : 31	240

ECCLESIASTES.

7 : 29	15
9 : 5	170
12 : 13, 14	41

ISAIAH.

9 : 6, 7	249
8 : 19, 20	169
11 : 6-9	241
13 : 19-22	99
23 : 3, 8	130
25 : 9	223

Text.	Page.
26 : 19	234
27 : 12, 13	62
29 : 13	26
29 : 13, 14	197
35 : 1-6	253
37 : 5-7	70
42 : 21	206
45 : 18	15, 67
51 : 11	253
54 : 1	242
58 : 13	46, 209
61 : 1, 2	179
61 : 21	179
65 : 17	252
65 : 25	241
66 : 1, 2	204

JEREMIAH.

4 : 4	26
10 : 11, 12	216
18 : 7-10	65
25 : 30	247
29 : 10-14	60
31 : 15-17	106, 234
31 : 31	54
31 : 31-34	41, 63
51 : 28-31, 37, 57, 58	100

EZEKIEL.

4 : 1-6	127
9 : 4-6	215
13 : 4-6	215
12 : 23	127
12 : 27	127
20 : 19, 20, 12	219
21 : 25-27	70
28 : 1-10	130
28 : 12-19	130
37 : 11-14	234
37 : 12-14	63
43 : 20-22	184

DANIEL.

1 : 1-7	89
1 : 3, 4	70
2	89, 90, 94, 110, 102, 183
2 : 9	72
2 : 24	84
2 : 28	71
2 : 28, 30	73
2 : 30	74
2 : 31-35	73
2 : 34	114
2 : 34, 44	95
2 : 36	74
2 : 37, 38	74, 86
2 : 39	75, 80
2 : 40	81, 182
2 : 41	83
2 : 42, 43	84
2 : 34	114
2 : 44	85, 87, 99, 243
2 : 44, 45	75
2 : 47	97
4	126
4 : 16, 23, 25, 32	125
5	75
5 : 18, 19	86
5 : 25	77
5 : 30, 31	79, 89, 90
7	81, 91, 94, 147, 163, 164, 165, 183
7 : 2, 3	215
7 : 4	110
7 : 5	111

INDEX OF SCRIPTURES QUOTED. 259

Text.	Page
7:6	92, 112, 113
7:1–7	131
7:7	112, 113, 182
7:8	114
7:9, 10	243
7:13, 14	43
7:13, 14, 27	88
7:17, 18	110
7:21, 22	97, 128
7:24	113
7:25	124, 126, 147, 222
8	81, 191
8:2	80
8:3, 4, 20	111
8:5–9	112
8:8, 9	182
8:10–12	183
8:14	150, 183, 189, 190
8:16	189
8:20–22	182
8:22	90, 112
8:24	114
8:27	190
9	127, 189, 190
9:24	191
9:24, 25	190
9:24–27	55
9:27	191
12:2	234

HOSEA.
13:14	234

JOEL.
2:1	224
3:15, 16	247

AMOS.
1:2	247

MICAH.
4:8	70

ZECHARIAH.
14:4, 5	246
14:8, R. V.	246

MALACHI.
4:1	240

MATTHEW.
1:21	32, 36, 172, 207
2:16–18	234
3:1, 2	101
3:9	66, 65, 107
5:1–9	207
5:3	101
5:5	30, 32
6:10	101
7:21	46, 206
7:21–23	36
9:12	50
10:1–8	167
10:7	101
13:28	16
13:38, 39	108
13:39–43	177
16:27	236
19:16, 17	207
21:33–43	107
21:43	66
22:9	12
22:21	197
23:37	107
21:3	225

Text.	Page.
24:4–8	225
24:9–14	225
24:14	102
24:21, 22	225
24:23, 24	225
24:24	167, 171
24:26, 27	225
24:29	226
24:30, 31	62, 177
24:32, 33	230
24:42	187
25:31–34	107
25:31–41	106
25:34	102
25:41	171
26:29	251

MARK.
1:14, 15	101, 191
2:27	208
13:24	226

LUKE.
1:32, 33	27, 105, 128, 244
2:1	81
4:16–21	179
10:17–20	167
12:31–37	250
14:14	235
19:12–15	243
19:27	243
19:38–40	108
21:29, 30	230
22:20	54
22:29, 30	251

JOHN.
1:1–3	15
3:16	172
4:20	56
4:21	57
4:21, 23	57
4:22	41
5:28, 29	237
6:40	173
7:22	49
8:33–39	46
8:38–44	65
8:39–44	108
8:44	17
8:56	20, 232
10:27, 28	172
10:28	32
10:29	250
11:23, 24	235
14:28	250
15:5	37
16:22	30
16:33	238
17:17	36
18:36	197

ACTS.
2:25–32	233
2:30	41
2:38	43
3:26	54
7:5	29
7:38	41, 57
13:46	54
15:14	239
17:23, 24	217
17:31	178, 206

TEXT.	PAGE.
19:26	219
23:6	235
24:15	236
24:25	179
26:6	19

ROMANS.

TEXT.	PAGE.
1:3	41
1:18–28	18
1:19, 20	217
1:21–23	217
1:23	172
1:28	217
1:28, 21	35
2:7	36, 172
2:14, 15	42
2:17–23	42, 46, 206
2:25	38
2:28, 29	26, 108
3	45
3:1, 2	57
3:2	41
3:3–19	41
3:9–19	40
3:12, 19	49
3:20	50, 207
3:24–28	36
3:31	206
4:11	13, 26, 216
4:11, 12	37
4:12	13
4:13	30
5:1–3	205
5:12	173
5:13	39, 44
5:20	50
6:9	251
6:23	172
7:7, 13	207
7:13	50
8:9	27
8:15	28
8:17	28
10:17	15
10:21	54
11:23	108
14:9	106
8:22, 23	238
8:38, 39	106
9:4	41
9:4, 5	57
9:5	41

1 CORINTHIANS.

4:5	182
6:1–3	182
15:22	173, 237
15:23–28	103
15:26	106, 234
15:27	104
15:42–53	237
15:42–54	180
15:50	106
15:51, 52	236
15:51–54	62, 172
15:54	236

2 CORINTHIANS.

6:2	179
11:14, 15	171
11:31	230

GALATIANS.

2:17	207
2:18	58

TEXT.	PAGE.
3:8, 9	20
3:9, 29	13
3:13, 14	39, 46
3:16, 17	50
3:16	27
3:17	41
3:24	50
3:26–29	55, 64
3:28	27
3:29	28, 30
4:25	250
4:25, 26	242
4:28	242
5:6	37
6:8	172, 237
6:16	218

EPHESIANS.

1:13	26
1:13, 14	31, 238
2:11–19	63, 108
2:11–22	59
2:13, 16	28
3:6	65
4:30	27

PHILIPPIANS.

2:12	36
3:5, 7	108

COLOSSIANS.

1:13–17	15
3:4	172, 236

1 THESSALONIANS.

1:3	37
4:13–17	231
4:13–18	224, 226
4:14–17	107
4:15–17	176
4:16, 17	62, 235
5:1–3	203
5:1–4	224
5:4	187, 230

2 THESSALONIANS.

1:11	37
1:6–10	95
2:1	62
2:1–9	124
2:3	222
2:9, 10	168

2 TIMOTHY.

1:10	172
3:1–5	225
3:1–9	168
3:12	31
4:1–8	223

TITUS.

2:13	236
2:14	48

HEBREWS.

1:1, 2	15
2:14	248
4:1, 2	25
6:11–19	20
8:1	102

INDEX OF SCRIPTURES QUOTED.

TEXT.	PAGE.
8:1, 2	53, 95
8:1-5	185
8:2	69
8:5	54
8:6-12	63
8:8, 9	64
9:7	52
9:15	185, 206
9:17	54
9:18, 19	54
9:23, 24	54, 185, 186
9:26	36, 207
9:28	223, 224
10:12, 13	103
10:25	224
11:2	15
11:6	37
11:8	21
11:8-13	233
11:9	29
11:10	241
11:17	30
11:17-19	232
11:35	13, 233
11:39, 40	231
12:2	102
12:22	247
12:25, 26	247

JAMES.

2:5	106
2:17, 20, 26	206
2:20	37
2:22	36

1 PETER.

1:22	36
2:5-9	48
2:9	49
2:11	30, 238
5:4	236

2 PETER.

1:19	100
2:4	171
2:6-8	39
3:5	239
3:5-7, 10, 13	238
3:7	239
3:10	239
3:13	240

1 JOHN.

2:16	217
3:4	37, 207
3:8	32
5:3	46
5:10	34
5:10, 11	173
5:17	37

JUDE.

6	171
9	130
13	237

REVELATION.

2:1-7	251
3:9	108

TEXT.	PAGE.
3:21	102, 128
4:1-5	186
5:13	254, 256
6:12-17	214
6:15-17	95
7:1-3	214, 215, 245
7:9	239
11:15-19	186
11:16-18	95
11:18	186
12	129, 147
12:6	126
12:9	130
12:14	126
12:17	131
13	203, 205, 223
13:1, 2	131
13:2	132
13:1-10	148, 156, 163
13:2, 3	162
13:3	147, 157
13:8	162
13:10	147
13:11	164
13:11-17	148, 212
13:11-18	179
13:12	165
13:13, 14	166, 170, 225
13:14	157, 165, 173
13:15	175
13:16, 17	175
14	181, 223
14:1-5	176
14:6, 7	177, 178, 179, 180, 186, 188, 191, 192
14:8	189, 202
14:9	177
14:9-11	176
14:9-12	205, 213, 214
14:14	177
15:7, 8	245
16	226
16:13, 14	225
16:14	171
16:14, 15	215
16:15	167, 171, 203
17:1-6	202
17:15	131, 164
17:18	242
18	188
19:6-9	250
19:10	131
20:2	17, 180
20:2-6	182
20:4-6	180
20:7-10	248
20:6, 13-15	237
20:15	240
21:1	241
21:1-5	33
21:2	248
21:4, 5	253
21:9	244
21:9-11	248
21:23, 24	252
21:24	67
22:1	246
22:2	250
22:11, 12	104, 181
22:12	236
22:14	207
22:20	236

INDEX OF AUTHORS QUOTED.

Anonymous, 135, 136, 193, 194, 195, 212, 221, 227, 228.
Appia, C., 199.
Barnes, Dr. Albert, 79, 82, 94.
Becker, 91.
Beyschlag, 211.
Bibliotheca Sacra, 210.
Bower, 116, 117, 118, 119, 121, 134, 138, 140, 146, 152.
Catholic Times, The, 161.
Chambers' Cyclopedia, 197, 198.
Chautre, M., 200.
Cormenin, 148.
Croly, 142, 154, 155.
D'Aubigne, Merle, 201.
Eck, 221.
Faucher, E., 200.
Gasparin, Count, 200, 201.
Gaussen, Prof. L., 83, 115.
Gibbon, 82, 91, 116, 119, 122, 123, 142, 144, 146.
Gieseler, 139, 143, 146, 211.
Henry, Matthew, 228.
Holtzman, 220.
Josephus, 61, 82, 125.
Justinian, 141.
Kuhn, Dr. Felix, 199.
Lives of the Popes, 159.
London *Telegraph*, 211.
Lowth, Bishop, 84.
Luther, Martin, 83.
Lyman, 112.
Machiavelli, 96, 118.
Maurice, Emperor, 198.
McClintock & Strong, 140, 159.
Melanchthon, 210.
Montague, Lord Robert, 194.
New American Encyclopedia, 160.
Newton, Sir Isaac, 148.
Olmstead, Prof., 229.
Robinson, 220.
Rollin, 78, 112.
Scheffmacher, P. J. J., Catechism of, 211.
Sozomon, 136.
Stanley, 136.
Stapfer, Edward, 199.
Sword and Trowel, 195.
Thoughts on the Revelation, 149, 165.
Vinet, Alexander, 197.
Von Ranke, 156, 158, 159.
Ward, Rev. Henry Dana, 229.
Weber, Dr. Geo., 82, 160.
Webster, Noah, LL.D., 227.

We invite you to view the complete
selection of titles we publish at:
www.TEACHServices.com

scan with your mobile
device to go directly
to our website

Please write or email us your praises, reactions, or
thoughts about this or any other book we publish at:

Info@TEACHServices.com

TEACH Services, Inc., titles may be purchased in bulk
for educational, business, fund-raising, or sales
promotional use. For information, please e-mail:

BulkSales@TEACHServices.com

Finally if you are interested in seeing
your own book in print, please contact us at

publishing@TEACHServices.com

We would be happy to review your manuscript for free.

www.ingramcontent.com/pod-product-compliance
Lightning Source LLC
Chambersburg PA
CBHW070536160426
43199CB00014B/2273